Studies in
Young Adult Literature
Series Editor: Patty Campbell

Studies in Young Adult Literature is intended to continue the body of critical writing established in Twayne's Young Adult Authors series and to expand it beyond single-author studies to explorations of genres, multicultural writing, and controversial issues in young adult (YA) reading. Many of the contributing authors of the series are among the leading scholars and critics of adolescent literature, and some are YA novelists themselves. The series is shaped by its editor, Patty Campbell, who is a renowned authority in the field, with a forty-year background as critic, lecturer, librarian, and teacher of YA literature. Patty Campbell was the 2001 winner of the ALAN Award, given by the Assembly on Literature for Adolescents of the National Council of Teachers of English for distinguished contribution to YA literature. In 1989 she was the winner of the American Library Association's Grolier Award for distinguished service to young adults and reading.

Titles in the Series

1. *What's So Scary about R. L. Stine?*, by Patrick Jones, 1998.
2. *Ann Rinaldi: Historian and Storyteller*, by Jeanne M. McGlinn, 2000.
3. *Norma Fox Mazer: A Writer's World*, by Arthea J. S. Reed, 2000.
4. *Exploding the Myths: The Truth about Teens and Reading*, by Marc Aronson, 2001.
5. *The Agony and the Eggplant: Daniel Pinkwater's Heroic Struggles in the Name of YA Literature*, by Walter Hogan, 2001.
6. *Caroline Cooney: Faith and Fiction*, by Pamela Sissi Carroll, 2001.
7. *Declarations of Independence: Empowered Girls in Young Adult Literature, 1990–2001*, by Joanne Brown and Nancy St. Clair, 2002.
8. *Lost Masterworks of Young Adult Literature*, by Connie S. Zitlow, 2002.
9. *Beyond the Pale: New Essays for a New Era*, by Marc Aronson, 2003.
10. *Orson Scott Card: Writer of the Terrible Choice*, by Edith S. Tyson, 2003.
11. *Jacqueline Woodson: "The Real Thing,"* by Lois Thomas Stover, 2003.
12. *Virginia Euwer Wolff: Capturing the Music of Young Voices*, by Suzanne Elizabeth Reid, 2003.
13. *More Than a Game: Sports Literature for Young Adults*, by Chris Crowe, 2004.
14. *Humor in Young Adult Literature: A Time to Laugh*, by Walter Hogan, 2005.
15. *Life Is Tough: Guys, Growing Up, and Young Adult Literature*, by Rachelle Lasky Bilz, 2004.
16. *Sarah Dessen: From Burritos to Box Office*, by Wendy J. Glenn, 2005.
17. *American Indian Themes in Young Adult Literature*, by Paulette F. Molin, 2005.
18. *The Heart Has Its Reasons: Young Adult Literature with Gay/Lesbian/Queer Content, 1969–2004*, by Michael Cart and Christine A. Jenkins, 2006.

19. *Karen Hesse*, by Rosemary Oliphant-Ingham, 2005.

20. *Graham Salisbury: Island Boy*, by David Macinnis Gill, 2005.

21. *The Distant Mirror: Reflections on Young Adult Historical Fiction*, by Joanne Brown and Nancy St. Clair, 2006.

22. *Sharon Creech: The Words We Choose to Say*, by Mary Ann Tighe, 2006.

23. *Angela Johnson: Poetic Prose*, by KaaVonia Hinton, 2006.

24. *David Almond: Memory and Magic*, by Don Latham, 2006.

25. *Aidan Chambers: Master Literary Choreographer*, by Betty Greenway, 2006.

26. *Passions and Pleasures: Essays and Speeches about Literature and Libraries*, by Michael Cart, 2007.

27. *Names and Naming in Young Adult Literature*, by Alleen Pace Nilsen and Don L. F. Nilsen, 2007.

28. *Janet McDonald: The Original Project Girl*, by Catherine Ross-Stroud, 2008.

29. *Richard Peck: The Past Is Paramount*, by Donald R. Gallo and Wendy Glenn, 2008.

30. *Sisters, Schoolgirls, and Sleuths: Girls' Series Books in America*, by Carolyn Carpan, 2009.

31. *Sharon Draper: Embracing Literacy*, by KaaVonia Hinton, 2009.

32. *Mixed Heritage in Young Adult Literature*, by Nancy Thalia Reynolds, 2009.

33. *Russell Freedman*, by Susan P. Bloom and Cathryn M. Mercier, 2009.

34. *Animals in Young Adult Fiction*, by Walter Hogan, 2009.

35. *Learning Curves: Body Image and Female Sexuality in Young Adult Literature*, by Beth Younger, 2009.

36. *Laurie Halse Anderson: Speaking in Tongues*, by Wendy J. Glenn, 2010.

37. *Suzanne Fisher Staples: The Setting Is the Story*, by Megan Lynn Isaac, 2010.

38. *Campbell's Scoop: Reflections on Young Adult Literature*, by Patty Campbell, 2010.

39. *Donna Jo Napoli: Writing with Passion*, by Hilary S. Crew, 2010.

40. *John Marsden: Darkness, Shadow, and Light*, by John Noell Moore, 2011.

41. *Robin McKinley: Girl Reader, Woman Writer*, by Evelyn M. Perry, 2011.

42. *Immigration Narratives in Young Adult Literature: Crossing Borders*, by Joanne Brown, 2011.

43. *They Suck, They Bite, They Eat, They Kill: The Psychological Meaning of Supernatural Monsters in Young Adult Fiction*, by Joni Richards Bodart, 2012.

44. *Stephenie Meyer: In the Twilight*, by James Blasingame Jr., Kathleen Deakin, and Laura A. Walsh, 2012.

45. *Chris Crutcher: A Stotan for Young Adults*, by Bryan Gillis and Pam B. Cole, 2012.

46. *Portrait of the Artist as a Young Adult: The Arts in Young Adult Literature*, by Lois Thomas Stover and Connie S. Zitlow, 2014.

47. *Virginity in Young Adult Literature after* Twilight, by Christine Seifert, 2015.

48. *Sexual Content in Young Adult Literature: Reading between the Sheets*, by Bryan Gillis and Joanna Simpson, 2015.

Sexual Content in Young Adult Literature

Reading between the Sheets

Bryan Gillis
Joanna Simpson

ROWMAN & LITTLEFIELD
Lanham • Boulder • New York • London

Published by Rowman & Littlefield
A wholly owned subsidiary of The Rowman & Littlefield Publishing Group, Inc.
4501 Forbes Boulevard, Suite 200, Lanham, Maryland 20706
www.rowman.com

Unit A, Whitacre Mews, 26-34 Stannary Street, London SE11 4AB

British Library Cataloguing in Publication Information Available

Library of Congress Cataloging-in-Publication Data

Gillis, Bryan, 1958–
Sexual content in young adult literature : reading between the sheets / Bryan Gillis and Joanna
Simpson.
pages cm. — (Studies in young adult literature ; no. 48)
Includes bibliographical references and index.
ISBN 978-1-4422-4687-4 (hardback : alk. paper) — ISBN 978-1-4422-4688-1 (ebook) 1.
Young adult literature—History and criticism. 2. Sex in literature. 3. Sex role in literature. 4.
Teenagers—Sexual behavior. 5. Young adult fiction—History and criticism. I. Simpson,
Joanna, 1980– II. Title.
PN1009.5.S48G55 2015
809'.9335380835—dc23
2014039649

∞ The paper used in this publication meets the minimum requirements of
American National Standard for Information Sciences Permanence of Paper for
Printed Library Materials, ANSI/NISO Z39.48-1992.

Printed in the United States of America

To my lifelong friend, Jeff Kemp. Thank you for teaching me how to be courageous.—B. G.

To my husband, Jason Simpson, for reminding me that perspective informs controversy.—J. S.

Contents

Preface ix

Acknowledgments xiii

1 Adolescent Identity Development 1
2 A Brief History of Sex Education in American Schools 11
3 Sexual Content and the Canon 17
4 Sexual Content in the Early Days of Young Adult Fiction: 1950s–1980s 37
5 Sex and Romance in Dystopian Young Adult Fiction 75
6 Sexual Content in Young Adult Romance 101
7 Sexual Content in Realistic Contemporary Young Adult Fiction 125
8 The Censorship of Young Adult Fiction 155

Bibliography 167
Index 175
About the Authors 179

Preface

Sexual Content in Young Adult Fiction: Reading between the Sheets reflects our desire to provide parents, teachers, and librarians with a better understanding of the role that sex in young adult fiction plays in the socioemotional and academic development of adolescents. The teens whom we know and teach have questions and concerns about sex, and most of their questions have little to do with basic biological facts. Instead, they are eager to learn about the social and emotional aspects of sexual feelings and sexual activity. Teachers, parents, and librarians are typically the best and most credible sources available for those students who seek this information, but often, neither the adults nor the teenagers are willing to have those conversations with each other. Consequently, much of the information that teens do acquire comes from their peers. The literature that students are exposed to in middle and high school offers an alternative, as it has the potential to provide opportunities for teen readers to process the complexities of sex in the safety of their own hearts and minds.

Young adult literature (YAL) has been instrumental in motivating our students to read, and it has had a profound effect on their reading abilities. As classroom teachers, we connect students with YAL because we know that the right book at the right time can trigger an avalanche of reading motivation. In our other role as preparers of future teachers, we preach the importance of making these books available to students because quality YAL possesses verisimilitude, and for many adolescents the presence of sexual situations in the books that they read contributes greatly to that semblance of reality.

Verisimilitude in literature not only motivates teens to read but also helps to improve their comprehension skills by enabling them to make critical text-to-text, text-to-self, and text-to-world connections. This sexual content also provides teachers with opportunities to teach language arts skills, such as tone, mood, and figurative language. For example, the sexual situations in which authors place their characters are often inextricably linked to key story elements (e.g., plot and character development). The hot tub scene in Jay Asher's *Thirteen Reasons Why*[1] illustrates this connectivity. The sexual explicitness in this scene is critical to an understanding of how far the main character, Hannah, has fallen as she considers suicide.

In *Young Adult Literature: From Romance to Realism*, Michael Cart makes the point that the difficulty lies not in defining the word *literature* but in trying to identify the audience.[2] What is a "young adult"? Is this even the proper term to use? Is *teen*, *adolescent*, or *juvenile* a more appropriate choice? The term *juvenile* typically carries a negative connotation, conjuring up images of immaturity or even criminal behavior. *Adolescent* is a psychology term and feels rather clinical. The term *teen* is used in many places; for example, Barnes and Noble has a teen literature section, and Teenreads is a popular review website for young adult literature. Ultimately, it may be no more than a semantics argument. For publishers' marketing purposes, teen and young adult readers fall between the ages of approximately twelve and eighteen. A relatively new category, "new adult," signifies readers between the ages of eighteen and twenty-five.

Young adult literature is typically defined by one or more of the following attributes or features: (1) The protagonist is a young adult; (2) the story is told from the perspective of a young adult; (3) the story is written in the voice of a young adult; (4) coming-of-age issues relevant to young adults are addressed; (5) the story is marketed to young adults; (6) the story is one that young adults choose to read.[3]

The potential for YAL to have a lasting positive impact on young adult readers depends on the connections that those readers make with the text; therefore, we feel that a definition that includes the first four of these attributes is critical, especially as we engage in discussions about a complex and controversial topic such as sex. A story that features a young adult protagonist, is told from the perspective of a young adult, is written in the language of young adults, and focuses on issues relevant to them offers the best opportunity for young adult readers to make those connections. Although we discuss several books that are defined by the last two attributes, these criteria can be problematic when considering what is and what is not young adult literature.

Marketing a book as "young adult" or "teen" does not necessarily make it so. For example, we recently visited the Teen Reads section at a Barnes and Noble bookstore in Atlanta, Georgia, and were surprised to see *Pride and Prejudice* nestled alongside Laurie Halse Anderson's *Speak*. The Jane Austen classic had been fitted with a new cover that looked surprisingly similar to the *Twilight* covers. And although Elizabeth Bennett is "not one and 20," the third-person narration does not create the tone and mood of adolescence. We would also argue that the dilemmas with which Elizabeth and her sisters struggle are hardly relevant coming-of-age issues for today's youth. We have seen other classics, such as George Orwell's *1984*, residing in the teen section at local bookstores. We are not suggesting that teens should not read these books—simply that they should not be classified as YAL.

Using *choice* as a category descriptor poses problems as well. First, the word suggests that virtually any book ever written may be included. In addition, several prominent young adult books have now been added to required middle and high school reading lists across the country (e.g., *Speak*). If these novels are assigned, do they cease to be YAL because the element of choice has been eliminated?

Whether an adolescent reader's purpose is to seek information, to connect and interact with what is happening in the story, or a combination of both, the sexual content encountered in the literature intended for young adults poses rewards and challenges for adolescents and the teachers, librarians, and parents who teach and promote this literature. Adolescents are rewarded with opportunities to strengthen their academic and socioemotional identities. Adults are challenged with identifying quality content and then creating and facilitating effective and responsible discussions about that content. In the following pages, through identification and discussion of quality literature targeted for young adults, we hope to demonstrate the importance of sexual content in young adult fiction.

NOTES

1. Jay Asher, *Thirteen Reasons Why* (New York: Razorbill, 2007).

2. Michael Cart, *Young Adult Literature: From Romance to Realism* (Chicago: American Library Association, 2011), 3.

3. Pam B. Cole, *Young Adult Literature in the 21st Century* (New York: McGraw-Hill, 2010); Alleen Pace Nilsen, James Blasingame, Kenneth L. Donelson, and Don L. F. Nilsen, *Literature for Today's Young Adults* (New York: Pearson, 2013).

Acknowledgments

Many thanks to Patty Campbell, series editor for Rowman & Littlefield, whose revision and editing expertise were invaluable. To Stephen Ryan, senior editor, who worked diligently to get the book published in a timely manner. Bryan would like to thank his beautiful wife, Nancy, for her endless support, and the entire crew at Daily Grind, Marietta, Georgia, for creating such a welcoming environment in which to write and for keeping him caffeinated. Joanna would like to thank the various teachers, librarians, and young adult authors who acted as the impetus for this research. She would also like to thank Gayle Deaver, Mark Williams, and Kelly Bragg for always returning e-mails; Darryl Hattenhauer for participating in lively Facebook chat debates on young adult literature; and Jason, her husband, for keeping her company while she stays up all night to write.

Chapter One

Adolescent Identity Development

DEFINING ADOLESCENCE

In 1904, G. Stanley Hall—the first president of the American Psychological Association and the man widely regarded as the founder of child psychology and educational psychology—published a two-volume work entitled *Adolescence*. According to Hall, adolescence occurred between the ages of thirteen to twenty-four and was defined by higher levels of attention seeking, engagement in risky behaviors, and a strong dependence on friendships. His research covered a range of topics, including physical maturation, cognitive development, sexuality, and psychopathology.[1] Before the publication of *Adolescence*, researchers in the fields of psychology and education had been engaged in discussions regarding individuals who had passed puberty but not yet reached what was perceived as adulthood,[2] but Hall is largely responsible for introducing the term into mainstream American culture.

The inception of adolescence in the late nineteenth century was rooted in three important changes that were occurring at the time: First, attendance at public and private schools was increasing, and students were being sorted by age; second, puberty was occurring at an earlier age, possibly due to changes in nutrition; third, job training for males was more time-consuming, resulting in a longer wait to get married.[3] As these newly labeled adolescents became more recognizable to the general public, so did their peculiar characteristics—specifically, their sexual urges.[4] Their interest in sex and the activity that accompanied

this interest indicated for adolescents "a new independence, a rechan-
neling of intense emotion away from parents and onto another object."[5]

Although Hall's contributions were groundbreaking in 1904, many
of his ideas are now viewed as incongruous with current research. For
example, Hall proposed that reading detective novels encouraged dangerous behaviors, including increased criminal activity and risky behaviors in regard to sex and alcohol use.[6] Most experts today also
disagree with Hall's notion that adolescence spans such a wide age
range. The compression of this age range can be attributed, in large
part, to the changing perception that Americans now have regarding
when one becomes an adult. Arnett, for example, states that the typical
range for adolescence is thirteen to eighteen years of age. He refers to
the eighteen- to twenty-five-year age range as a separate developmental
stage called *emerging adulthood*.[7] Age range notwithstanding, nearly
all adolescents experience key development changes during their transition from childhood to adulthood.

IDENTITY DEVELOPMENT

Adolescence is a time when identity development and relationship
building are critical. Positive and negative life experiences play a vital
role in the development of an adolescent's identity. However, it is not
only the experiences themselves but also how they are perceived and
processed that influence this development. If the majority of an adolescent's experiences are processed in a positive manner, greater opportunities exist for the development of a healthy identity. A combination of
environmental factors and societal expectations influence how an adolescent perceives and ultimately processes these life experiences.

The environments that adolescents occupy play an important role in
their perceptions of experiences and the development of a healthy identity. Homes, schools, neighborhoods, and workplaces are all examples
of environments that influence adolescents' perceptions and processing
of life experiences as either positive or negative, depending on how an
adolescent functions within these environments. The environments also
interact so that the connections between work and home or neighborhood and school also influence experiential outcomes.[8] Living, working, and playing in environments that are perceived as positive provide
the best opportunities for adolescents to create a healthy identity.

A positive environment is one that is supportive and understanding: a space where adolescents feel inspired, experience realistic expectations, and receive adequate caring attention from parents, teachers, and mentors.[9] In a perfect world, these environments would all function positively. Unfortunately, judgment, ridicule, and indifference often operate in these same spaces, contributing to a potentially negative environment.[10] It is also during this stage of life that adolescents view the school as more of a home than their actual place of residence. The perception of home shifts from the bedroom or family room to the classroom or the cafeteria, and parents and siblings are replaced in importance by peers. The increased importance of this new family introduces social pressures that can create even more confusion.[11]

Adolescents are navigating an incredibly complicated social world. According to social identity theory, individuals possess multiple social identities that are related to the various groups in which they perceive membership. Social situations within these various groups trigger unique social identities, or ways of thinking, feeling, and acting based on the most salient perceived group memberships at the time. For example, a teen may act one way around a group of friends at school, another way around that same group of friends at church, and still another way around family. They are attempting to navigate their worlds in a socially acceptable manner while trying to establish and commit to an identity. This search for identity is the paramount psychosocial experience for adolescents. Puberty disrupts the predictability and understandings that an individual has developed as a child and so creates "role confusion."[12] Adolescents are attempting to integrate what they believed themselves to be as children, their newly discovered libidos, and visions of their future selves. As they are constructing these identities through social experiences, they may compulsively overidentify with a specific group. The formation of such groups or cliques, as well as other types of exclusionary behaviors, function as a defense against identity confusion.

> The adolescent mind is essentially a mind of the moratorium, a psychosocial stage between childhood and adulthood, and between the morality learned by the child, and the ethics to be developed by the adult. It is an ideological mind and, indeed, it is the ideological outlook of a society that speaks most clearly to the adolescent who is eager to be affirmed by peers, and is ready to be confirmed by rituals, creeds, and programs, which at the same time define what is evil, uncanny, and inimical.[13]

When negative environmental and societal factors adversely affect an adolescent's identity development, he or she may abandon or hide a previously adopted identity and pursue interests that lead to identities—gender, sexuality, religion, ethnicity—that are perceived as more socially acceptable. Positive identities are shaped in nonjudgmental spaces where adolescents are encouraged to explore their identity options safely. This type of exploration can help reduce risk-taking behaviors. Adolescents who are encouraged to explore other identities and consider alternative points of view have a tendency to rely less on peer influence, and those who commit to an identity engage in significantly less risk-taking behaviors, such as substance abuse and general deviancy.[14] Safe, nonjudgmental exploration enables them to understand consequences associated with specific behaviors, and as a result, they are less likely to participate in unhealthy lifestyle choices.

SEXUAL IDENTITY DEVELOPMENT

Adolescents define their sexuality by how they communicate their identities to the world. Sexual identity begins to develop when an adolescent associates with a specific gender—"the socially constructed roles, behaviours, activities, and attributes that a given society considers appropriate for men and women"[15]—and with a sexual orientation: the physical, emotional, sexual, and romantic attraction patterns toward other people.[16]

Gender identities are influenced by parents, family, and peers. Behaviors stereotyped by society as either masculine or feminine are passed down from generation to generation, and these stereotypes shape adolescents' perceptions of what it means to be a man or a woman. For example, a father may discourage his son from crying after the boy skins his knee, telling him that it is not "manly." A mother may tell her daughter not to use certain language because it is not "lady-like."[17] Conversely, parents may establish an environment that encourages sons to play with dolls, a behavior viewed by society as feminine, but later those sons may grow into young men who play football, a behavior viewed as masculine. Due to these influences, preadolescent gender identities tend to be fluid. Once an awareness of gender has been developed, however, a child's perception of self becomes more concrete and begins to function as the primary filter through which he or she experiences the world. These experiences are then assimilated into the sexual identities that adolescents will later construct.

Sexual identity develops in stages, and although definitive scientific research exists suggesting that this development is genetic,[18] an individual's acceptance or rejection of his or her sexual identity is heavily influenced by social factors, including exposure to input from peers, adults, and various forms of media. Healthy and unhealthy sexual identities are formed through adolescents' constructions of their self-images through experiences from within the meaningful environments in which they live and interact. Once they have gathered this arsenal of experience, they must accept their sexual identity.

The first stage of sexual identity acceptance is an attraction to a specific gender. Next, the individual identifies with people in the larger society whom they view as being like—close friends, members of favorite bands, actors, and celebrities. Finally, dating occurs, and if these interactions are positive, identity acceptance occurs.

Once a sexual identity has been accepted, it tends to remain consistent. However, if the adolescent perceives the majority of his or her experiences as harmful, a negative self-image may develop. This can result in a rejection of part or all of an existing sexual identity. Forced to navigate between sexual orientations, genders, attractions, and self-images, acceptance of the final stage of sexual identity may never be reached.[19] It is also important to note that many homosexual adolescents choose to hide their sexual identities, "coming out" later than their heterosexual peers, thus giving the impression that a perceived sexual identity can change at any time in life.

Research on adolescents who identify as lesbian, gay, bisexual, transgendered, queer, intersex, and questioning (LGBTQIQ) suggests that these individuals develop in the same way as their heterosexual peers.[20] They are attempting to reconcile their individuality with the expectations of the group to fit in. However, they are under additional pressure because homosexuality is still not embraced by American society as a whole. In fact, it is often referred to as an abnormal sexual preference.[21] Feeling abnormal only compounds the difficulties and confusion that they are already experiencing. This lack of acceptance often results in bullying and an overwhelming pressure to "go straight." As a result, a greater chance exists that homosexual adolescents will engage in what they perceive as negative sexual experiences. Many feel compelled to hide their desires and, in some cases, their actual gender.

INFLUENCES ON SEXUAL IDENTITY DEVELOPMENT

Adolescents' interactions with media—television, movies, music, and print—play a critical role in their sexual identity development. Popular culture media represents aspects of real-life sexual behavior and provides sexual scripts for young adults. As exposure to these images increases, identity perceptions can quickly spiral out of control. For example, when a girl sees an advertisement for a weight loss product that features a slender female walking on the beach in a bikini or a male views a television commercial that depicts drinking beer as a method for men to meet beautiful women, both males and females can feel as though they must operate in a specific manner to be accepted by a particular social group.

Cable and satellite television companies offer extensive catalogs of film, television programming, and music from which to choose. Portable computerized devices such as smartphones and tablets give users easy access to this content. This ability to discreetly choose and view content in anonymous settings has given adolescents power that they heretofore did not possess. They are also being exposed to a plethora of sexual content at a much earlier age than previous generations. All of this *input* can have a major impact on adolescents' sexual identity development.

The Internet is a one-stop shopping center for all this content and is therefore frequently used by adolescents as a resource for sex-related issues.[22] From research on body functions to sexually charged online chats and cybersex, the opportunities for an adolescent to learn and explore sexual content are endless. The abundance and accessibility of sexually explicit materials and the impact that exposure to them is having on adolescents' sexual attitudes and sexual behavior form a major concern for parents and educators.[23] Note, however, that adolescents' engage in online activities for other reasons than the viewing of sexually explicit content. Chat room conversations and social media interactions are just two ways in which they create sexually relevant content that helps them construct their sexual identities.[24] Opportunities for positive sexual identity development through these types of activities seem promising, and more research is this area is needed.

The literature that adolescents read has the power to influence sexual identity. Hubler's study of gender revealed that the traditional femininity found within children's literature plays a significant role in the construction of female identity. Females who read books about the gender roles that other females play will choose to identify with these characters and the various traits they possess—for example, outspoken, strong, independent, caring, different, quiet, passive, dependent, compliant, timid. Exposure to these types of literature enables females to reflect on the process of gender role socialization and take an active role in the construction of their sexual identity. Furthermore, literature that provides examples of rewards and repercussions that female characters experience as a result of the sexual choices that they make has the potential to positively contribute to the construction of the adolescent reader's sexual identity, often in ways that will feel safer than experiencing the rewards and repercussions themselves.[25]

Smith and Wilhelm conducted extensive research on boys and literacy and found that boys encounter many developmental and social deterrents to reading. As a result, experiences with literature occur far less frequently among males.[26] Influenced by Smith and Wilhelm's research, Jon Scieszka created a literacy program entitled Guys Read.[27] Scieszka states that many girls read books that have been recommended to them by their peers. This rarely happens with boys. Oftentimes, book titles recommended to boys are generated from the adults in their lives and so focus on topics perceived as masculine (e.g., sports, war, and competition). This approach has the potential to reinforce stereotypes, behaviors, and attitudes that are not beneficial to an adolescent's gender identity perceptions or sexual identity development. To combat this stereotyping behavior, Scieszka advocates for teachers and parents to offer boys choices in selecting reading material. He also encourages boys to discard books that they do not have an interest in reading.[28] These practices have the potential to create safe spaces for males to develop healthy sexual identities.

Literature can also provide a safe space for exploration. For example, many adolescents who identify as homosexual have a difficult time reconciling their sexuality and often must do so alone. Since the publication of the first young adult novel to deal with issues of sexual identity, John Donovan's *I'll Get There, It Better Be Worth the Trip*, more than 200 novels have been published that deal with LGBTQIQ characters and conflicts.[29] Living vicariously through these characters and the struggles that they face allows readers to safely explore their sexuality in a nonthreatening environment.

Parents, teachers, and peers all have a tremendous influence on adolescents' sexual identity development. For example, one study on females' abilities to recognize sexism—defined as discrimination based on gender—found that parents, teachers, and male and female peer groups were all guilty of academic and athletic sexist practices, in both word and deed.[30] Surprisingly, teachers were identified as the most frequent offenders, specifically in regard to girls' academic abilities. For males, gender typing was found to be more common among fathers than mothers, particularly "in the socialization of traditionally male-dominated achievements."[31]

Once these gender roles have been established in the home and the school, it becomes more of a struggle for an adolescent to explore his or her sexuality options safely. Conversely, when teachers, parents, and mentors provide safe, supportive, and nonjudgmental environments where adolescents are allowed to explore their identity options, healthy sexual identities can be formed.

NOTES

1. Jeffrey J. Arnett, "G. Stanley Hall's Adolescence: Brilliance and Nonsense," *History of Psychology* 9, no. 13 (2006): 186.

2. Kenneth Keniston, *Youth and Dissent: The Rise of a New Opposition* (New York: Harcourt Brace Jovanovich, 1971), 4–5.

3. Jeffrey P. Moran, *Teaching Sex: The Shaping of Adolescence in the 20th Century* (Cambridge, MA: Harvard University Press), 2000, 15.

4. Moran, *Teaching Sex*, 20.

5. Moran, *Teaching Sex*, 21.

6. Arnett, "Brilliance," 187.

7. Jeffrey J. Arnett, "Emerging Adulthood: A Theory of Development from the Late Teens through the Twenties," *American Psychologist* 55, no. 5 (2000): 469–80.

8. Tracy L. Cross and Andrea Dawn Frazier, "Guiding the Psychosocial Development of Gifted Students Attending Specialized Residential STEM Schools," *Roeper Review* 32 (2010): 34.

9. Roland S. Persson, "Experiences of Intellectually Gifted Students in an Egalitarian and Inclusive Educational System: A Survey Study," *Journal for the Education of the Gifted* 33, no. 4 (2010): 548.

10. Persson, "Experiences," 549.

11. Cross and Frazier, "Guiding," 34.

12. Erik H. Erikson, *Childhood and Society*, 2nd ed. (New York: Norton, 1963), 262.

13. Erikson, *Childhood and Society*, 262–63.

14. Tara M. Dumas, Wendy E. Ellis, and David A. Wolfe, "Identity Development as a Buffer of Adolescent Risk Behaviors in the Context of Peer Group Pressure and Control," *Journal of Adolescence* 35, no. 4 (2012): 917–27.

15. World Health Organization, "What Do We Mean By 'Sex' and 'Gender'?" http://www.who.int/gender/whatisgender/en/.

16. Angela Oswalt, "The Development of Sexual Orientation," http://www.sevencounties.org/poc/view_doc.php?type=doc&id=41179&cn=1310.

17. Oswalt, "Development."

18. Simon LeVay, *Queer Science: The Use and Abuse of Research into Homosexuality* (Cambridge, MA: American Psychological Association, 1996).

19. Harold D. Grotevant, "Adolescent Development in Family Contexts," in *Handbook of Child Psychology: Social, Emotional, and Personality Development*, ed. N. Eisenberg (New York: Wiley, 1998), 3:1097–149; Harold D. Grotevant and Catherine R. Cooper, "Patterns of Interaction in Family Relationships and the Development of Identity Exploration in Adolescence," *Child Development* 56 (1985): 415–28.

20. Eric Dube and Ritch C. Savin-Williams, "Sexual Identity Development among Ethnic Sexual-Minority Male Youths," *Developmental Psychology* 35 (1999): 1389–98.

21. Tomer Shechner, "Gender Identity Disorder: A Literature Review from a Developmental Perspective," *Israel Journal of Psychiatry and Related Sciences* 47, no. 2 (2010): 42–48.

22. Al Cooper and Eric Griffin-Shelley, "The Internet: The New Sexual Revolution," in *Sex and the Internet: A Guidebook for Clinicians*, ed. Al Cooper (New York: Brunner-Routledge, 2002), 2.

23. Debra K. Braun-Courville and Mary Rojas, "Exposure to Sexually Explicit Web Sites and Adolescent Sexual Attitudes and Behaviors," *Journal of Adolescent Health* 45, no. 2 (2009): 156–62; Jane D. Brown and Kelly L. L'Engle, "X-Rated: Sexual Attitudes and Behaviors Associated with U.S. Early Adolescents' Exposure to Sexually Explicit Media," *Communication Research* 36 (2009): 129–51; Michael Flood, "Exposure to Pornography among Youth in Australia," *Journal of Sociology* 43 (2007): 45–60; Venhwei Lo and Ran Wei, "Exposure to Internet Pornography and Taiwanese Adolescents' Sexual Attitudes and Behavior," *Journal of Broadcasting and Electronic Media* 49 (2005): 221–37; Jochen Peter and Patti Valkenburg, "Adolescents' Exposure to Sexually Explicit Material on the Internet," *Communication Research* 33 (2006): 178–204; Janis Wolak, Kimberly J. Mitchell, and David Finkelhor, "Unwanted and Wanted Exposure to Online Pornography in a National Survey of Youth Internet Users," *Pediatrics* 119 (2007): 247–57.

24. Cooper and Griffin-Shelley, "The Internet," 2.

25. Angela E. Hubler, "Beyond the Image: Adolescent Girls, Reading, and Social Reality," *NWSA Journal* 12, no. 1 (2000): 84–99.

26. Michael Smith and Jeffrey Wilhelm, *Reading Don't Fix No Chevys: Literacy in the Lives of Young Men* (New York: Heinemann, 2002).

27. Jon Scieszka, GuysRead.com.

28. Scieszka, GuysRead.com.

29. Michael Cart and Christine A. Jenkins, *The Heart Has Its Reasons:Young Adult Literature with Gay/Lesbian/Queer Content, 1969–2004* (Lanham, MD: Scarecrow Press, 2006), xv.

30. Campbell Leaper and Christia Spears Brown, "Perceived Experiences with Sexism among Adolescent Girls," *Child Development* 79, no. 3 (2008): 685–704.

31. Leaper and Brown, "Perceived Experiences," 698.

Chapter Two

A Brief History of Sex Education in American Schools

A prominent life insurance expert [commented], "They called it a congress on school hygiene, but it was in reality a conference on sex education; there wasn't a section of the congress that at some point in its program did not jump the track to discuss certain phases of the sex problem." This was literally true. One of the largest audiences of the entire congress, numbering several thousand persons, assembled to hear President Eliot and the other speakers on the program of the annual meeting of the American Federation for Sex Hygiene. That the public is now thoroughly interested in the sex problem in all its various phases is certain. [1]—Fourth International Congress on School Hygiene, Buffalo, New York (November 1913)

This editorial, from the *American Journal of Public Health*, is an excellent insight into the social hygiene movement that began during the latter part of the nineteenth century and gained momentum in the early twentieth century. Social hygienists believed that "scientific promotion of well-being in childhood could prevent adult dysfunction." [2] Their goal was the promotion of a sex education agenda that would be supported and validated by advisors both moral and medical—a program that would call for the Victorian principles of self-discipline and social responsibility. Although many of the accusations associated with the perceived downfall of this Victorian morality were directed at women—prostitution and the spread of venereal disease, for instance—the sex education agenda seemed to be aimed primarily at males.

The Victorian morality that was prevalent in the late nineteenth and early twentieth centuries—the term *Victorian* elicits prudishness and repression—prescribed these concepts of self-discipline and social responsibility and was a major influence on most of what was then being marketed as sex education. The following description provides a canvas on which the early sex education programs were created:

> Women were considered the weaker, more innocent sex. She had little to no sexual appetite, often capturing all the sympathy and none of the blame over indiscretions. Men represented the fallen, sinful, and lustful creatures, wrongfully taking advantage of the fragility of women. However, this situation switched in the latter half of the period; women had to be held accountable, while the men, slaves to their katabolic purposes and sexual appetites, could not really be blamed.[3]

The early programs warned of the dangers of engaging in sex outside of marriage, but their primary target in the war against lack of self-control was masturbation, or "'self-abuse' as it was euphemistically known."[4] A prime illustration of the belief that masturbation had deleterious effects on males in particular can be found in the 1897 sex education book *What a Young Boy Ought to Know*, written by Sylvanus Stall, a retired Lutheran minister. *What a Young Boy Ought to Know* was not the first book of its kind, but it "set the tone for the sex education of teenagers for fifty years."[5] After several chapters dealing with God's purpose for reproductive organs, Stall proceeds to warn against masturbation, defining the act as "the manner in which the reproductive organs are injured in boys by abuse."[6] He explains that masturbation can lead to "idiocy, and even death. . . . Boys often have to be put in a straitjacket or their hands tied to the bedposts or to rings in the wall."[7] The *Journal of the American Medical Association* (1901) recommended the book, stating in part, "We find nothing from which to dissent, but much to commend."[8]

Victorian morality held that a man's sexual behavior was the key to his character. Engagement in impure activities such as masturbation would adversely affect his physical and mental health. Thus, educating against the ills of masturbation was a primary goal of early sex education. However, in 1917, the growth and standardization of these programs were bolstered when the United States made its formal declaration to enter the Great War. The military recognized the need to warn its men against the danger of prostitution, which many felt was the leading cause of venereal disease. The newly appointed secretary of war, Newton Baker, recognizing that the areas surrounding military bases were breeding grounds for prostitution, created the Commission on Training Camp Activities. Its purpose was to train soldiers in the areas of sexual education and social hygiene.[9] One of the commission's more interesting findings was that venereal disease was a more significant problem in civilian life than in military life. The findings estimated that five of every six soldiers who were infected had contracted the disease before military life.[10]

The U.S. Public Health Service quickly got on board to assist in the standardization of sex education materials. In 1918, it created a department dedicating public resources to sex education in public schools. The Venereal Disease Division's primary focus, as the name suggests, was to educate students about the dangers and risks of sexual activity.[11] The proponents of sex education in the schools were not as concerned with educating students, however, as they were with attempting to change America's sexual behavior, which many perceived as dangerous and immoral, and the schools were the ideal place to influence the most lives at a most critical age. By teaching about the dangers of masturbation and sex outside of marriage, it was believed that students would hear and heed the message.

In the late 1930s, Alfred Kinsey challenged this moral approach, stating, "The sex instruction which is gradually creeping into our science classrooms is animated by a desire to impose particular systems of morality, and as such, does not belong in our science teaching."[12] Kinsey's subsequent research, *Sexual Behavior in the Human Male* (1948) and *Sexual Behavior in the Human Female* (1953), revealed through extensive surveys that both male and female sexual behavior had not been accurately reflected, thus challenging the established moral code as the social ideal.[13] These findings were largely ignored when it came to sex education in the schools, which continued to focus on morality and instill the fear of masturbation, pregnancy, and venereal disease.

Flash forward to the 1970s. The ability to access condoms and other birth control methods without parental consent—thanks to the Supreme Court ruling *Griswold v. Connecticut* in 1965[14]—made it possible for adolescents to disassociate sexual intercourse and pregnancy as a natural cause and effect, thus lessening some of the fears associated with contracting a venereal disease. This, combined with the sexual revolution taking place at that time, motivated an attempt by some sex educators to promote more realistic and liberal sex agendas. Most schools did not buy into these types of programs, and they quickly disappeared.

The most common sex education approach continued to be diagrams of the sexual body parts and descriptions of their functions, followed by lurid examples of the dangers of any form of sexual activity outside of marriage.

By the mid-1980s, the fear of venereal disease and unwanted pregnancy was overshadowed by the fear of HIV and AIDS. In the early 1990s, many school districts began implementing sex education programs that focused exclusively on the prevention of contracting HIV, some as early as the first grade.[15] In the early grades, teachers were asked to emphasize how bodily fluids such as blood and saliva can transmit HIV. It is not until junior high that there is even a mention of sexual activity as a possible transmitter of HIV. Abstinence-only programs made a big comeback at this time, spearheaded by conservative Christian groups with strong political ties, such as Focus on the Family. Fueled by the fear of AIDS and a fallacious belief that sex education led to sexual indulgence, proponents were able to sell school districts on the idea that abstinence programs would thwart the sexual liberalism that they believed had resulted in the AIDS epidemic.[16]

During the George W. Bush administration, abstinence-only programs became the favored recipient of federal funds. From 1996 to 2005, nearly $1 billion in state and federal funding was allocated for abstinence-only education, despite a lack of evidence supporting the effectiveness of this approach.[17] But with the implementation of the federal No Child Left Behind program in 2001, school districts had too much on their plates in terms of required academic curriculum to concern themselves with sex education. By the late 1990s, many schools had abandoned sex education programs. Although discussions of sexual functions became part of required health classes in many schools, sex was not a central focus.

Is the future of sex education in America destined to repeat its mistakes? As recently as September 2013, a school district in Tulsa, Oklahoma, began implementing a plan to teach what they referred to as "comprehensive" sex education in the seventh, ninth, and eleventh grades. This program was a direct response to Oklahoma's status as the fourth-highest state for teen pregnancies. Citing the ineffectiveness of abstinence-only programs, Tulsa Public Schools spokesperson Steve Mayfield stated that to his knowledge, sex education classes that include information about contraception and STD protection have never been taught in Oklahoma schools.[18] Kim Schutz, the director of Oklahoma's Campaign to Prevent Teen Pregnancy, stated, "We really view the teen pregnancy prevention program as a dropout prevention program. This is really going to help students stay in school, finish school, go on to college, get good jobs, make Tulsa a better place to live."[19] In this case, "comprehensive," at least in terms of purpose, may be a bit overstated if the goal is simply to reduce teen pregnancy.

What has stayed consistent throughout the history of sex education is that it is less about a search for the truth and more a reflection of society's response to changes in sexual behavior.[20] Librarian and young adult literature expert Patty Campbell's statement in 1986 still holds true today:

> The most useful lesson to be learned from the history of sex education is humility. We will never get it right once and for all. Sexual styles and attitudes and behaviors and problems will continue to change, so that what seems to us today to be the ultimate word will appear out of date in ten years and ridiculous in twenty. Advice will continue to lag behind reality, because the people who write it form their sexual opinions twenty years earlier than the people who need it.[21]

The failure of sex education programs in schools to have any sort of measurable effect on students' sexual behavior may be attributed to several factors: the amount of time spent teaching the subject matter as a percentage of the overall curriculum is miniscule; the accountability for learning the content is nonexistent; and most important, there is a significant difference—we might go so far as to say disconnect—between the transmission and reception of sexual information and the accurate transference of that information to sexual behavior. In other words, just because students know what a condom is used for does not mean that they will use one.[22]

NOTES

1. "The Social Hygiene Movement," *American Journal of Public Health* 3, no. 11 (1913): 1154.

2. Theresa R. Richardson, *The Century of the Child: The Mental Hygiene Movement and Social Policy in the United States and Canada* (Albany: State University of New York Press, 1989), 3.

3. Elizabeth Lee, "Victorian Theories of Sex and Sexuality," http://www.victorianweb.org/gender/sextheory.html.

4. Jeffrey Moran, *Teaching Sex: The Shaping of Adolescence in the 20th Century* (Cambridge, MA: Harvard University Press, 2000), 10.

5. Patty Campbell, *Sex Guides: Books and Films about Sexuality for Young Adults* (New York: Garland, 1986), 7.

6. Campbell, *Sex Guides*, 10.

7. Campbell, *Sex Guides*, 10.

8. Campbell, *Sex Guides*, 10.

9. Nancy K. Bristow, "Commission on Training Camp Activities," in *Encyclopedia of War and American Society*, ed. Peter Karsten (Thousand Oaks, CA: Sage, 2005), http://knowledge.sagepub.com/view/war/n72.xml.

10. Allan M. Brandt, *No Magic Bullet: A Social History of Venereal Disease in the United States since 1880* (New York: Oxford University Press), 1987, 115.

11. Moran, *Teaching Sex*, 75.

12. "Sex Education Opposed as Unscientific," *School Science and Mathematics* 41, no. 355 (1941), 114; in Moran, *Teaching Sex*, 96.

13. Moran, *Teaching Sex*, 135.

14. Cornell University Legal Information Institute, "Griswold vs. Connecticut," 2013,   http://www.law.cornell.edu/supct/html/historics/USSC_CR_0381_0479_ZO.html.

15. New York and California both have HIV/AIDS prevention programs in place. California, as one example, has administered an HIV/AIDS program since 1992. California Department of Education, Comprehensive Sexual Health and HIV/AIDS Instruction, http://www.cde.ca.gov/ls/he/se/faq.asp.

16. Moran, *Teaching Sex*, 214.

17. Rebecca Wind, "New Studies Signal Dangers of Limiting Teen Access to Birth Control Information and Services: Researchers and Medical Experts Urge New Congress and State Legislatures to Heed Data," media release, January 18, 2005, https://guttmacher.org/media/nr/2005/01/18/index.html.

18. Rebecca Klein, "Tulsa Schools to Include Sex Education in Regular Curriculum for   the   First   Time,"   *Huffington   Post*,   September   4,   2013,   http://www.huffingtonpost.com/2013/09/04/tulsa-sex-education_n_3867876.html?utm_hp_ref=politics.

19. David Ferguson, "Oklahoma School District Giving Up on Abstinence-Only Education,"   September   4,   2013,   http://www.rawstory.com/rs/2013/09/04/oklahoma-school-district-giving-up-on-abstinence-only-education/.

20. Moran, *Teaching Sex*, 230.

21. Campbell, *Sex Guides*, 179.

22. Moran, *Teaching Sex*, 222.

Chapter Three

Sexual Content and the Canon

The term *canon* is derived from the Old English and Latin word meaning "church law" or "measuring line." The term is used to describe works that are considered sacred and genuine, or it can refer to the criteria by which works are judged.[1] The Western canon is a collection of literature that has been traditionally accepted by scholars as having shaped Western culture. There has been much debate over what should be included in the canon, with Harvard and the University of Chicago both establishing lists of books that they have deemed worthy. Traditionally, this collection has been considered required reading for incoming freshmen at the college/university level, although much of it is now found in sixth- through twelfth-grade classrooms across the country.

The formation of the canon began in 1891, when the National Council of Education met and appointed the Committee of Ten. The commissioner of education and nine men from leading universities across the country came together to restructure secondary education. They made recommendations on how the curriculum should change to better prepare students for entry into their universities. The Eliot report—named for the president of Harvard, Charles Eliot—outlined college entrance requirements for such subjects as Latin, geometry, and American history. They focused on details such as how much time should be spent on any one subject and what credits would be necessary for entering college. This was also the first attempt in America to

prescribe curriculum and the first attempt to list literature that secondary students should read before entering a university.

Harvard Classics was released in 1909. Approximately forty years
later, the University of Chicago created the Great Books of the Western
World program. The original series, published by Encyclopedia Britan-
nica, contained fifty-four volumes, but the list making has continued. It
was last updated in 1990 and now contains sixty volumes. According to
the editors, the three criteria necessary for a work to be considered part
of the canon are as follows: first, it must have historical value and be
relevant to contemporary issues; second, it must reward rereading;
third, it must be a part of the great conversation of great ideas. Great
Books notes that there are 102 of these great ideas, and for a work to be
considered, it must be relevant to at least 25 of them.[2] We were unsuc-
cessful in our attempts to locate these ideas and were informed by
several English professor colleagues that only the editors have access to
them.

YAL scholars have posed valid arguments for its inclusion in the
traditional literary canon or at least for its place alongside the canon in
classrooms. In *From Hinton to Hamlet: Building Bridges between
Young Adult Literature and the Classics*, Sara Hertz and Donald Gallo
encourage teachers to search for common themes that quality YAL
works share with the classic texts. For example, a teacher preparing a
three-week unit on *Lord of the Flies* might first assign the more accessible *Whale Talk,* by Chris Crutcher, focusing on the themes of the
abuse of power, good versus evil, peer pressure, and so on. When
students are then introduced to *Lord of the Flies*, they have had time to
wrestle with these themes and become more familiar with what to
expect when they read Golding's work.[3]

Pam Cole argues that the classics and YAL need not be viewed as
oppositional. She suggests that this conflict occurs in part because the
two are taught as separate courses in teacher preparation programs and
are taught to different groups of students in schools, with honor students being given access to the classics while YAL is offered up to
struggling readers.[4] If our goal as teachers is for students to comprehend what they read through textual analysis, to make connections with
deeper meanings, and, ultimately, to become effective critical thinkers,
the canon and YAL both offer opportunities for this learning to occur.

Others have suggested that for quality YAL titles to be considered
as having equal value as canonical literature, scholars must begin to
apply research methodology and literary theory to these books. In her

2006 article entitled "Literary Theory and Young Adult Literature: The Open Frontier in Critical Studies," Cindy Lou Daniels calls on literary critics to "take charge" and begin writing about YAL through a critical lens,[5] defined as "the discussion of literature undertaken in order to interpret its meaning and to evaluate its quality."[6]

A select few YA novels have become required school reading. Two examples are S. E. Hinton's *The Outsiders* and Laurie Halse Anderson's *Speak*, which can be found on middle school and high school reading lists across the country. Will more young adult novels become a part of this newly formed canon? This is certainly possible if, when choosing YAL to include on their reading lists, school district decision makers consider the three criteria used by Great Books to determine the classic canon. The young adult genre is filled with literature that possesses historical value, is relevant to contemporary issues, rewards re-reading, and most definitely has the potential to be part of the great conversation of great ideas.

For the purposes of this chapter, we will be looking solely at the classics that students in middle and high school are required to read. Most of these works were originally marketed to adults, and many of them contain sexual content. In addition, while numerous YAL titles are being challenged and removed from school bookshelves across the country, the books that compose the canon remain in classrooms, relatively unchallenged. The "this is what we've always done" mentality may be partly responsible for this, while the difficulty in comprehending the language may prevent many parents—the primary instigators of challenges—from realizing that these books contain sexual content.

Surprisingly, when we asked teachers from across the country how they dealt with discussions of sexual content in the canon (see Thoughts from Educators at the end of this chapter), most of them told us that they avoided the subject completely.[7] Many cited concerns over creating conflict with either administration or parents as the primary reason. In addition, although we are not convinced that avoiding the subject will prevent students from being aware, we do understand teachers' reticence in wanting to be the ones who are responsible for introducing a discussion about sex into the classroom. In this chapter, we attempt to lessen those fears by demonstrating that the inclusion of sexual content from the canon can be a beneficial teaching tool.

SPEAKING OF SEX

William Shakespeare: *Romeo and Juliet* and *Hamlet*

Shakespeare's work is fertile ground for teaching literary techniques. His use of simile, metaphor, dialogue, puns, and imagery is masterful. The effectiveness of these techniques often relies on sexual references. Consider the following frequently cited books dedicated to the subject:

- *Filthy Shakespeare: Shakespeare's Most Outrageous Sexual Puns*[8]
- *A Dictionary of Shakespeare's Sexual Puns and Their Significance*[9]
- *Shakespeare's Sexual Language: A Glossary*[10]
- *Shakespeare & Sexuality*[11]

Perhaps the most significant barrier to teaching Shakespeare is the complexity of his poetic language. This presents teachers with decisions about what and how they choose to translate the readings for students. Teachers may be reluctant to facilitate discussions that include sex, but these discussions can increase students' motivation to read and strengthen their comprehension skills. Geoff Sheehy, a high school English teacher in South Dakota, has composed several rules for teachers of Shakespeare. Rule 5 reads,

> Don't hide anything from them. When the Nurse makes a dirty joke, I don't hide it from students. Students love it and it helps them understand crucial relationships later in the play. I don't mean I explain every double entendre or crude pun, but seeing how obsessed the Nurse is with sex not only amuses us, it deepens our appreciation for how she later betrays Juliet. The Nurse's inappropriate jokes and the Capulets' servants' immature brawling hook and amuse my students, drawing them into the play; then, when the mood changes and tragedy enters, they are affected and even overwhelmed by it. Surely Shakespeare did this to us on purpose, and I would lessen the text if I hid these things from high school students.[12]

Romeo and Juliet might be Shakespeare's most accessible work, and it is taught to students as early as sixth grade. The dramatic structure that Shakespeare uses in *Romeo and Juliet*, the shifts between comedy and tragedy to heighten tension, and the addition and expansion of minor characters, such as the nurse and Mercutio, add to the dramatic impact of the story. Much of the comic relief is found in puns. The pun—"a play on words based on the similarity of sound between two words with different meanings"[13]—had humble beginnings. Shakespeare was often criticized for his use of them, but a good pun was always well received by the largely lower-class audience for whom his plays were performed, and they are now considered a staple of English literature.

Act 1, scene 1, of *Romeo and Juliet* opens with an abundance of sexual puns that no teacher should ignore. The meanings behind the sexual interchanges between the servants of the Capulet and Montague households are critical to the readers' understanding of the severity of the insults being thrown, as well as to their recognition of the use of puns. *No Fear Shakespeare* provides this translation of a conversation between two Capulet servants:

> **Sampson (original text):** 'Tis all one. I will show myself a tyrant. When I have fought with the men, I will be civil with the maids. I will cut off their heads.

> **Translation:** It's all the same. I'll be a harsh master to them. After I fight the men, I'll be nice to the women—I'll cut off their heads.

> **Gregory:** The heads of the maids?

> **Sampson (original text):** Ay, the heads of the maids, or their maidenheads. Take it in what sense thou wilt.

> **Translation:** Cut off their heads, take their maidenheads (virginity)—whatever. Take my remark in whichever sense you like.

> **Gregory (original text):** They must take it in sense that feel it.

> **Translation:** The women you rape are the ones who'll have to sense it.

> **Sampson (original text):** Me they shall feel while I am able to stand, and 'tis known I am a pretty piece of flesh.

> **Translation:** They'll feel me as long as I can keep an erection. Everybody knows I'm a nice piece of flesh. [14]

In the Folger's Shakespeare Library version of *Romeo and Juliet*, Sampson's lines "'Tis true, and therefore women, being the weaker vessels, are ever thrust to the wall. Therefore I will push Montague's men from the wall and thrust his maids to the wall" are explained in the notes in this way: "Here begins a series of sexual puns on 'thrust,' 'heads,' 'stand,' 'tool,' 'weapon.'"

In addition to the sexual references, in act 3, scene 5, readers find Romeo and Juliet in bed together after consummating their love. This scene is humorous because Romeo and Juliet try to deny that it is morning, knowing that Romeo will have to leave; it is also poignant because readers understand that this is the last time that the two star-crossed lovers will see each other. In this passage, Juliet denies the arrival of day and begs Romeo to stay:

> Yond light is not day-light, I know it, I;
> It is some meteor that the sun exhal'd
> To be to thee this night a torch bearer and light thee on thy way to Mantua.
> Therefore stay yet, though need'st not be gone.

Teachers who pair a version of the film with the text (in our humble opinion, the Franco Zefferelli version is the truest to the text) will have a difficult time avoiding a discussion of what happened before that scene, especially after students watch Romeo climb out of bed in his full naked glory.

The sexual content in *Romeo and Juliet* serves to heighten the dramatic effect of the story. Contemporary adolescents know that the most powerful insults are the ones directed at family, and in many cultures, this effect is amplified when the insults are directed by men toward women. As Geoff Sheehy points out, the use of bawdy language and sexual references serves to enhance students' understandings of the story and helps them to grasp the character's motivations. Students will struggle with recognizing and understanding puns if they are not privy to the meaning of a word such as *maidenhead* and how that word interacts or plays with the word *head* to create the pun. If a teacher does choose to explain the opening scene of *Romeo and Juliet* sans the explication of sexual puns, students need only go to the Internet, where many Shakespeare-related websites are available for their perusal.

Hamlet, another of Shakespeare's frequently taught plays, contains several scenes in which the prince pursues Ophelia in a sexual manner (typically translated as "courting"). Shakespeare's use of sexual puns is intended to add some relief to the overall mood of death and destruction that fills this play. Act 3, scene 2, illustrates the flirting that goes on between Ophelia and Prince Hamlet:

Hamlet (original text): Lady, shall I lie in your lap?

Translation: Can I lie on top of you? (They are in a public place.)

Ophelia: No, my lord.

Hamlet: I mean, my head upon your lap.

Ophelia: Ay, my lord.

Hamlet (original text): Do you think I meant country matters?

Translation: Did you think I wanted to have sex? (By placing the emphasis on the first syllable, the audience hears the word *cunt*.)

Ophelia (original text): I think nothing, my lord.

Translation: I can't acknowledge your sexual innuendos because I am an unmarried maid who isn't supposed to know that much about sex.

Hamlet (original text): That's a fair thought to lie between maids' legs.

Translation: That's exactly what is supposed to be in between your legs. (This is in response to her mention of nothing, which was a slang term for vagina. Hamlet's comment also serves to reinforce his *country* pun.)

Ophelia (original text): What is, my lord?

Translation: Stop it.

Hamlet (original text): Nothing.

Translation: Your vagina.[15]

Shakespeare included adult humor in his plays because they were written to be performed for adult audiences. Because the audiences understood the puns, they generated laughter, which was Shakespeare's intention. The complexity of Shakespeare's texts enables teachers to avoid discussions about sex, but this in turn prevents students from fully comprehending and appreciating the plays. If we are to teach Shakespeare to our students, we must teach with the context of audience and purpose in mind. When we choose to teach any piece of literature that was originally directed toward adult audiences, we are obligated to respect our students enough to offer it to them in an adult manner.

Geoffrey Chaucer: *The Canterbury Tales*

The Middle English language in *The Canterbury Tales* is difficult for most students to decipher without help from the teacher; therefore, it is critical that readers have a clear understanding of the context in which the tales are set. The pilgrimage is the vehicle that allows the characters to tell their stories each night around the campfire. These travelers are suffering the hardships of a long journey and desperately need some entertainment to help ease their burdens. In this type of setting, stories must be elaborate, exciting, and even exaggerated. Each storyteller wants to share the most memorable story. Chaucer, like Shakespeare, was writing for an adult audience; thus, the descriptions of sex are lewd, and the conduct of some of the men is vulgar. It is important that contemporary readers are provided with this background information to accurately analyze the characters and comprehend the stories.

Although many of the tales are sexual, *The Miller's Tale* is the most overt in its references. Lines 91–92 tell readers of a man named Nicholas, who enjoys conducting illicit love affairs:

> This clerk was cleped hende Nicholas.
> Of derne love he coude and of solas.

Chaucer tells us here that Nicholas was skilled ("cleped hende") in the pursuit of secret love ("derne") and solace ("solas"). *Solace* refers to the cure for love sickness—that is, having sex.[16] In medieval times, young bachelors believed that the only way to cure the illness of missing someone was to have sex with someone else (convenient, eh?). This did not necessarily mean employing a prostitute, although there were many available. Translation: Nicholas was very skilled at having illicit (secret) sex, likely with someone other than his spouse.

The word *cuckold*, a man who is cheated on by his wife, first appears in lines 117–18:

> For she was wilde and yong, and he was old
> And demed himself ben lyk a cokewold.

John is afraid that his wife, Alisoun, will make him a "cokewold" because he is getting older and is unable to satisfy her sexually. In lines 173–75, Nicholas says that he will die from this illness if he does not have sex with Alisoun (John's wife):

> And prively he caughte hire by the queynte,
> And seyde, "Y-wis, but if ich have my wille,
> For derne love of thee, lemman, I spille."

This is a rather romantic verse for the times. A man is professing his absolute need of a woman. Less romantic, of course, is how Nicholas describes grabbing Alisoun's "queynte" (genitals or, specifically, her cunt).[17] In lines 200–201, Nicholas goes on to say that he slapped Alisoun's butt ("lendes wheel").

> When Nicholas had doon thus everydeel,
> He thakked hire aboute the lendes weel,

The final section, lines 747–48, include "swyved," a vulgar term for sex. Nicholas not only has sex with Alisoun but does so in John's bed and feels no remorse.

> Thus swyved was this carpenteris wyf
> For al his keping and his jalousye.

The tale ends by explaining that despite's John's best attempts, he was cuckolded. The Miller goes on to explain that all men will be made cuckolds by their wives, and it is in their best interests to allow their wives to keep their private lives to themselves. *The Miller's Tale* provides teachers with opportunities to discuss how the inclusion of sex in setting and dialogue (specifically, the Miller's choice of story) illuminates character and develops plot.

THE MORAL OF THE STORY

Gustave Flaubert: *Madame Bovary*

Gustave Flaubert wrote one the first novels depicting extramarital sex. He and his publisher were put on trial for the violation of public morals soon after the release of *Madame Bovary*. Both were acquitted, but the trial caused Flaubert to protest what he perceived as detestable middle-class public morals.[18] In the dedication section of the republication of the novel, Flaubert thanks his lawyer for getting him acquitted. He continued to speak out against public morals in subsequent publications.

Madame Bovary tells the story of Emma Bovary, a married woman educated in a convent who has an affair with a wealthy man named Rodolphe. The following passage describes the initiation of the affair. It feels tame by today's standards but at the time was considered one of the most risqué scenes in the novel: "The cloth of her habit caught against the velvet of his coat. She threw back her white neck, swelling with a sigh, and faltering, in tears, with a long shudder and hiding her face, she gave herself up to him."

Later in the novel, Rodolphe dumps Emma, and Léon Dupris, a law clerk who has been lusting after her, orchestrates a rendezvous with her at a church she is visiting. Emma likes and respects Léon, and she eventually allows him to pull her away from the church. He suggests that they take a cab (carriage) ride around the park, and Emma half-heartedly and unsuccessfully attempts to resist Léon's charms: "Oh, Léon! Really—I don't know whether I should . . . !" she simpers. Then in a serious tone: "It's very improper, you know." Flaubert then gives readers a two-page description of the couple's cab ride. Flaubert doesn't actually show us what is happening in that cab, but it does not take long for readers to draw some solid conclusions:

> From his seat the coachman now and again cast a desperate glance at a café. He couldn't conceive what locomotive frenzy was making these people persist in refusing to stop. He tried a few times, only to hear immediate angry exclamations from behind. . . . Along the river from amidst the wagons and the barrels, along the streets, the bourgeois on the corners stared wide-eyed at this unheard of spectacle—a carriage with drawn blinds that kept appearing and reappearing, sealed tighter than a tomb and tossing like a ship.

The passage concludes with this: "Finally, at about six-o'clock, the carriage stopped in a side street near the Place Beauviosine. A woman got out and walked off, her veil down, without a backward glance."

Madame Bovary made such an impact on society that "a year after the publication of the novel, cabs in Hamburg, Germany, could be rented for sexual dalliance; they were known as 'Bovaries.'"[19] This was certainly not a result that Flaubert intended. He wrote the novel to protest public morals in France during the 1850s, and he felt that the book adequately portrayed life in Paris at the time. He found the outward displays of sex in Paris to be disgusting and did not hide this fact.

He has since been hailed as a realist. Ironically, Flaubert was put on trial for the same indecencies that he despised. All of this suggests the importance of discussing the author's purpose, which necessitates a discussion of sex.

This classic tale offers readers a realistic peek into the sexual attitudes and mores of 1856 France. An understanding of these attitudes and mores is critical to a reader's understanding of the story. Furthermore, classroom discussions that focus on fictional attitudes toward sex—specifically, sex outside of marriage—will provide students with opportunities to make historical and contemporary text-to-text, text-to-self, and text-to-world connections, resulting in a much more effective learning experience than that of a "just say no" abstinence-only sex education approach. That readers do not witness the sexual act is no excuse to ignore its existence.

Nathaniel Hawthorne: *The Scarlet Letter*

The Scarlet Letter is set during the time of the Puritans and tells the story of Hester Prynne, who becomes pregnant while her husband is residing in America. The story opens with Hester walking out of prison holding a baby. Rather than reveal the name of her sexual partner, Hester accepts the punishment of the town alone and is forced to wear a scarlet-colored "A" on her clothing. Readers later discover that the man with whom she committed adultery was the town minister, Dimmesdale. As in *Madame Bovary*, readers do not witness any sexual acts in *The Scarlet Letter*, but the opening scene makes it clear that Hester's baby was not conceived by immaculate conception. The theme of adultery becomes magnified when readers discover that Hester's partner was the town minister—who then does not take responsibility for his actions.

Hawthorne is known as one of the dark Romantics because his stories often have moral messages with deep psychological complexity that focus on evil and the sin of humanity. Hawthorne was a direct descendent of Judge Hathorne (great grandfather), who presided over the Salem witch trials. Judge Hathorne was the only judge who never repented for his actions, and he continued to proclaim that the nineteen women who were murdered deserved to die for their sins.

Hawthorne frequently wrote about female protagonists who suffered hardships. His motivation for writing these stories, at least in part, comes from the intense guilt that he felt because of his family name. He went so far as to change the spelling of his name to include a "W," a poor attempt to disguise the familial relationship.[20] Much of Hawthorne's work includes allegories that contain Puritan inspiration. To understand the author's perspective, it is important that readers explore the problems that he had with religion and the way that women were treated at the time.

For example, in the prologue to *The Scarlet Letter*, entitled "The Custom House," Hawthorne describes himself as the narrator who discovers the story of Hester Prynne. His point of view serves as his fictional commentary on the realities of the Puritan times. The author's sympathetic treatment of Hester and her sin of adultery reflects his purpose: to reveal the unfair treatment of women and the blame placed on them. Hawthorne's classic provides great opportunities for discussions on family, relationships, and accountability. As the criterion for inclusion in the canon states, *The Scarlet Letter* contains big ideas that are still worth considering.

Dante Alighieri: *The Divine Comedy* (*Inferno*)

Inferno (Italian for "Hell") is the first part of Dante Alighieri's three-part epic poem *The Divine Comedy*. Dante wrote the poem in the fourteenth century as an allegory of his journey through Hell, guided by Virgil, the blind Roman poet. In *Inferno*, Hell is described as having nine circles. In the first circle, Limbo, virtuous pagan souls wander aimlessly. The second circle is reserved for those who have committed the capital sin of lust—adulterers and those who have participated in "sensual love." Lust is the first sin to be punished in Hell. Souls in the second circle are blown around in a violent storm.

Sexual acts are not graphically described in *Inferno*, but clear distinctions of love, sex, and lust are explored. Those who fall in love, get married, and have sex are viewed as virtuous. Those who commit adultery while married or experience lust without action are "carnal sinners who subordinate reason to desire."[21] Although it appears as though Dante views this sin as the first to be punished (likely representative of the original sin of Adam and Eve), he places this circle of Hell the farthest from Satan, marking it as the least serious offense.

Sex is also mentioned in the seventh circle, where Dante discusses the punishment for sodomy (sex between two males). In Dante's time, sex between adult and adolescent males was common, but it was condemned by the Christian church. Those who suffer here must face the third ring of the seventh circle, where they wander a barren plain of sand ignited by flakes of fire.

In the eighth and ninth circles, the two lowest circles of hell, Dante deals with those who have committed different types of fraud. The two circles are connected by a bridge that separates those who commit fraud on strangers from those who commit fraud on close acquaintances. This section becomes sexual when Dante includes those who sell false love—flatterers, pimps, and prostitutes—in his definition of fraud. The pimps and prostitutes are whipped by horned demons, while the flatterers are dipped in excrement.

If students are to understand *Inferno*, they will need to process all that transpires in each circle of Hell, including the role that sex plays in several circles. Dante is meticulous in his descriptions of the differences between lust and love. With proper explication, readers will not misunderstand what he believes to be the differences between right and wrong. He leans heavily on Christianity and his interpretation of the Bible, specifically his moral judgments on sex, offering teachers a logical contextual starting point for instruction.

This judgmental approach may cause some teachers to avoid any discussion that involves sex, but it seems incomprehensible that a discussion of Hell can take place without some mention of sex and its place in any society. *Inferno* is an allegory that points to characteristics of the people and the society of Dante's age. His journey through Hell represents his—and every human being's—experience with weaknesses and sinfulness. *Inferno* is part of the canon because the big ideas that it confronts are still big ideas today. This masterpiece offers teachers the chance to engage students in meaningful discussions about societal attitudes toward sex while introducing and reinforcing the concepts of allegory and symbolism.

Leo Tolstoy: *Anna Karenina*

Written in the nineteenth century, *Anna Karenina* tells the story of a young married woman who has an extramarital affair with an even younger man, gives birth to his child, then commits suicide because she thinks that her lover is cheating on her. Adultery and betrayal are major themes.

In the opening scene, Anna arrives home only to find her family in turmoil over the discovery of her brother's womanizing ways. Anna is then seduced by Vronsky, who is eager to marry her if she will just leave her husband. Anna becomes increasingly possessive of her spouse, imagining that he is having affairs. Kitty, Anna's sister-in-law, believes that she is in love with Vronsky and is hurt by his obsession with Anna. Anna at first refuses Vronsky's advances but then gives in and begins an affair with him. After confessing the affair to her husband and having Vronsky's child, her sexual and passionate relationship with Vronsky begins to fade:

> And though she felt sure that his love for her was waning, there was nothing she could do, she could not in any way alter her relations to him. Just as before, only by love and by charm could she keep him. And so, just as before, only by occupation in the day, by morphine at night, could she stifle the fearful thought of what would be if he ceased to love her.

Anna Karenina was written as a romantic novel for adults. Several characters in the story participate in complicated sexual relationships that serve to humanize the themes of deceit and adultery. Teachers who want to engage in critical discussions that focus on characters' motivations, plot development, and author's purpose should not overlook the sexual content.

THE MYTH OF SEX

Sophocles: *Oedipus* and *Antigone*

Oedipus the King, *Oedipus at Colunus*, and *Antigone* all feature Oedipus, a classic tragic hero in Greek mythology. These plays are often taught in conjunction with other pieces from Greek mythology that focus on the themes of humanity's flawed nature and an individual's powerlessness against destiny.

Oedipus's life begins badly. His father, the king, hears of a prophecy predicting that Oedipus will murder him, so shortly after his birth, he nails his son to a mountainside and leaves him to die. Oedipus is found and raised by shepherds, having no idea that his birth father and mother are the king and queen. Oedipus eventually rises to power, where he ultimately kills his father and, fulfilling the other half of the prophecy, marries his mother, the queen. He has sex with his mother and has four children with her before realizing that she is his mother and that he killed his father. The queen then takes her own life, and Oedipus drives pins into his eyes to blind himself.

The character of Oedipus inspired Sigmund Freud's psychoanalytical condition, the Oedipus complex, which he described as a boy's childhood desire to kill his father and marry and have sex with his mother. The mother half of the Oedipus complex is arguably the most commonly referred to in discussions. Thankfully, Sophocles does not include graphic sex scenes in these plays, but sex is a significant reason why the plays are considered tragedies. Acknowledging the role that sex plays can lead to discussions on psychological development and societal mores.

Homer: *The Iliad* and *The Odyssey*

Aphrodite, the goddess of love and desire, is one of the main characters in *The Iliad*. In several scenes, she inspires sex by giving aphrodisiacs to other women. She also causes the Trojan War by promising a married woman to another man, which causes them to have an affair and fall in love.

One particularly sexual and violent scene describes Zeus bragging to his wife about sleeping with at least thirty other women while they were married. Zeus also discusses raping women, particularly Leda, Helen's mother. He also rapes Europa and Ganymede, a young boy. Zeus is not the only character who commits rape. King Laius (from the stories of Oedipus) rapes Chrysippus (a male). The crime of Laius—a term applied to all male rape—spawned the prophecy about Laius's son Oedipus, who is responsible for the deaths of Laius's entire extended family.

The Odyssey centers on Odysseus's acts of infidelity. Odysseus is doomed by the gods, for various reasons, to remain at war and apart from his wife. He is first trapped by Calypso, who is described as "a nymph, immortal and most beautiful, who craves Odysseus for her own." She proves to be the perfect mate, and Odysseus remains with her for seven years. It is only after other gods get involved and force Calypso to stop having sex with Odysseus that he is able to leave her island. Hermes brings the news to Calypso, and she responds:

> You gods are unbearable in your jealousy: you stand aghast at goddesses who openly sleep with men, if ever one of them wants to make a man her bedmate.[22]

Once Odysseus leaves Calypso in an attempt to return to his wife, he lands on the isle of Circe. Odysseus and his men participate in an orgy, gorging themselves on food and having sex with multiple women. Circe understands that the travelers miss their homes, but these desires can be assuaged with alcohol, sex, and drugs—and Circe, being a witch, knows her drugs. While they are drugged, she turns all of Odysseus's men into grunting swine, the epitome of men in sexual heat. This is likely the derivation of the term *sexist pig.*[23]

Classroom teachers often pair film versions[24] of these epics with the texts as a way to bolster student comprehension. The films contain a number of sex scenes; therefore, anyone choosing to use the films will be compelled to address the content or edit it out. Doing the latter would severely impede a student's comprehension of the stories.

THOUGHTS FROM EDUCATORS

We asked middle and high school teachers and university professors who prepare teachers[25] to answer the following question: How do you address the sexual content in the literature that you teach to students?

Bob, a teacher education professor, expressed an unwillingness to address sexual content:

> Sex in literature is the last thing I would know about. I've avoided it in my classes because there are always some people who get offended, usually for different reasons. So, you can't win. As a practical matter, professors and teachers self-censor. Professors, because you'll run afoul of competing versions of political correctness, and teachers because they will get accused of everything imaginable.

Elaine, a ninth-grade English teacher shared similar sentiments:

> When I teach *Speak*, we don't discuss the rape or sexual content at all. The focus is primarily about what happens when a girl is bullied and how difficult it is to deal with being condemned by your peers in high school. That is a much more important and relevant topic in today's time. In addition, parents are much less likely to complain about us teaching a lesson on bullying over a lesson on rape or rape culture.

Keith, a Shakespeare scholar and teacher educator, said,

We discuss the ambiguities of language in Shakespeare's day (for instance, stand could mean "to stand" while it could mean "to have an erection"). Shakespeare, I show students, was playing with the multiple meanings of language, and his audience would have been attuned to this reality. Having been a high school teacher myself, I often have conversations with teacher candidates about how to handle the sexual content. We discuss why Shakespeare seems to "get a pass" from the book-burning crowd because he's Shakespeare, even though his works are full of references to body parts and sex (just take a peek at *Romeo and Juliet*, that fixture in most ninth-grade classrooms!). My discussions with practicing teachers are often fascinating, as some of them—depending on their school district—must navigate treacherous waters to teach books with even a hint of sexual content. I feel teachers have a responsibility to model for students how to talk maturely about sexual content in literature, thinking about it in relation to the story being told and what it adds to the narrative arc of a character.

Mary, a high school English teacher, commented,

I present sex as the author has presented it, but after discussing the scene/content with the class, I offer my interpretation of the content and discuss why I think it is valuable and necessary to the overall structure of the novel. Sex is a predominant theme that is weaved through the fabric of society. Unfortunately, our society has made it taboo. Literature is no exception. Teachers deal with teenagers who are in the early stages of their sexual explorations. Each year, thousands of students are getting pregnant, yet people are afraid to talk about sex with this group. I know that some teachers will skip the subject altogether. Sadly, I don't believe this helps. Discussion leads to thought. Thought leads to growth.

Dennis, another high school English teacher, stated,

I hope I present sexual content as the author intends it. Sexuality allows the human species to continue; naturally, then, the sexual urge must be one of man's strongest urges. The books I teach deal in small ways with the power and consequences of lust, with the power and consequences of loveless marriages, with the coexistence of life and death, and with confusion over the power of attraction and physical need. Frequently, sex is not even the primary theme in these books. Sexuality is simply acknowledged as one of the forces that acts upon humans.

Although we have selected quotes here that represent both sides of the argument for teaching sexual content, the majority of participants that we surveyed indicated that they avoid teaching sexual content in both YAL and the canon. This seems counterproductive to us. We agree with Keith that the sexual content in canonical literature was intended to be meaningful to its intended audience (adults), and if teachers are requiring their students to read these works, then they have a responsibility to be mindful of each author's purpose, as well as the setting and historical context of each novel. If we are requiring students to read adult content, then we should treat them as adults or choose alternative texts.

Most canonical literature was written so long ago that it contains dead language and scenarios that are far removed from present-day adolescent experiences. This can cause younger, more inexperienced readers to miss much of an author's intended meaning. Teachers who choose to avoid any discussions of sex can certainly benefit from their readers' lack of experience, by relying on the complexity of language to hide references that they are unwilling to uncover for their students. However, because the lasting positive impact that literature has on readers depends on the connections that they make with those texts, don't we owe it to our students to fully engage them in the experience?

NOTES

1. Online Etymology Dictionary, http://www.etymonline.com/index.php?term=canon.

2. Mialton Meyer, *Robert Maynard Hutchins: A Memoir* (Berkeley: University of California Press, 1993), 305.

3. Sarah K. Hertz and Donald R. Gallo, *From Hinton to Hamlet: Building Bridges between Young Adult Literature and the Classics*, 2nd ed. (Westport, CT: Greenwood Press, 2005), 28, 59–60. See also, Joan Kaywell, ed. *Adolescent Literature as a Complement to the Classics: Addressing Critical Issues in Today's Classroom* (Lanham, MD: Rowman & Littlefield, 2010).

4. Pam Cole, *Young Adult Literature in the 21st Century* (New York: McGraw-Hill, 2009), 513.

5. Cindy Lou Daniels, "Literary Theory and Young Adult Literature: The Open Frontier in Literary Studies," *ALAN Review* (winter 2006).

6. David L. Russell, *Literature for Children*, 5th ed. (Boston: Pearson, 2005), 48.

7. All teacher survey results were obtained via e-mail communications between August 8 and September 20, 2013.

8. Pauline Kiernan, *Filthy Shakespeare: Shakespeare's Most Outrageous Sexual Puns* (New York: Gotham, 2008).

9. Frankie Rubinstein, *A Dictionary of Shakespeare's Sexual Puns and Their Significance* (New York: Palgrave Macmillan, 1995).

10. Gordon Williams, *Shakespeare's Sexual Language: A Glossary* (New York: Bloomsbury Academic, 2006).

11. Catherine M. S. Alexander and Stanley Wells, eds., *Shakespeare and Sexuality* (New York: Cambridge University Press, 2001).

12. Geoff Sheehy, "A Teacher's Writes: One Teacher's Thoughts on Life, Literature, and Learning," blog, http://ateacherswrites.wordpress.com/2009/03/04/how-to-teach-shakespeare-to-high-school-students-a-few-basics-from-one-who-does-it/.

13. William Harmon and Hugh Holman, *A Handbook to Literature*, 10th ed. (New York: Pearson, 2006), 423.

14. Sparknotes, "No Fear Shakespeare, *Romeo and Juliet*," nfs.sparknotes.com/romeojuliet.

15. Sparknotes, "No Fear Shakespeare."

16. Laura C. Lambdin, *Chaucer's Pilgrims: An Historical Guide to the Pilgrims in "The Canterbury Tales"* (Westport, CT: Greenwood, 1999).

17. Online Etymology Dictionary, http://www.etymonline.com/index.php?term=cunt.

18. Henry James, *Notes on Novelists* (New York: Charles Scribner's Sons, 1914).

19. Barnaby Conrad, *101 Best Sex Scenes Ever Written: An Erotic Romp through Literature for Writers and Readers* (Fresno, CA: Quill Driver, 2011), 7.

20. In Arthur Miller's *The Crucible*, Hawthorne's great grandfather stars as one of the presiding judges who condemned the twenty-six women and five men to death. In addition to the witch trials, a subplot of adultery is once again present here, thus making this an excellent companion piece.

21. Dante, "Inferno," 5.38–5.39.

22. Homer, *The Odyssey*, public domain.

23. "Sexual Fables: Homer's Women," http://sexualfables.com/homers_women.php.

24. Such as Francis Ford Coppola's *The Odyssey*, starring Armand Assante, 1997, and Mario Camerini's *Ulysses*, starring Kirk Douglas, 1955.

25. The teachers we surveyed were from Arizona, Georgia, Nebraska, Washington, and New York.

Chapter Four

Sexual Content in the Early Days of Young Adult Fiction: 1950s–1980s

THE TRAILBLAZER:
MARGARET ALEXANDER EDWARDS (1902–1988)

Margaret Edwards was a leader in the development of library services to teenagers. Although Edwards retired in 1962—five years before the establishment of a young adult genre[1]—her relentless commitment to get the right books into the hands of teens, books that would broaden their experiences and help them seek truth, was groundbreaking and controversial.[2]

The term *young adult* was introduced to the library world in 1937 with the publication of *The Public Library and the Adolescent*.[3] The author, recognizing the need for a public library space for teens in the wake of its burgeoning popularity, wrote the book primarily as an instructional guide for cataloging book collections for young adult rooms. Edwards recognized that the books being offered in these rooms did not provide teens with the types of experiences that she felt were necessary, so she went to great lengths, including rushing around her huge library and searching through the stacks to find something appropriate (at least according to one of her coworkers).[4]

Edwards did not avoid the topic of sex when trying to locate the right book for a teen, but because the young adult genre was then nonexistent, she often found these books in the adult stacks. In her seminal work *The Fair Garden and the Swarm of Beasts: The Library and the Young Adult* (1969), Edwards lists her suggestions for novels that contain sexuality, including *Wuthering Heights, Gone with the Wind*, and *Of Human Bondage.*

More significant than her choice of books, however, were her thoughts on sexual content in the literature that young adults should read. Edwards had this to say on the subject of sex and literature for adolescents:

> Many adults seem to think that if sex is not mentioned to adolescents, it will go away. On the contrary, it is here to stay and teenagers are avidly interested in it. They will find out all they can about it and wise adults will make available reliable books that tell them what they wish to know. There are excellent factual books on the market, but the best novels on the subject go beyond the facts to the emotional implications of love. Too many adults wish to protect teenagers when they should be stimulating them to read of life as it is lived. When a story is true to life and well written, the teenager will do well to arm himself with whatever experience such a book has to give him. . . . The best books, old and new, have a richer and more subtle message about sex for the adolescent than he will hear from his peers. Certainly, they will supplement whatever truths he may glean from a conscientious but sometimes tongue-tied parent.[5]

THE CONSEQUENCES OF BEING A
(FICTIONAL) SEXUALLY PROMISCUOUS TEEN

The first authors to include sexually active teens in their novels devoted the majority of pages to the aftermath of *the act*. The sex scene itself was often avoided altogether or presented through the point of view of the female character, whose thoughts and actions focused less on the physical act and more on the emotional impact of what was occurring. The primary consequence of premarital sex in these early novels was pregnancy, which then triggered a massive loss of opportunities—high school graduation, college, a promising football career, friends . . . the list goes on. All these stories contained elements that served to create the illusion that the 1950s and 1960s were sexually conservative decades. Even as the research of Kinsey and Masters and Johnson was exposing misperceptions regarding the frequency and variety of sexual behaviors that were actually occurring behind closed doors, these books attempted to portray adolescence—just as G. Stanley Hall had done in the early twentieth century—as a time of risk taking, fraught with dire consequences. Furthermore, it was the responsibility of parents and teenagers alike to curb such behavior, lest lives be ruined.

Two and the Town, by Henry Gregor Felsen (1952)

Margaret Edwards called *Two and the Town* "one of the first teenage novels to deal with the boy and girl who 'had to get married'" and said of the story, "The boy's resentment at losing a chance to play college football, the girl's embarrassment at being asked by the school principal not to come back to school, and the coming of the baby are skillfully handled."[6] Although Edwards supported the book, the American Library Association panel ultimately decided that Felsen's story was "too hot to handle."[7] A 2013 rereading of *Two and the Town* reveals several reasons why today's readers might consider this cautionary tale of the relationship between high school seniors Buff and Elaine more of an instruction manual on what not to do than realistic young adult fiction.

The third-person omniscient narration in *Two and the Town* jumps in and out of the characters' thoughts, sometimes from one sentence to the next. The narrator's voice is decidedly adult, and because the parents of both teens are given significant "air time," the novel provides many opportunities for sage wisdom and advice. On several occasions, readers witness both Buff's and Elaine's parents discussing their children's well-being after the teens have left the scene. The dialogue of the adults does not serve to develop their characters or those of the teens but instead provides the narrator with opportunities to preach. For example, in the following passage, Elaine's father tells his wife why he feels that it is important that Buff come to the house and meet them before they allow him to date their daughter: "It's not safe to let girls out the way so many parents let them run. They have feelings and no judgment, these young ones."[8]

At times, the teens' thoughts feel more like those of hurt and resentful parents than those of teenagers. Here, Buff ponders his parents' role in his life: "They were his parents, people who saw that he was fed, clothed, provided with a home, educated, supplied with money when needed, protected when in trouble. In exchange, they were allowed to restrict his freedom when they wished to; had the right to ask him questions about his activities . . . to expect that he mow the lawn, run errands, wash the car."[9]

Buff is the star football player for his high school football team. After his team loses the big game, he sees his girlfriend Carol dancing with a player from the opposing team and, feeling betrayed, looks to Elaine, the only girl who seems to be sympathetic toward him at that moment. Buff and Elaine drive to a deserted part of town, where he proceeds to kiss her. The narration makes it clear that Buff is in the moment and does not care about Elaine as much as he cares that there is someone, anyone there to comfort him. Elaine, however, truly cares for Buff. We are told that she likes what is happening between them but feels the need to resist. Finally, Elaine realizes that "Buff was beyond rational thinking,"[10] and "the act" takes place.

> And Elaine, sensing at last that Buff was beyond reason, that he was in the grip of his emotions, wondered where to draw the line, felt she had gone too far already, and wanted to cry out and save herself. But she had waited too long, and when she cried faintly she didn't know whether she cried halt or hurry. She became as furiously unrestrained as Buff himself, made one last, frightened effort to break away, and, in a situation where Carol would have laughed and saved herself, Elaine wept and was lost.[11]

This was quite the racy passage in 1952, not due to the description or, more accurately, the implication, but due to the age of the participants. The fact that Buff and Elaine were both still in high school is referenced frequently by virtually every adult in the story. This was to be the first of many sexual situations in which the female is in love and "allows" sex to happen while the male is portrayed as simply pursuing his animal urges.

Once Elaine discovers that she is pregnant, readers are made aware of her pregnancy in this one line: "The doctor was definite, and that left only one course of action."[12] The consequences resulting from the pregnancy then begin to rain down upon the two teenagers. Buff and Elaine are forced to marry; their friends shun them; and Elaine is pulled from school. She begins to sense that Buff is resentful about being forced into marriage, his future hopes for college football ruined. As they are embarking on their honeymoon, Elaine looks at Buff and thinks,

> To be forced into marriage with a boy who hated her—to be forced to live together, to see each other all the time, reminding each other of the unhappiness they had brought upon themselves. . . . They made us

marry to protect me from shame, she thought. But what greater shame than to live with a boy who hates you, who will hate your baby. [13]

Buff and Elaine are set up in a vacant house owned by her father's construction company. Buff frequently comes home late, often drunk, and he encourages Elaine to stay at home. For example, when she offers to come watch him play in a company softball tournament, Buff discourages her, embarrassed to be seen with a pregnant woman. Buff eventually runs away from his responsibilities and joins the marines but is injured during boot camp. When he returns home, he is no longer a boy but a wiser man, suddenly prepared to take care of his new wife and baby. Despite being ostracized by friends and forced to "grow up" before they were ready, and despite their—according to the book's cover—"Teen-age emotions out of control"—Buff and Elaine keep their baby and try to make a go at a happy marriage.

A Girl Like Me, by Jeanette Eyerly (1966)

Robin James is an intelligent, perceptive, but not extremely popular high school teenager who is introduced to and becomes friendly with Cass, a girl who runs with the "fast" crowd. Cass suggests that Robin go on a blind date with her and her friend Randy and her boyfriend, Brewster Bailey Winfield III. Robin soon discovers that Randy and others in the fast crowd—people with names such as Pris Gosling and Biz Dudevant, names that try too hard to sound aristocratic—are dangerous people to be around. Randy is clearly only interested in getting physical with Robin, but Robin adeptly manages to fend him off. Eventually, Robin's parents forbid her to see him, but Randy persists. One evening after Robin's parents leave the house, Randy appears at Robin's door:

> "Listen baby. Quit clowning. Let's give the thing we've got going a chance. Why else do you think I've been hanging around your house for the last three nights, waiting for a chance to see you alone. All alone."
>
> For a moment, Robin felt dizzy, confused, a little ill. . . . Somewhere out there . . . the perfect boy would come along. He would know her when he found her—and she would know him. Although at this distance she could not hope to see his face, one thing was clear. It wasn't Randy. . . .
>
> "Sorry, Randy," she said softly. "Not tonight. Not ever." With a firm hand she closed the little brass door. [14]

Once Robin has been established as a strong and morally credible character, readers soon discover that Cass is not as forceful or persuasive with Brewster. From a brief reference, we learn that Cass and Brewster "hooked up" at a party, when Robin was looking for the couple so that she could get a ride home. Cass and Brewster had suddenly disappeared, and no one knew where they were. A couple of months later at school, Robin finds Cass sick in the girl's bathroom. She has missed two periods.

Robin searches the phone book for a doctor so that Cass can confirm the pregnancy. On the way to the appointment, they stop by a five-and-dime store to purchase a cheap wedding ring and then sign in at the doctor's office using the name Mrs. Bailey, both attempts to fool the doctor into believing that Cass is married. The doctor sees through the ruse, and Cass is forced to tell her parents. She is immediately sent to a hospital for unwed mothers.

A Girl Like Me is told from Robin's point of view, and because she is a responsible teen who makes wise, moral decisions, she is given the role of judgmental narrator. As a result, her narration feels a bit less parental and overbearing (just a little) than the narration in *Two and the Town*. Cass and Brewster do not continue their relationship once she is sent off to live at the hospital—a hospital that, from its description, feels more like the mental ward from *One Flew over the Cuckoo's Nest* than a nurturing, caring place for unwed mothers.

Ultimately, Cass, like Elaine, will not consider abortion. But when Brewster finally comes to visit her and offers marriage, Cass reveals her plans to put her new baby up for adoption:

> "*Your* kid? Don't make me laugh!" Cass said. Her bitter caroling laugh shattered the silence of the room, then from somewhere the control that she had so briefly lost returned. "He's not going to be your kid, Brew," she said, softly. "And he's not going to be my kid, either. He's going to be the kid of somebody who gets married to stay married. Somebody who will love him whether he's a great athlete or not."[15]

Mr. and Mrs. Bo Jo Jones, by Ann Head (1967)

In 1967, a young adult genre known as "the new realism" was born. What set this genre apart from preceding novels featuring teens as the main characters were the voices of those characters. Though not immune to the devastating consequences that always seemed to follow teens' bad choices, the new realism gave young adults an adolescent voice instead of an adult voice hidden inside an adolescent's body. Several hard-hitting novels written for teens were released that year, including S. E. Hinton's *The Outsiders*, Robert Lipsyte's *The Contender*, and *Mr. and Mrs. Bo Jo Jones*. *Bo Jo Jones* was originally marketed as an adult novel, but less than a year later, it was released as a paperback and marketed to high schoolers.[16] On the front cover of the paperback edition beneath the title was this quote: "She's sixteen, he's seventeen, a pregnant bride, a bewildered groom . . . playing a grown-up game with adult consequences."[17]

Ann Head's novel does share several similarities with *Two and the Town* and *A Girl Like Me*. Two teens, emotions out of control, have sex and pay the price—pregnancy and its consequences. Parents function as the voices of reason and morality, while the teens struggle to make what they feel are the right choices. The reason that *Bo Jo* feels more like young adult fiction can be largely credited to the character of July, the female narrator of the story, who feels and sounds more like a teenager (albeit a very mature one) than either Robin or Elaine. In the opening line of the story, July tells us, "With much talk about teen-age marriages, I feel, for whatever it may be worth to some young people on the brink of same, that I should tell about mine."[18] This serves to establish July as a responsible narrator, and although she is one of the teens who "lost control," her narration is believable to teen readers due to her newly achieved status as a wiser character reflecting on her (and Bo Jo's) successes and failures.

Several scenes in *Bo Jo Jones* have a familiar ring to them. When Bo Jo arrives to take July out on a date, her mother's comment sounds very similar to the views on dating shared by Buff's dad in *Two and the Town*: "Wait a minute," Mother said. "I've a message for your friend out there. Tell him that we like to meet the boys you go out with *before* you go out with them." Then she asks, "Are you ashamed of him?"

The scene in which readers discover that July is pregnant is surprisingly similar to what happens in *A Girl Like Me*. Once July suspects that she is pregnant, we are told,

> The next day I hopped a bus for Westcott, which is about fifty miles away, bought myself a wedding ring at the dime store, and picked a doctor out of the telephone directory. . . . He wasn't fooled by the wedding ring or by the phony name I gave with the "Mrs." attached. . . . He told me to go home and tell my parents the truth.[19]

Here is where the story veers away from earlier versions of the pregnancy theme. Bo Jo and July *choose* to get married (they elope): "We
wrapped it up three days later on a Saturday in a town over the line in
Georgia, where we'd heard they'd marry anybody sober enough to
stand up and lie about their age."[20] And when their parents offer them a
way out, by attempting to convince them to annul the marriage, Bo Jo
and July refuse. After much consternation on the part of both sets of
parents, the newly married couple is set up in a garage apartment
owned by a relative.

Although they do not experience the same level of ostracism from
their peers as Buff and Elaine did, Bo Jo is forced to quit school and
take a menial job at the bank. The few friends that visit July are judgmental and unsupportive. High school friend Mary Ann, upon discovering that July really is pregnant says, "You of all people . . . you always
seemed so clever and sure of yourself." July's new married friend Lou
hates kids and decides to get an abortion when she learns that she is
pregnant—then runs away to New York.

July is also ostracized by her family. Just as Buff was embarrassed
to have Elaine come to his softball game because everyone would see
that she was pregnant, July's sister is embarrassed to be seen with her at
their brother's little league baseball game. The couple frequently fights,
and like Buff, Bo Jo comes home drunk on at least one occasion.

Through it all, however, the couple perseveres. Unfortunately, a
much worse fate awaits July and Bo than being stuck in a loveless
marriage with a baby or being forced to give the baby up for adoption.
Their baby is born prematurely, and several days later, as she lies in her
hospital bed, July receives the news: "I worried all day and all night. I
worried up until eleven a.m. the next morning when Dr. Harvey and Bo
Jo came to tell me that the baby was dead."[21]

The story does have a somewhat, if not happy, at least hopeful
ending, another characteristic that came to define this new genre called
realistic young adult fiction. Despite both sets of parents' strong urg-
ings that the couple get divorced and start fresh after they lose the baby,
Bo Jo and July decide to stay together, and readers are given hope that
they just may make it.

My Darling, My Hamburger, by Paul Zindel (1969)

The sex act, a resulting pregnancy, and the flood of consequences that
follow are all on display in *My Darling, My Hamburger*, with one

major twist. Neither marriage nor adoption is chosen as the final solution. Abortion is the answer to Liz's unwanted pregnancy. Sean and Liz are dating, and readers are told that although Liz cares deeply for Sean, she is not ready to move past the heavy-petting stage: "She loved being near him. He made her feel secure and happy. When he touched her hand or pressed against her, she was certain there was a special chemistry between them. If only he could be satisfied with what they had been doing—at least for now."[22]

Sean is portrayed as a caring guy, although he does have a bit of a temper. Unfortunately, he cannot seem to control his sexual urges (sound familiar?), nor does he feel like he should. He explains to his friend Dennis why he is frustrated with Liz for not wanting to have sex:

> Nature arranged it so that we have the equipment. And the need. So we'd better find a way, or we're going to do something as bad as suffocating. If you ask me, that's why there are so many sickies in the world. Everybody gets suffocated as teenagers.[23]

Liz breaks it off with Sean for a time, but after realizing how much she cares for him, she writes a note professing her love. The note is intercepted, presumably by Sean's alcoholic father, and when Liz does not hear from Sean, she decides to go to the dance with Rod, a bad boy who dropped out of school after getting a freshman girl pregnant. Liz decides that she will start a rumor by letting Rod take her into one of the classrooms at the school during the dance, aware that several of the gossip girls are watching. But when she tries to stop Rod from going where she would not let Sean go, Rod becomes forceful. As luck would have it, Sean arrives in the nick of time to rescue Liz from Rod.

Zindel's novel is a departure from previous pregnancy novels in that the implied sex scene is not caused by a sudden rage of male hormones but by a decision made in response to a parent's adverse reaction. As Sean and Liz are driving home, Sean's car gets a flat tire. It is midnight, and Liz realizes that she needs to call her parents and let them know that she is safe. At this point, it has been made clear to readers that sex will not be happening on this night. But when Liz calls home, her mother puts stepfather on the phone:

> "You're late."
>   Liz was glad to hear him. If he only knew how much she wanted to be home instead of in that freezing phone booth.

"We had a flat," Liz said. "It's a bit complicated, but I had a fight with the boy that took me to the dance . . . " Liz slowed her voice, then stopped. She felt she was saying all the wrong things.

"Get home here!"

The tone of his voice made her heart sink.

"Do you hear me, you little tramp?"

Liz froze. Slowly she removed the receiver from her ear and looked at it disbelievingly. Without a word, she put it back on the hook. [24]

After a few moments back in the car with Sean, Liz makes her decision: "She looked at him. She knew she had been wrong. She was no longer frightened about building the world in which she wanted to live. . . . 'I'm in no hurry to go home anymore.' she said. 'Not anymore.'" [25]

Liz tells Maggie that she is pregnant, but she chooses not to tell Sean, and the next time that the couple is alone together, readers witness a very uncomfortable scene as a result of dramatic irony—the reader's knowledge of Liz's pregnancy combined with Sean's lack of knowledge. Poor Sean, now thinking that he has the green light for sex, is turned away. When Liz finally does tell Sean, he tells her that he will marry her, and Liz is thrilled; but once again, the evil parents intervene. This time it is Sean's alcoholic father. When Sean goes to him for advice about a "friend" who got a girl pregnant, the father tells Sean that the boy should send the girl on a "Puerto Rican vacation" because the doctors down there do that sort of thing (abortions). [26]

Sean follows through on his father's advice, telling Liz that he does not want to marry her and giving her $300 for the abortion. Rod finds the doctor, and he and Maggie drive Liz to get the abortion. When Rod drops Liz at her house, she is bleeding and in pain. The rest of the story is told from Maggie's point of view, and we learn that Liz now wants nothing to do with Sean, Maggie, or anyone from her previous life.

Zindel's novel characterizes teenage sexual relationships—more prominently than previous pregnancy novels—as resulting from the male's uncontrollable desires and emotions (love). Instead of parents who try to enforce some sort of moral code, we see a father who cares only about money and booze and a stepfather who thinks that his daughter is a whore. Other abortion novels followed—for example, *Bonnie Jo, Go Home* (1972), by Jeannette Eyerly, in which a Midwestern girl travels all the way to New York to get an abortion. The abortions in these novels are typically portrayed as horrifically painful and emotionally damaging experiences. However, as Patty Campbell notes, "after the legalization of abortion in 1973, the subject was less dramatic and therefore appeared less frequently."[27]

Are You in the House Alone? by Richard Peck (1976)

Gail is a nice girl from a middle-class family. Her boyfriend, Steve—a raging male-hormone stereotype—is from a blue-collar family. Gail and Steve are in a sexually active relationship (Gail is on the pill). Soon after the story begins, readers see Gail losing interest in Steve. Steve seems oblivious to this, evidenced by the fact that he tries to convince her to go to his family's cabin for the sole purpose of having sex.

Phil is the town's golden boy. He comes from a rich family and is perceived by the townsfolk as extremely conservative. So when Gail begins finding obscene notes in her locker, no one suspects that the culprit might be Phil. The adults in the story, even the counselor, do not believe Gail when she comes forward, even when she produces the sexually suggestive notes. Then the creepy phone calls begin. Eventually, Phil shows up at Gail's house one evening when she is alone:

> He pushed his face against the side of my head and whispered into my ear, "And don't worry. I don't want you to do anything you haven't already done, Gail. You've had more experience in certain matters than I have. And this is your chance to share it." . . . "Let's both enjoy this, why not? You've already lost what you've got to lose."[28]

Phil rapes Gail and hits her with the fireplace poker, and she blacks out. The rest of the story is a series of Spanish inquisitions in which Gail's character and claims of rape are called into question, due to her previous sexual activity and the belief that Phil's moral character is beyond reproach. Gail's mother initially chooses not to report the rape, but Gail eventually goes to the doctor for an exam. A police officer shows up to question her. After Gail tells the officer about the threatening notes and phone calls, he responds, "You're kind of grown up to let a thing like that worry you, aren't you?"[29] And when she describes Phil's arrival at her house, the officer says,

> "So somebody comes to the door, and you let him in, and he pulls a gun on you, right?"
> "No, I mean, I let him in, but he didn't have a gun."
> "A knife, maybe?"
> "No."

"Now wait a minute, honey. Let me get this straight in my mind. You open the door to a perfect stranger and without threatening you, he rapes you, right?"[30]

The lawyer that Gail's father hires is not much help either. He tells her that the medical report proves only that something happened, and he proceeds to list several other caveats that would be necessary to prove that a rape occurred: "If the assailant had forced his way in . . . if he'd been a stranger . . . if you'd been a virgin . . . if you hadn't been on birth control pills, because that's part of the medical report . . . if you'd been screaming and hysterical and incoherent throughout the police interview."[31]

We viewed *Are You in the House Alone?* at least initially as just another "consequences of having premarital sex" novel, but not everyone, especially during the time that it was written, agreed with us. *Kirkus* categorized Peck's book as a "chiller":

> Distortingly harsh, and insofar as Peck presents this as an accurate profile of rape and its aftermath, readers might conclude that it's futile for any victim to seek protection or justice. As we expect this to be read as a chiller rather than a case study, we'll rate it medium cool—fast-paced and frighteningly accurate but without the quality of inevitability that keeps one awake after lights out.[32]

The story also gained somewhat of a cult following after being made into a television movie in 1978 (with Dennis Quaid as Phil). The television incarnation was also constructed and marketed as a chiller or horror movie. The film version begins with Gail being taken to the hospital after being raped. Flashbacks then lead us back to the incident, with red herrings strewn everywhere, specifically the various men with whom Gail comes in contact along the way. This story arc does create a bit of suspense leading up to the night in question, but it also serves to magnify what *Kirkus* referred to as the "distortingly harsh . . . profile of rape and its aftermath."

OTHER NOTABLE EARLY YOUNG ADULT FICTION WITH SEXUAL CONTENT

Free Not to Love, by Anne Emory (1975)

Emery's novel is worth mentioning because it is one of many that surfaced in the 1970s in which a high school girl has sex (believing that the boy loves her), but instead of being clobbered with consequences—pregnancy, public humiliation, abortion, even rape—she simply discovers that her first sexual experience was not love at all, and through a series of relationships and conversations with both sexes, she realizes that she must wait for the "right" guy to come along before having sex again.

Dori's story begins on an island that she had visited as a child, where she is now doing some soul-searching, and where she realizes that sex is not the answer to loneliness. In a series of flashbacks, we learn that Lennie is the boy whom she is trying to forget. In this scene, Dori has sex with Lennie for the first time:

> He began kissing me again, holding me close and making love, until a kind of emotional tide took over in a way I had never expected. I could not have pulled away, all I wanted was to be closer. He carried me to the bed, and all I thought was, when you feel like this, how can it be wrong? It's got to be the most beautiful thing in the world. So . . .
>
> It was not what I expected after all. I thought there should have been some great crashing high, and evidently Lennie had a great time. For me . . . nothing happened. After all the loving and the buildup, I was left feeling afterward as if love was over. I wanted more loving then, for warmth and reassurance, but Lennie didn't understand. Everything faded so fast. I thought, was this all there was to it?
>
> Mostly, I just wanted to cry.[33]

Like Elaine in *Two and the Town*, Dori is unable to restrain her passion, but whereas Elaine felt that what she was doing was wrong, Dori engages willingly, believing that it is love. That perception changes quickly when she realizes that all Lennie wants is sex: "Lennie wanted me to go home with him a couple of days a week. But I never saw him in between those days anymore. It seemed now as if the only thing Lennie really wanted when we were together was to go to bed. And he was always busy on the days between."[34]

Dori wishes that Lennie would do something, anything to demon-strate his love for her. She wants a commitment, and in a complete shift from the pregnancy novels that we have discussed, Dori thinks,

> It was a very mixed-up time, and I thought about marriage a lot. It would be more satisfying to try to build on a permanent commitment like that. I kept wishing Lennie would say something that showed he felt that way too. I even wished I was pregnant, because that could lead to something more permanent than the way things were now. [35]

Free Not to Love is representative of many YA novels that began to appear in the mid- to late 1970s that demonstrated a shift in the cultural mores of the times. Females were more willing to engage in sex before marriage if they felt as though they were in a loving and committed relationship. Dori wishes that she would get pregnant, wishes that she was married, but once she comes to her senses, she makes a conscious choice (as opposed to being forced into one) and walks away from the relationship.

This is not to suggest that Emery has written a story that most teens will believe. Her time on the island is spent getting advice from anyone and everyone—including a talk from her grandmother on birth control. *Free Not to Love*, as the title suggests, spends most of its pages preach-ing about the responsibilities of sex and how to make the right deci-sions. In the end, Dori returns from the island determined to wait for true love and, thankfully, without a baby.

I'll Get There, It Better Be Worth the Trip, by John Donovan (1969)

Just as novels such as *The Outsiders* and *The Contender* defined what we now refer to as realistic young adult fiction, Donovan's *I'll Get There, It Better Be Worth the Trip* initiated the genre of gay teen litera-ture by introducing readers to Davy Ross, a thirteen-year-old boy who moves to Manhattan to live with his estranged mother after his grand-mother dies. It seems that Davy's only friend is his dachshund, Fred, until he meets Douglas Altschuler. Similar dysfunctional home lives contribute to their friendship, and then one afternoon while playing on the floor with Fred, the two boys take the friendship a step further: "First he licks my face, then Altschuler's, and back and forth between us. I think that this unusual feeling I have will end, but in a minute the three of us are lying there, our heads together. I guess I kiss Altschuler and he kisses me. It isn't like that dumb kiss I gave Mary Lou Gerrity in Massachusetts before I left. It just happens."[36]

Readers witness another kiss, but the physical part of the relationship goes no further. What makes *I'll Get There* groundbreaking is the candid way in which Donovan addresses (at the time) the taboo topic of homosexuality. For example, on several occasions, Davy tries to convince himself that there is nothing wrong with what happened: "Don't get me wrong, I'm not ashamed. There was nothing wrong about it, I keep telling myself."[37]

When Davy's mother comes home one day and finds the two boys passed out on the floor with their arms draped over one another—as a result of sampling her whiskey—she loses control, assuming that their relationship must be more than just platonic.

> "Davy, Davy," she says, "truth."
> I nod.
> "Nothing . . . unnatural . . . happened this afternoon with you and Douglas, did it?"
> "No," I say.
> "Or ever?"
> "What do you mean, 'unnatural'?"
> "I want the truth, Davy."[38]

Davy's father is called in to discuss the situation with him, and he handles it with aplomb:

> "Is he a special friend, Davy?"
> "Sure. Altschuler. I told you about him."
> "I'm not prying, Davy," my father says, "so don't get mad. We don't talk about personal things much, but sometimes it can't be avoided. I guess you have a crush on your friend, is that it?"
> "A crush?" I ask. I get red in the face. "I don't know." I can't think of another word. "I'm not queer or anything, if that's what you think," I say.
> Now my father gets red in the face. "I'm sure you're not, Davy. I don't want to make a big case out of this."[39]

Davy's father goes on to explain that differences are what makes the world go around, and he points out that when people are too narrow-minded, they can become dangerous. Unfortunately for Davy, it was 1969, and there were consequences for being gay. Dad's talk is interrupted when Davy realizes that his mother, who had taken Fred for a walk, has been gone for quite some time. He glances out the window to see Fred running loose without his leash, and by the time Davy can get to him, Fred has been struck by a car and dies in Davy's arms. Davy spends the next few chapters blaming Douglas and their "queer" encounter for Fred's death, but to Donovan's credit, Davy comes to his senses in the end, and he and Douglas agree that they will "respect each other."[40]

LGBTQIQ literature has come a long way in the forty-five years since the release of *I'll Get There*. There is no denying that although we may not quite be *there*, we have made a tremendous amount of progress. What Donovan accomplished with this novel is significant. Without being preachy, he was able to write a story that realistically confronted the teen emotions and feelings that accompany sexual discovery.

FICTION FEATURING TEEN CHARACTERS MARKETED FOR ADULTS

The term *new adult*, coined in 2009, is commonly used to describe the target audience for novels with characters in their late teens or early twenties who are transitioning from adolescence into adulthood. In the 1950s and 1960s, these characters appeared from time-to-time in fiction marketed to adults. These novels, which were being read by young adults despite their adult label, serve to illustrate how the adult world saw teen sex in adult fiction, in contrast to how the adult world thought teens should see sex in the books written for teens.

The Young Lovers, by Julian Halevy (1955)

The Young Lovers is the story of two twenty-year-olds, Eddie Slocum and Pamela Oldenburg. Eddie, a sophomore at NYU, pursues Pamela from the opening pages, and she quickly becomes enamored with his intelligence and wit. Pam's parents are divorced, and her mother drinks and writes suicide notes. Eddie's father was killed in the war, and he hates his stepfather. After spending some time together and following a presex conversation on Eddie's bed—in which Pam tells him that she mostly dates older men, some of them married—their passion erupts. The sex scene is certainly not avoided as it is in other novels that we have discussed; in fact, the lovemaking goes on for three entire pages.

Notice, however, how the narrator's stilted prose affects the tone of the scene:

> Desire came to him timidly, and he welcomed it with a leaping of the spirit and hosannas. He put his hand inside the kimono and cupped her sweet firm breast, erect and butting into his palm. She held his hands against her, and when he lowered his head, she offered her breasts willingly to his lips. Desire coursed through him like an army with banners. Exultantly, he felt himself proud and eager, and imagined himself lion-like in his hunger.[41]

Later, Eddie—like many male characters discussed in this chapter and others—struggles with the mechanics of sex: "His first attempts were fumbling. He thrust blindly, searching—abandoning himself to an unknown, driving force. She cried out, and her pain frightened him. He froze, torn between the frantic, straining urge to beat through the barrier between them and his far stronger will to spare her hurt."[42] The "barrier" and the "hurt" that the narrator is referring to is Pam's hymen (she is a virgin). Finally, Eddie climaxes:

> Then from the hidden resources of his being, he felt the coming of a mighty tide. It caught him up and swept him in a great soaring wave, leaving behind all burdens like ships bobbing on the surface of the sea, bearing him far, far inland, where the swirling waters of an unknown, underground river burst forth into sunlight and flung him high. His vision blurred in a bright sparkling burst of ecstatic sun and spray, and fainting, he fell downwards.[43]

A spectacular level of self-awareness for a twenty-year-old, wouldn't you say? Aside from two "breast" references, a reader trying to make sense of these passages without any additional context clues might find it difficult to discern that the couple is even having sex. In the *Kirkus* review of *The Young Lovers*, the atmosphere created through the use of this language is described as a "cloud cuckoo land of young love, absolute and reckless and radiant."[44] We actually enjoyed reading these poetic renditions of sexual activity. What did surprise us, however, was that, eventually, this story headed down the same path as all the others in this section. Pam learns that she is pregnant, and Eddie gets drafted into military service. Eddie pouts, and Pam wonders if she should saddle Eddie with a baby that he is clearly not mature enough to care for. In the end, Eddie goes off to war, and Pam, very pregnant, awaits his return:

The train was beside them too soon, the door opening relentlessly, nothing and everything still left to say. He began to cry. The seconds fled. He kissed her blindly, tore his hand free, and stepped into the car just ahead of the advancing door.

As the train rolled forward, he looked back at her standing alone on the platform, her hands thrust rigidly into her pockets as if to keep them from going out to him. She dwindled in size. Gathering speed, the train whipped around a curve.[45]

I Am the Beautiful Stranger, by Rosalyn Drexler (1965)

I Am the Beautiful Stranger is the disturbing tale of Selma, an extremely intelligent girl who—through a narration style similar to but not nearly as adept as Holden Caulfield in *The Catcher in the Rye*—tells the story of her brutal initiation into adulthood. Selma, thirteen when the story begins and fifteen at its conclusion, describes in graphic detail how her parents, her friends, and her home and school environments all contribute to her bleak situation. The following passage provides one example. Selma's mother, who frequently offers Selma to older men, introduces Selma to her cousin, who is described by Selma as "that old and licentious man about town":[46]

> When I was thirteen, Mother took me to see my second cousin Marshall Baxter. He felt me up while I sat next to him on a love seat in his hotel suite. I didn't know what to do, so I didn't do anything. Mother wanted me to sing for him, to persuade him to get me a screen test. Marshall was a well-known Hollywood comedian, but he certainly wasn't going to thrust me into the lap of fame. What I want to say is that I think Marshall Baxter is a kind of sex maniac, because whenever I went to see him after that he unzipped his fly.[47]

The back cover of the paperback edition of *I Am the Beautiful Stranger* includes reviewer blurbs suggesting that the book is being marketed to adults. *Village Voice* stated, "Marvelous . . . a thinking man's Lolita . . . the coolest of current heroines." A *New York Herald Tribune* blurb reads, "Selma's shocking adventures are nothing like the way we nice girls from sheltered homes behaved, yet we recognize in them our fantasies, our gossip, and our speculations." The comparisons to *Lolita* are suspect, as the narrator in *Lolita* is an older male who lusts after a young girl. Despite the adult tone of the reviews, the fact remains that the narrator/protagonist is a thirteen-year-old girl who confesses to enjoying the attention that she receives from men. *Kirkus*

Reviews addressed the narrator issue by noting a lack of an identifiable audience for the book: "The problem is the lack of wide reader identification—her milieu, lower class Jewry in upper Manhattan, and a series of sexual encounters that range from fantasy to commercial, perverse vulgarity."[48] The review is missing a key element of reader identification: the age of the protagonist.

One example of the "vulgarity" occurs when Selma's cousin Marshall introduces her to a millionaire whom she refers to as the Baron:

> The drinks come. We drink and talk—my aspirations: college, dance, drama. He listens while he toys with my tits. . . . He wants to know what I do with my boyfriends. He thinks I'm sex on wheels. I tell him "that's private." "You can tell me," he whispers and goes to his knees, kissing my panties under the dress. I pull away and leave him kissing the air. . . . "C'mere," he shouts, and twists my arm. This time he means business. He opens his fly and orders, "Kiss it!" He is meaner than his penis. It looks relatively sober. I feel affection for it and do as he orders.
>
> Then we go out and have a swell time at the Copa where everyone knows him.[49]

Selma's acceptance of a clearly dysfunctional environment is proof that her character has given in to the realities of her situation. She sums up her philosophy in this way: "Nobody would guess what a stimulator I am. I wear very prudish clothes, but I am constantly preparing activities (in my mind) to spur men on. The more I excite the emptiness, the better I'll get paid, and I enjoy myself too."[50] Selma's philosophy and her resulting behavior should be disturbing to readers, but the reviews seem to indicate that Selma is no more than a promiscuous teen and that we should enjoy reading about her "shocking adventures."

The author, Rosalyn Drexler, is also an accomplished artist who, in the early sixties just before the publication of *I Am the Beautiful Stranger*, created a body of paintings known as *The Love and Violence* series, which depicted abusive relationships between men and women. Some of the titles include *Rape* (1962) and *I Won't Hurt You* (1964). In 2007, she released a book of prints that included these works: *I Am the Beautiful Stranger, Paintings of the '60's.*[51]

Last Summer, by Evan Hunter (1968)

Although Evan Hunter (born Salvatore Lombino) did not write for young adults, he did write about them. His first literary success was

The Blackboard Jungle (1954), a novel about a young teacher whose ideals are crushed after he begins teaching in an urban high school inhabited by quite a few aggressively hostile teens. Hunter began his career as a teacher, and *The Blackboard Jungle* was semiautobiographical. Later in life, he wrote under the pseudonym Ed McBain, and he is credited for creating and popularizing the police procedural novel. He is also responsible for many successful screenplays, including *The Birds*, the classic 1963 film that he and Alfred Hitchcock adapted from Daphne du Maurier's story.

Last Summer is the story of three high school sophomores who spend a summer vacation together on the fictional Atlantic coast island of Greensward. As with *The Blackboard Jungle*, Hunter creates aggressively hostile characters in Peter, David, and Sandy. The narrator is an older and wiser Peter looking back on the events of that particular summer. After Peter and David meet Sandy, they hang out on the beach, sneak beers from their parents' refrigerators, and sail around the island. Both boys find Sandy extremely attractive, and she seems to enjoy sexually teasing them—going topless at the beach, asking them questions about their sex lives while playing truth or dare, and allowing them to feel her up in the movie theater. In this scene, the boys sit on either side of Sandy in the theater as they watch a visually arousing film. Peter reflects,

> Sandy clasped her hands in her lap, sitting very still, watching the screen . . . and it was then that I realized that David's hand was under her sweater. I dropped my own hand to her waist, remembering that she had not allowed me to do this to her when we were alone together in the forest, found the bottom edge of her sweater, and eased my hand under it and up over her ribs to her bra. [52]

Peter's narration enables readers to feel the sexual tension that builds between the boys and Sandy. David and Peter are willing to follow Sandy anywhere, in the hopes that she might once again bare her breasts, let them touch something, or maybe even let them do more.

But Sandy has a dark side. When the boys first meet her, she is trying to help an injured seagull that she has found. She quickly convinces the boys to help her nurse it back to health, but later, when the bird appears to have fully recovered, Sandy refuses to let it off the leash that she has made for it. The bird bites her, and the boys later find the bird with its skull crushed.

Last Summer is separated into two parts: "The Gull" and "Rhoda." The second part of the story begins with the trio meeting Rhoda, an awkward, rather prim and proper girl who is also spending her summer on the island. She likes Peter, and the trio, led by Sandy, decide to bring her into their group. They discover that Rhoda is afraid of the water and has never learned to swim, as a result of her mother's death by drowning. Like the seagull, Rhoda is a wounded creature whom the trio want to "make healthy." Armed with the knowledge of what happened to the seagull, readers understand that things do not look good for Rhoda.

After witnessing a particularly brutal act in which the trio, with Rhoda as an unwilling accomplice, con an older man into a blind date with Sandy and then leave him to be beaten by a gang of thugs, Rhoda has had enough. She tries to talk to Peter about the incident, but he has been swept up in the sexual chemistry that the trio have created. Peter assumes that this will be the last that he sees of Rhoda. David decides that he and Peter should try to go all the way with Sandy, and he buys condoms at the drugstore. They plan to meet with Sandy in a secluded spot in the forest, but unbeknownst to the boys, Sandy invites Rhoda to join them. The four of them trek to their spot, and David, Peter, and Sandy begin drinking.

> She lifted the half-full bottle she was holding in her hand, and suddenly poured beer onto her breasts and into the front of her bikini top. "Ahhhhh," she said, "that's better," and tossed the empty bottle away. "But now my top is wet," she said, giggling. "Peter, my top is wet."
> "Okay," I said.
> "Don't you like girls who say things like 'My top is wet'?"[53]

Rhoda immediately becomes uncomfortable and wants to leave. The situation escalates: "'Thank you,' [Sandy] said, and made a pretty little curtsy. She finished the beer, carefully put the empty bottle down on the ground, and took off the top of her suit."

Rhoda continues to plead with Peter to take her home. David and Sandy both encourage Rhoda to take her top off. The following passage sums up Peter's inner struggles between his newly discovered masculinity and his waning sense of decency:

> I thought This is outrageous and then immediately realized I was only relating to Rhoda's shock and not to any belief of my own. This is *marvelous*, I thought, this is stimulating and daring, and was immediately overcome by fresh guilt when Rhoda plaintively touched my arm, but

> I could not take my eyes from Sandy. This is shameless, I thought, and
> the thought excited me, and I was thrilled and then embarrassed by my
> masculine response, and I thought I'd better get Rhoda out of here
> before something terrible happens, and then I began to anticipate what
> might happen.[54]

The buildup of sexual tension, combined with the cruelty and scorn
that the three teens seem to elicit from one another, creates a shocking
conclusion. Hunter uses just short of three pages to describe the rape of
Rhoda. It begins with David and Sandy telling Rhoda that she should
take her top off:

> David . . . his fists clenched, a contorted look on his face, rose in one
> swift smooth sudden motion to seize Rhoda from behind while Sandy
> pulled the bra top down. Her breasts burst free, she tried to raise her
> hands to cover them, but David grabbed both her wrists and Sandy
> slapped her hard across the face, twice, the way she had slapped her that
> night we'd found her crying on the dune.[55]

What follows is a detailed description of David and Sandy pulling
off Rhoda's bathing suit, Rhoda calling for Peter while Peter stands
idly by. The passage concludes with the following:

> She gave a final futile twist as we forced her legs apart, trying to turn
> over on the poncho and away from him as he walked to her, and stood
> above her, and suddenly crouched, poised.
>   We did it to her.
>   He did it to her first, and then I did.
>   I was last.[56]

Perhaps the description on the inside of the original book cover sums
up the story best: "The opening is as bright as summer, as calm as a
cobra dozing in the sun. But, as summer and compassion wane, the
author strips away the pretense of youth and lays bare the blunt, prime-
val urge to crush, defile, betray. The tragic, inevitable outcome exposes
the depths of moral corruption and the violation of the soul."[57]

Last Summer was made into a film only a year after the release of
the book in 1969, and it starred Barbara Hershey and Richard Thomas.
The popularity of the film created a renewed interest in the book,
especially the teenage demographic. Like many other books discussed
in this chapter, *Last Summer* was never marketed as young adult fiction—but when has that ever stopped adolescents from reading what is

a finely crafted story that contains realistic depictions of sexually curious teens?

GROUNDBREAKING YA AUTHORS

Judy Blume

It would be difficult to imagine that there are kids who grew up in the United States over the past forty years who have not heard of Judy Blume. Children's and young adult titles such as *Are You There God? It's Me, Margaret, Tales of a Fourth Grade Nothing, Blubber*, and *Tiger Eyes* are still flying off the shelves years after their initial releases. Blume has also written three adult novels—*Summer Sisters, Smart Women*, and *Wifey* (all *New York Times* bestsellers). She has sold more than eighty-two million copies of her books, and they have been translated into thirty-two languages. Her list of honors includes the American Library Association Margaret A. Edwards Award for Lifetime Achievement, the Library of Congress Living Legends Award, and the National Book Foundation's Medal for Distinguished Contribution to American Letters. Most recently, Blume received the ALAN Award for outstanding contributions to the field of adolescent literature. Here, we discuss two of her most influential and controversial young adult novels: *Then Again, Maybe I Won't* and *Forever*.

Then Again, Maybe I Won't (1971)

Then Again, Maybe I Won't is the story of Tony, a thirteen-year-old who is forced to move to a new community after the financial success of his father's new invention. Tony's stress level increases as he watches his parents succumb to the temptations of the nouveau riche. His mother becomes a social climber, and his father throws money at their problems. One perk of Tony's new community, however, is the view that he is afforded from his bedroom of the neighbor girl, Lisa:

> That's when I discovered I could see Lisa's room from my room. I don't know why I never thought of it before. I guess I've been so busy pulling down my shades to make sure she can't see me it never entered my mind that I could see her. With all my lights turned off and with her lights turned on, I can see everything she's doing. And what she was doing was getting undressed. [58]

Then Again is a departure from the previous novels that we have discussed because it is told from a realistic male point of view. The ways in which Tony confronts his budding sexual desires are devoid of harsh lessons and dire consequences. Tony is simply an adolescent attempting to comprehend his newly discovered sexuality. For example, after peeping on Lisa, he begins to have wet dreams. Upon waking from one of these dreams, Tony thinks, "Oh God! There is something wrong with me. *Really* wrong. Dr. Holland doesn't know what he is talking about! I am *so* sick. This proves it."[59] And yet, he continues to watch, even asking for a pair of binoculars for Christmas.

Blume manages to avoid the creepiness factor that would seem inevitable in a story whose main character is a peeping Tom. She accomplishes this by making Tony sympathetic. For example, notice what Tony attends to as he tries out his new binoculars:

> My hands were really shaking. I couldn't even hold my binoculars steady. The view was great. Just great! It was like she was standing right in front of me. I could even see the expression on her face. She was smiling. She has a terrific smile. The first thing she did was try on the green stretch sweater. She turned around and around in front of her mirror. She doesn't have to worry. She's beautiful from every angle. I wanted to tell her that . . . I love her, I think.[60]

Poor Tony hasn't ever spoken to Lisa at this point, but he thinks he loves her. Is Tony misguided? Yes. Is this a natural response for a thirteen-year-old boy who is trying to unravel the mysteries of his budding sexuality? Yes again. When Tony does finally talk to Lisa, he discovers that she likes to drive her Corvette at unreasonably high speeds and that she smokes. It appears as though this humanization of Lisa will cause Tony to stop looking through her window, but Blume leaves us with this closing passage:

> I think what I'll do is—I'll go home and put my binoculars away on the top shelf of my closet—over in the corner—so they're hard to get.
>   Then again, maybe I won't.[61]

Forever (1975)

As discussed in chapter 1, well-written young adult fiction has the power to influence sexual identity. The problem, as Patty Campbell noted back in 1986, is that when sex appears in fiction—as opposed to its clinical presentation in a scientific manual—it will be perceived as erotic: "To require books that teach the techniques and emotions of sex *not* to be arousing is as paradoxical and nonsensical as to prohibit cookbooks from inspiring hunger."[62] *Forever* was the first novel for young adults that accurately portrayed responsible teenage sexual behavior—that is, if you believe that there is such a thing as responsible teenage sexual behavior.

Forever was a landmark YA novel for many reasons. Blume's love story deals with teenage sexuality in an open, responsible, and descriptive manner. The characters discuss STDs and contraception, but it never comes across as contrived or preachy. Blume makes strong connections between sex and love, as opposed to sex and horrible consequences. But what truly sets *Forever* apart from its predecessors is Blume's attention to the mental, emotional, and physical portrayals of Kathy and Michael. They are honest and open with each other. They are at times scared, vulnerable, and appropriately curious about the physical and emotional aspects of sex. It is particularly refreshing to see an adolescent male motivated by more than simply his basic animal urges.

When questioned, fans and critics of the book most often recall the sexually explicit scenes in which Kathy and her boyfriend Michael physically explore their feelings for each other. Often criticized as overly graphic, these scenes are more awkward than romantic or stimulating. For example, when they finally make the decision to "do everything," neither of them appears to know what they are doing:

> "Are you in . . . are we doing it?"
> "Not yet," Michael said, pushing harder. "I don't want to hurt you."
> "Don't worry . . . just do it!"
> "I'm trying, Kath . . . but it's very tight in there."
> "What should I do?"
> "Can you spread your legs some more . . . and maybe raise them a little?"
> "Like this?"
> "That's better . . . much better."
> I could feel him halfway inside me and then Michael whispered, "Kath . . ."
> "What?"
> "I think I'm going to come again."[63]

Kathy and Michael finally do get it right, and in this, perhaps the most erotically charged scene in the story, both characters seem comfortable in their skins. Notice, however, that Blume does add a nice little touch at the conclusion of the passage, possibly to remind us that these are still teenagers:

> This time Michael made it last much, much longer and I got so carried away I grabbed his backside with both hands, trying to push him deeper and deeper into me—and I spread my legs as far apart as I could—and I raised my hips off the bed—and I moved with him, again and again and again—and at last, I came. I came right before Michael and as I did I made noises, *just like my mother*. Michael did too.[64] (italics added)

Kathy's recognition of the noises that her mother makes, right at the moment of climax, serves to diffuse the erotic tone of the passage and remind readers that these are teenagers.

In addition to *Forever*'s sexual content, the novel was controversial because of the perceived age group to which it was being marketed. Before the release of *Forever*, Judy Blume had been known for her preteen novels, such as *Tales of a Fourth Grade Nothing*, *Blubber*, and *The Pain and the Great One*. Imagine the shock when parents discovered that *Forever* was something completely different. The irony, of course, is that Kathy and Michael's relationship does not last forever. Blume's story of sexual discovery will be, however, forever credited for allowing YA authors to further explore sex in all its manifestations.

Norma Klein

Best known for young adult fiction that explores such controversial social issues as sexism, contraception, and adolescent sexuality, Norma Klein is also responsible for more than a dozen adult novels, two collections of short stories, and several children's picture books. From 1972 until her untimely death at age fifty in 1989, Klein wrote more than thirty novels, many of which contained teenage characters as protagonists. Despite their initial classifications as adult fiction, many soon became extremely popular with teens. In an exhaustive book on her life and works published one year before her death, she is referred to as "a superstar. In the young adult field, her name recognition is enormous with young readers, their teachers, librarians, and book dealers. Perhaps only Judy Blume has a more devoted following."[65]

Klein was not interested in portraying sex in her young adult fiction as merely a physiological act. Her treatment of adolescent sexuality explores the mental and emotional effects of sex on an adolescent's state of being.[66] To her credit, Klein created male and female characters who desire sex and who act on those desires. The females are often the initiators. Many of her critics at the time argued that the teenage characters in her novels who engaged in sex lacked a sense of commitment toward each other. Klein believed, however, that her portrayal of an adolescent's sexual encounter should be about capturing one of the many essential experiences in which they must engage as they search for meaning in their lives. This perspective is not at all surprising from a writer who was the daughter of a Freudian psychologist.[67] Klein's young adult novels demonstrate her belief that although sex and love are an amazing combination, having sex does not mean that one has to pledge his or her undying love.[68]

Klein had no reservations about writing explicit sex scenes: "I'm not a rebel, trying to stir things up just to be provocative. I'm doing it because I feel like writing about real life."[69] Perhaps *Kirkus* summed up Klein's books best in this review of her 1983 novel *Beginner's Love*: "With that title and the Norma Klein byline, you probably already know exactly what you're getting: a casually confided tale of high-schooler, sex/love, in a Manhattan/YA style that's R-rated (with a dollop or two of X)."[70]

Klein's sexually explicit scenes typically involve characters who are eighteen and older, although some are still in high school. Although much of her story plotting relies on more than a few contrived circumstances, she must be applauded, along with Judy Blume, for redefining gender roles in YA that had previously been characterized in stereotypical Victorian fashion: females constantly being coerced by males who are unable to control their animalistic sexual urges. Two of her most popular novels for teens are discussed here.

It's Ok If You Don't Love Me (1977)

New Yorker Jody Epstein meets Midwesterner Lyle Alexander at the research lab where she is working for the summer. Jody and Lyle are each eighteen, and they love playing tennis but do not seem to have too much else in common. Jody is outspoken and assertive and has some sexual experience. Lyle is much more straight-laced and is a virgin. Jody's mother and her boyfriend have very open conversations with Jody on topics ranging from having children to population control and vasectomies. When Lyle is present, he is clearly uncomfortable participating in these discussions.

Early in the story, Jody takes Lyle to her room, and readers see the couple's differing attitudes toward sex: "All of a sudden Lyle said, 'Jody, would you mind if I—' and then we started kissing each other. It's funny with being horny. Sometimes you just know you're in that kind of mood, and in some ways, I don't like that because I've gone out with boys I didn't even like very much and ended up making out with them out of sheer horniness."[71]

They continue to make out, and Lyle slips his hand underneath Jody's blouse—then,

> After we had continued in that vein for a while, Lyle reached down and slipped his hand below my waist, under my jeans, down to my under-pants. He kept going till he reached my vagina. But then it was funny. He put his hand on it just for, like, one second, and then he took his hand away. "Listen, I'm sorry," he said.
>
> "What about?"
>
> "I didn't . . . I really swear I didn't come here tonight planning on this."[72]

Lyle continues to apologize.

> "Lyle, will you quit apologizing? I *mean* it."
>
> "Do you really not mind?"
>
> "Well, why would I do it if I minded?"
>
> He looked puzzled, like that had never occurred to him. "I just don't want you to think that I don't respect you or anything," he said.[73]

Later, Jody shares her views on sex with readers:

> When I was little, like ten or eleven, I'd read these books about teen-age romances with the parts where the girl would say, "You can touch my right breast, but not my left" or "You can put your hand two inches up there, but not two inches down here" and "We can do that on the third date but not the second." It all seemed like some weirdly elaborate code that I assumed I would suddenly understand when I got to be six-teen. . . . But the funny thing is, I *still* don't understand it. I suppose I feel that if I like someone enough to do anything with them, even kiss them, I don't see such a difference between that and all the rest.[74]

Jody is a stark departure from earlier female teen characters who begrudgingly gave in to sexual activity as a result of extreme pressure or force from the male or as an impulsive response to feelings of love toward the male. Kathy in *Forever* does not begin to approach the experience and comfort levels that Jody demonstrates. Jody does, however, remind us of Kathy in this passage, the first time that she and Lyle go all the way:

> We must have talked about it too much, or maybe it was just both of us being so nervous, but the actual act wasn't that much. That is, Lyle took his penis and pushed it into me, but he came so fast I didn't even have time to try and come myself. In some ways it reminded me of those books they give you in grade school about sex education where they usually have a line, "The father puts his penis in the mother's vagina." That was more or less precisely what happened. [75]

Klein, like Blume, creates an uncomfortable yet realistic first-time sexual encounter here. We would not anticipate scenes such as these conjuring feelings of arousal in teens. In fact, Klein's friends often told her, "Your books may be about sex, but they are not sexy books." [76] These realistic scenes are not created as teaching tools; they are Klein's attempt to represent real life.

Beginner's Love (1983)

Beginner's Love is described by the book's publisher as "the story of two adolescents who find excitement and joy in a new relationship but must balance this with the problems that arise when two people who are old enough for passion are too young to deal with its complications." [77] The narrator is Joel, a shy seventeen-year-old senior at the Willard School for Boys. Joel meets Leda at the movies and soon learns that Leda is not shy at all. For example, while attending an outdoor Simon and Garfunkel concert, they notice a couple writhing underneath a blanket, and Leda remarks, "God, I wish they'd stop. They're making me so horny." [78]

Later that evening, at Leda's house, Joel tells readers that Leda "unhooked her bra and threw that on the floor and got out of her jeans. She was just wearing a pair of bikini underpants with little strawberries on them. She looked at me and struck a pose, her hand on her hip. 'Ta da!' she said. 'Preview of coming attractions.'" [79] Soon, Joel and Leda lay down on her bed:

> "Do you want me to touch you?" she asks.
> "Sure," I said.

> She slipped her hand under my underpants and put it on my cock.
> She touched it gently like she was afraid it would hurt me or something.
> "Is that okay?" she asked.
> "Yeah, it's great." I was having trouble talking. I was scared I might
> pass out or something. Then she began stroking it up and down. It's
> funny. In a way, it wasn't as good as when I do it myself because if
> you've jerked off enough, obviously, you learn how to make yourself
> come pretty quickly. But the fact that it was Leda doing it made me so
> excited, I felt like I was going to go crazy.[80]

A couple of weeks after this first sexual encounter, they meet again,
both aware that they will consummate their relationship. Joel does what
many adolescent males before him have done:

> Okay, so I did a classic thing. I absolutely couldn't help it. I entered her
> and it felt so great, just the *idea* that we were really doing it, plus the
> feeling, just everything, that I came. There's no way on earth I could've
> held off. When I was finished, I lay there on top of her, embarrassed.[81]

Klein does an effective job of conveying a seventeen-year-old adolescent male's fear and excitement while in the throes of a sexual
encounter. He and Leda seem destined to enjoy a loving, long-term
relationship. Unfortunately, Joel has a problem. He loves the attention
that he receives from Leda, and he really loves the sex. But along with
Leda's considerable sexual prowess comes the knowledge that she has
been with a few other men before Joel. At first, this seems like a fairly
normal male teen reaction. *Why not ask the girl with whom I just had
sex how many other partners she has had?* However, this is where the
story becomes less believable due to Klein's characterization of Leda.
Leda, as loving as she is, does not understand that openly discussing
previous boyfriends (especially ones who were older and married) and
her sexual experiences with them might pose a problem for a seventeen-year-old boy. So Leda does discuss her previous encounters in
detail, often at the most uncomfortable moments. For example, immediately after she and Joel have sex for the first time, Leda asks, "Was it
hard getting in? Ramon said I was tight or something."[82]

Joel contributes to the problem by continually asking questions that
he clearly should not be asking of Leda, especially armed with knowledge that she is going to answer. Leda eventually becomes pregnant, as
a result of her forgetting to wear her diaphragm, and after an abortion,
Joel goes to college and Leda finds another boyfriend.

Reading Klein's novels today, we are struck by the explicitness of her descriptions of sex, even when measured by modern standards, and by the amount of inner monologue and self-reflection that she includes. Her female characters are to be applauded for their strength and willingness to explore their sexuality. Perhaps at least one of us, however, was a bit uncomfortable at times reading the self-reflections of some of her male characters—Joel, for one—most likely due to the truth found within those lines.

Phyllis Reynolds Naylor

The twenty-eight book *Alice* series is a great example of how literature for young adults can address a variety of sexual topics in a respectful manner. The series begins with *The Agony of Alice* (1985) and concludes with *Now I'll Tell You Everything* (2014). In *Agony*, readers learn that Alice's mother died when she was four, that she lives with her father and her brother, and that she is entering the sixth grade. This transition into adolescence, combined with her lack of access to female role models, causes Alice to continually seek out answers that will help her cope with the anxieties associated with adolescence. Much of this anxiety focuses on sex.

With the exception of the third- through fifth-grade prequels—*Starting with Alice*, *Alice in Blunderland*, and *Lovingly Alice*—the *Alice* series follows the eponymous protagonist through her junior high and high school years. Characters in the junior high novels[83] do not engage in any sex acts but rather ask questions and have discussions about sex and sex-related subjects—body parts, wedding nights, pregnancy, abortion, and healthy versus unhealthy babies. This allows Naylor's characters to maneuver the sexual landscape without placing them in the actual situations. Furthermore, she manages to do this while avoiding a clinical or preachy tone.

Alice is surrounded by characters who possess varying degrees of knowledge and perspective, and all of them are more than willing to engage her in sexual discussions. Each time her closest friends—Pamela (sexually liberal) and Elizabeth (sexually conservative)—her father, her brother, or her brother's girlfriends share their opinions, Alice and readers are given opportunities to discern and evaluate the sexual information being discussed.

For example, as Alice gets older, much of the firsthand sexual information that she gets, for better and for worse, comes from Pamela's sharing of her sexual experiences. These scenes allow readers to evaluate and explore sexual decision making from perspectives both physical and emotional. They can then process the characters' choices on the basis of their own viewpoints. This creates a safe space that allows readers to explore sexuality at an age when most of their information comes from peers. The next few pages provide specific examples of Alice's adventures in sexual wonderland.

In *Alice in Lace,* Alice and her eighth-grade classmates are given assignments in health class that require each of them to tackle an *adult* situation and devise a solution. Pamela's assignment? She is pregnant. She decides to call several abortion clinics, and she discovers that they will perform an abortion only in the first three months and that she may need to have her parents' permission. Because Pamela's character is more liberal (and not really pregnant), readers can evaluate her consideration of abortion through this lens. Alice and Patrick's assignment is to plan a wedding. Alice asks her brother Lester about the wedding night, and he shares, to Alice's dismay, that some couples do not even turn off the lights when they have sex.

In *Outrageously Alice*, Alice reads a *Cosmopolitan*-type magazine, and after considering questions such as "Have you ever mentally undressed a stranger?" she decides to ask her brother for some answers. At a party, Alice is pulled into a dark closet and kissed (she later discovers that it was her boyfriend, Patrick). Alice's friend Elizabeth thinks that Alice has been violated and refers to the incident as "the next thing to being raped."[84] As is the case with Pamela, readers can evaluate Elizabeth's comments based on the establishment of her more conservative character and can then process her use of the word *rape* through that filter. All of these scenes provide readers safe-space opportunities to learn about sex and the consequences thereof.

Naylor's use of humor is another way in which she creates this safe space for readers. For example, in *Outrageously Alice*, when Alice asks Crystal, her brother's ex-girlfriend, about the possibility of discovering on your wedding night that you do not like sex, Crystal explains, "Well you don't have to do everything, either. You can tell your husband what you like and what you don't, and then you can try something else. . . . There are a lot of ways to make love. Not everybody uses the missionary position, you know."

Later, Alice has a conversation with her dad and brother in an attempt to figure out what Crystal meant by "missionary":

"I thought missionaries were preachers," I said finally.

"Huh?" said Lester.

"This is a topic of conversation, Lester," I said primly. "I just want to know what they do."

"They don't usually preach as much as they go to foreign countries and teach people how to do things a little better," said Dad.

"Sort of like sex therapists?" I asked.

"*What?*" said Lester.

"They show people the right positions and everything?" Dad and Lester stared at me.

"Are we talking religion here, or are we talking sex?" asked Dad. [85]

Alice's father goes on to explain the missionary position and how it got its name, [86] a good example of how Naylor shares accurate information within the context of the story. Naylor's junior high *Alice* books serve as an "everything you always wanted to know about sex but were afraid to ask," and Alice is not afraid to ask.

Despite this respectful treatment, however, the *Alice* series, specifically the junior high novels, has been the target of numerous challenges over the years. According to the American Library Association, books from the series were among the top ten challenged in 2001, 2002, 2006, and 2011. Considering that "the number of challenges reflects only incidents reported" and that "for every reported challenge, four or five remain unreported," this is quite a significant statistic. [87] One factor that may influence the controversy surrounding these books is the target audience. Middle school readers like to read up—that is, read about characters that are one to two years older. As a result, the junior high *Alice* books tend to be very popular with fifth and sixth graders, and this may explain many of the challenges, which most often originate with parents.

Fortunately or unfortunately, depending on your point of view, many girls who read these books today are much more informed than Alice's character. Nevertheless, although today's fifth- and sixth-grade readers may know the answers to some of the questions that Alice poses, the books still portray a character who is dealing with sex in an intelligent and respectful manner. We asked Naylor how she went about creating Alice's sexually inquisitive character:

> In my twenty-eight-book *Alice* series, the only constant I kept in mind was to be truthful, to present Alice and her friends and their concerns in as real a manner as possible, keeping in mind, of course, that this is subjective. But I know what my closest friends and I talked and worried

about, and from the letters I receive from readers, I know that their
feelings are very much the same, and though today's teens have far
more decisions to make than we did, they also have many more acceptable choices. [88]

As Alice moves on to high school, she is still asking questions, but
now readers begin to see and hear about characters, including Alice,
who are actually engaging in sex. In *Alice on Her Way*, Alice (now a
sophomore) participates in a church Sunday school class that addresses
sexual topics. A first activity has students walking around the classroom trying to identify sex-related words that have been written on
pieces of paper and taped to their backs. Words such as "semen,"
"vagina," and "clitoris" make the students uncomfortable, and the
scene made some parents uncomfortable as well—but not just for the
sexual content. Although "sexually explicit" was one of the reasons
given for the many challenges to *Alice*, "religious viewpoint" also appeared several times. [89] It is not surprising that Alice has generated so
many challenges, given that Naylor frequently features two of the most
controversial subjects in YAL: religion and sex.

It is also in *Alice on Her Way* that Pamela describes one of her
sexual experiences. When Alice asks Pamela what she and Brian did on
their date after going to dinner, Pamela replies,

> "We parked."
> *"Yeah?"*
> "and did . . . whatever."

After some prodding, Pamela admits, "Okay. So I gave him a hand
job." [90] Later, Pamela tells Alice that she gave a guy a "blow job,"
explaining that it made her happy to make him happy. [91] Once again,
readers are able to experience sexual situations vicariously, thus creating a safe space to process information.

It is in her sophomore year that Alice becomes sexually active.
Sam—who is a nice but needy boy, according to Alice—feels her
breasts and puts his fingers under the waistband of her panties. She is
surprised that she feels wet. Although she admits that she likes the
feelings associated with sexual touching, she does not like Sam's
neediness and breaks up with him. In *Dangerously Alice* (junior year),
Alice sexually stimulates herself following a date with Tony, stopping
him after he touches her beneath her clothes: "My own fingers caressed

my breasts under the blanket. Then my stomach, then between my legs, and finally I finished what Tony had begun in the car."[92]

Later, Tony invites Alice to his house and attempts to escalate their previous encounter:

> Then he was unzipping my jeans, tugging at the sides till they were down past my hips, and his hand was inside my underwear, finding my slippery place. I felt the swelling sensation in my vagina.
> "Oh, baby, you're creaming for me," he said. "You want it as much as I do."
> He didn't say he wanted *me*, I noticed. He wanted *it*. So did I, honestly, but not, I think, with Tony.[93]

The "it" that Tony and Alice are referring to, of course, is the act of penetration. Alice's character recognizes, here and in other scenes, that sex involves more than the act of penetration, and she acknowledges that she likes how sex feels and that she wants to explore further possibilities, but she also realizes that, for her, *who* and *where* are as important as *how*. Later, she reflects on the episode in Tony's bedroom:

> I liked sex, that's certain. I liked a boy to kiss my breasts, to run his hands up and down my sides, to thrust his tongue in my mouth, to explore my slippery place and finger me. I was eager, I'll admit, for whatever came next. But I was going to be choosy. It wouldn't be lying sideways, with my bra yanked up like a rape scene. It wouldn't be with a guy who . . . was adding me to a long list of girls, condom at the ready.[94]

Finally, in *Intensely Alice*, Alice is forced to contend with her sexual desire for Patrick, whom she truly does care for. They ultimately agree to satisfy each other through mutual masturbation.

In all the *Alice* books, Phyllis Reynolds Naylor created a safe environment in which she presents issues surrounding adolescent sex from a perspective both physical and emotional. These books give readers many opportunities to explore the world of sexual possibilities. Naylor had this to say about why it was important for her to include sexual content in the *Alice* books:

> It was a huge part of our consciousness—our changing bodies, how we looked in our clothes, things we overheard from our parents' bedrooms, stories about girls who were more adventurous than we were, and most of all, the sexual feelings we experienced with our boyfriends. And I

know from the letters and emails I get from readers, that many girls get a charge out of sexually exciting their boyfriends, intentionally or not; that they, like their boyfriends, get very aroused in their love play and are conflicted on how to resolve it. For fans of TV reality programs like *Teen Mom*, which I watch, one would think that teens never give birth control a thought until after they become pregnant. But I know from some agonizing emails I get, that others are scared half out of their minds when they have missed a period. I can only be the girl that Alice has become, and to me, it seemed that she and Patrick would resolve their sexual arousal on that bench in *Intensely Alice* with mutual masturbation—a safe alternative for a loving couple who communicate well with each other. Contrast this with Pamela's panic when her period is late, and Elizabeth's initial reluctance to face her own sexual feelings, and I think that I've dealt honestly with three normal girls, all of whom must make decisions that may be very different from each other's.[95]

NOTES

1. *The Outsiders* (1967), written by a then sixteen-year-old Susan (S. E.) Hinton, is considered by many to mark the beginning of YAL as a genre; Patty Campbell, in Margaret Edwards, *The Fair Garden and the Swarm of Beasts: The Library and the Young Adult*, reprint (Chicago: American Library Association, 1994), vii.
    2. Campbell, in Edwards, *The Fair Garden*, xii.
    3. Eric Leyland, *The Public Library and the Adolescent* (London: Grafton, 1937).
    4. Campbell in Edwards, *The Fair Garden*, xii.
    5. Edwards, *The Fair Garden*, 54–55.
    6. Edwards, *The Fair Garden*, 61.
    7. Edwards, *The Fair Garden*, 62.
    8. Henry Gregor Felsen, *Two and the Town* (New York: Pennant, 1952), 24.
    9. Felsen, *Two and the Town*, 28.
    10. Felsen, *Two and the Town*, 70.
    11. Felsen, *Two and the Town*, 70–71.
    12. Felsen, *Two and the Town*, 80.
    13. Felsen, *Two and the Town*, 98.
    14. Jeanette Eyerly, *A Girl Like Me* (New York: Berkley Highland, 1966), 52–53.
    15. Eyerly, *A Girl Like Me*, 126.
    16. Michael Cart, *Young Adult Literature: From Romance to Realism* (Chicago: American Library Association, 2011), 192.
    17. Ann Head, *Mr. and Mrs. Bo Jo Jones* (New York: Signet, 1968).
    18. Head, *Bo Jo Jones*, 1.
    19. Head, *Bo Jo Jones*, 21.
    20. Head, *Bo Jo Jones*, 27.
    21. Head, *Bo Jo Jones*, 167.
    22. Paul Zindel, *My Darling, My Hamburger* (New York: Harper Crest, 1969), 24.
    23. Zindel, *My Darling*, 51–52.
    24. Zindel, *My Darling*, 92.
    25. Zindel, *My Darling*, 93.
    26. Zindel, *My Darling*, 123.

27. Patty Campbell, *Sex Guides: Books and Films about Sexuality for Young Adults* (New York: Garland, 1986), 233.

28. Richard Peck, *Are You in the House Alone?* (New York: Viking, 1976), 107.

29. Peck, *Are You?* 125.

30. Peck, *Are You?* 125.

31. Peck, *Are You?* 131.

32. *Kirkus Reviews*, review of *Are You in the House Alone*, https://www.kirkusreviews.com/book-reviews/richard-peck/are-you-in-the-house-alone/.

33. Anne Emery, *Free Not to Love* (Philadelphia: Westminster Press, 1975), 43–44.

34. Emery, *Free*, 46.

35. Emery, *Free*, 46.

36. John Donovan, *I'll Get There, It Better Be Worth the Trip* (Woodbury, MN: Flux, 2010), 150.

37. Donovan, *I'll Get There*, 158.

38. Donovan, *I'll Get There*, 169.

39. Donovan, *I'll Get There*, 173.

40. Donovan, *I'll Get There*, 199.

41. Julie Halevy, *The Young Lovers* (New York: Dell, 1955), 72.

42. Halevy, *The Young Lovers*, 74.

43. Halevy, *The Young Lovers*, 74.

44. *Kirkus Reviews*, review of *The Young Lovers*, https://www.kirkusreviews.com/book-reviews/julian-halevy/the-young-lovers/.

45. Halevy, *The Young Lovers*, 319–20.

46. Rosalyn Drexler, *I Am the Beautiful Stranger* (New York: Dell, 1965), 72.

47. Drexler, *I Am*, 71.

48. *Kirkus Reviews*, review of *I Am the Beautiful Stranger*, https://www.kirkusreviews.com/book-reviews/rosalyn-drexler-4/i-am-the-beautiful-stranger/.

49. Drexler, *I Am*, 72, 73.

50. Drexler, *I Am*, 108.

51. Rosalyn Drexler, *I Am the Beautiful Stranger, Paintings from the '60's* (Pace Wildenstein, 2007).

52. Evan Hunter, *Last Summer* (New York: Doubleday, 1968), 79.

53. Hunter, *Last Summer*, 238.

54. Hunter, *Last Summer*, 240.

55. Hunter *Last Summer*, 242.

56. Hunter, *Last Summer*, 244.

57. Hunter, *Last Summer*.

58. Judy Blume, *Then Again, Maybe I Won't* (New York: Yearling, 1986), 73.

59. Blume, *Then Again*, 93.

60. Blume, *Then Again*, 106.

61. Blume, *Then Again*, 164.

62. Patty Campbell, *Sex Guides: Books and Films about Sexuality for Young Adults* (New York: Garland, 1986), 217.

63. Judy Blume, *Forever* (New York: Simon Pulse, 2003), 97.

64. Blume, *Forever*, 130.

65. Allene Stuart Phy, *Presenting Norma Klein* (Woodbridge, CT: Twayne, 1988), 37.

66. Phy, *Presenting*, 23.

67. Phy, *Presenting*, 23.

68. Phy, *Presenting*, 51.

69. NYTimes.com, "Norma Klein, 50, a Young-Adult Novelist," last modified April 27, 1989, http://www.nytimes.com/1989/04/27/obituaries/norma-klein-50-a-young-adult-novelist.html.

70. *Kirkus Reviews*, review of *Beginner's Love*, https://www.kirkusreviews.com/book-reviews/norma-klein-16/beginners-love/.

71. Norma Klein, *It's OK If You Don't Love Me* (New York: Fawcett Juniper, 1977), 38.

72. Klein, *It's OK*, 39, 40.

73. Klein, *It's OK*, 40.

74. Klein, *It's OK*, 44.

75. Klein, *It's OK*, 132.

76. Phy, *Presenting*, 23.

77. Norma Klein, *Beginner's Love* (New York: Dutton, 1983).

78. Klein, *Beginner's Love*, 59.

79. Klein, *Beginner's Love*, 62.

80. Klein, *Beginner's Love*, 63.

81. Klein, *Beginner's Love*, 88.

82. Klein, *Beginner's Love*, 88.

83. *The Agony of Alice, Alice in Rapture, Sort of Reluctantly Alice, All but Alice, Alice in April, Alice In-Between, Alice the Brave, Alice in Lace, Outrageously Alice, Achingly Alice, Alice on the Outside, The Grooming of Alice.*

84. Phyllis Reynolds Naylor, *Outrageously Alice* (New York: Atheneum, 1997), 34.

85. Naylor, *Outrageously Alice*, 88–89.

86. Missionaries talked to the natives of foreign countries about giving up what they felt were unusual sexual practices. The only acceptable position was woman on bottom, man on top.

87. American Library Association, "Frequently Challenged Books of the 21st Century," http://www.ala.org/advocacy/banned/frequentlychallenged/21stcenturychallenged.

88. Bryan Gillis, e-mail interview with Phyllis Reynolds Naylor, April 26, 2013.

89. American Library Association, "Frequently."

90. Phyllis Reynolds Naylor, *Alice on Her Way* (New York: Atheneum, 2005), 113.

91. Naylor, *Alice on Her Way*, 222.

92. Phyllis Reynolds Naylor, *Dangerously Alice* (New York: Atheneum, 2007), 147.

93. Naylor, *Dangerously Alice*, 216.

94. Naylor, *Dangerously Alice*, 219.

95. Bryan Gillis, e-mail interview with Phyllis Reynolds Naylor, April 26, 2013.

Chapter Five

Sex and Romance in Dystopian Young Adult Fiction

The term *utopia*—from the Greek meaning "no place" and "good place"—first appeared in Sir Thomas More's treatise *Utopia* in 1516. Utopia is an imaginary island with a perfect social and political system where everyone is treated fairly. Plato, Machiavelli, Samuel Johnson, Samuel Butler, and many other prominent thinkers have attempted to create utopias, but the task has proven impossible for various reasons. First, a utopia must be a place where all are compatible. Next, the political process—which by necessity will be woven into the social structure—must be foolproof. Then, morality must be defined in a way that makes it an absolute. Even if these first three tasks can be accomplished, getting everyone to agree will be impossible. Ultimately, dystopias are created instead because it is much easier to get people to agree on what is wrong with a society.[1]

Machiavelli's *The Prince* is an example of the paradox of utopia. His so-called utopia illustrated that freedom and justice for individuals and law and order for a society cannot coexist because the needs of the individual and the needs of a society are, by definition, mutually incompatible. In the real world, every time that a utopia is attempted (e.g., the Crusades, imperialism, Nazi Germany), the results have been disastrous.

Young adult dystopian novels contain elements of science fiction, fantasy, and, more recently, plenty of romance. Set in the future and defined by deprivation, oppression, or terror, fiction about dystopias is popular with adolescents because the protagonists in these novels are placed in situations in which they must demonstrate transition from adolescence to adulthood, one of the key characteristics of young adult literature. These characters must make tough choices and the consequences at that age can seem monumental. In short, a dystopia is synonymous with high school life.

Dystopias in literature typically depict complete societal meltdowns. They can be caused by the failure of a utopia or an existing government system; a magnification of a current real-world societal concern, such as overpopulation or nuclear war; a catastrophic natural disaster, like an earthquake or a collision with an asteroid; a pandemic that results in some sort of mutation, such as a zombie apocalypse; or even an alien invasion. Dystopias offer a lens through which we can view our present circumstances, providing "fresh perspectives on problematic social and political practices that might otherwise be taken for granted or considered natural and inevitable."[2]

Sex is a dominant social and political topic in dystopian literature. How a dystopia is created and how it currently functions dictates the significance, frequency, and intensity of sexual activity within that dystopia. Under an authoritarian government, sexual activity and procreation are often rigidly monitored as a way to gain control over the people. This may be done to increase or decrease the population, manipulate the type and/or quality of the individuals being created within that society, or, in the case of sexual activity for reasons other than procreation, as a way to either promote pleasure and happiness or extinguish behaviors that have the potential to cause unpredictable behavior.

For example, in Huxley's *Brave New World*, "the World State" controls the traits in fetuses, creating their citizens in test tubes so that they will conform to specific castes. Once these babies are "born," their beliefs and behaviors are conditioned through subliminal (and not so subliminal) messaging. Uninhibited and frequent sex with multiple partners is encouraged (citizens have been conditioned to take contraceptives), but relationships are outlawed. In Ayn Rand's *Anthem*, male and female living spaces are separated. The genders have meetings where they have sex orgies to populate the species. Again, monogamy and relationships are forbidden. In *The Giver*, babies are euthanized if they possess any physical or mental problems that interfere with the community's predictable life patterns.

Many of the books we discuss here—classic and YAL—do not contain scenes that most readers will consider sexually explicit. We include them because a well-written scene describing an adolescent's sexual experience need not always detail every action and body part— although, when done well, this too can be a positive instructional experience for readers. The proper tone and mood (e.g., a description of even a kiss) can be extremely sexually charged. By positioning a romance within the context of a dystopia, the emotional intensity and urgency that engulf the characters have the potential to engage adolescent readers, thus enabling them to better understand what sexual intimacy feels like. These are emotions that adolescents will likely not hear about from their parents or learn in a sex education class.

GOVERNMENT-CONTROLLED SEX: *1984, DELIRIUM, THE FOREST OF HANDS AND TEETH*

In this type of dystopia, the government monitors and regulates sexual activity. In Orwell's *1984*, sex between Party members is forbidden; the Anti-Sex League promotes the sublimation of the libido; and Party scientists research ways to eliminate the orgasm. The government controls every aspect of human life, including the one act (sex) that can lead to intimate relationships that have the potential to place personal loyalties ahead of those of the government. Children are brainwashed to believe that sex is disgusting, not pleasurable, and should be engaged in only as a means to procreate. As a result, sexual drives become repressed, and sex is viewed as necessary only as a responsibility to the Party.

In the following passage, Winston reflects on why he believes that the Party has made sex illegal:

> The aim of the Party was not merely to prevent men and women from forming loyalties which it might not be able to control. Its real, undeclared purpose was to remove all pleasure from the sexual act. . . . Sexual intercourse was to be looked on as a slightly disgusting minor operation, like having an enema.[3]

Winston embarks on a journey to awaken his sexually repressed self. Initially motivated by passion and sexual curiosity, he ultimately discovers love.

Many YAL dystopias function under similar restrictions as those present in *1984*. In *Delirium*, Lauren Oliver creates a world in which love is considered a disease known as Amor Deliria Nervosa. The symptoms are categorized in four phases, each phase more critical than the previous:

> Phase One—perspiration, sweaty palms . . . reduced mental aware-
> ness . . . impaired reasoning skills; Phase Two—fixation; loss of other
> interests . . . disruption of sleep patterns . . . paranoia; Phase Three—
> complete breakdown of rational facilities; Phase Four—emotional and
> physical paralysis; death. [4]

At the age of eighteen, citizens undergo an operation to "cure" them of the disease. Boys and girls live separately until they are cured, and upon completion of their education, they are paired with a mate whom they will marry for the purpose of procreation. The government strictly prohibits any fraternization between the sexes before the operation. If a teen falls in love before the age of eighteen and the symptoms of Amor Deliria Nervosa are evident, the operation can be performed sooner, although mental complications often occur as a result. In this opening passage, Lena, a few months shy of her eighteenth birthday, considers the operation:

> I don't like to think that I'm still walking around with the disease
> running through my blood. Sometimes I swear I can feel it writhing in
> my veins like something spoiled, like sour milk. It makes me feel dir-
> ty. . . . After the procedure I will be happy and safe forever. That's what
> everybody says, the scientists and my sister and Aunt Carol. I will have
> the procedure and then I will be paired with a boy that the evaluators
> choose for me. In a few years, we'll get married. . . . Safe and free from
> pain. [5]

The only male-female interaction that the government occasionally overlooks is a casual and temporary pairing between a cured and an uncured, because a cured does not possess the desire to have sex or feel love and therefore will not pose a threat. When Lena meets Alex, they are able to interact—albeit discreetly—because Alex has fooled the government into believing that he is cured.

The cure for the disease not only eliminates the capacity for roman-tic love but also extinguishes the ability to love anything—family, friends, even music. Lena tells readers that after the cure, "music doesn't move people the same way."[6] It makes sense that the govern-ment would want to eliminate a love of music, as it has historically been perceived as a stimulator for sexual expression. When Lena's rebellious friend Hana first tells of the illegal coed parties taking place in secret locations throughout the community—parties where kissing and sexual intercourse are prevalent—she first describes the music. "And you should *hear* the music. Incredible, amazing music, like nothing you've ever heard, music that almost takes your head off, you know? That makes you want to scream and jump up and down and break stuff and cry."

Hana's rebellion is motivated by her desires, her need to experience the pleasures that music, dancing, and sex provide. As Lena and Alex spend more time together, readers see that their desires—unlike Hana's and unlike Winston's in *1984*—are fueled by love. Their love manifests itself in this, the most explicit scene in the book:

> And of course, we kiss. We kiss so much that when we're not kissing it feels weird, like I get used to breathing through his lips and into his mouth. Slowly, as we get more comfortable, I start to explore other parts of his body too. The delicate structure of his ribs under his skin, his chest and shoulders like chiseled stone, the soft curls of pale hair on his legs. . . . Even crazier is that I let him look at me, too. First I'll only let him pull my shirt aside and kiss my collarbone and shoulders. Then I let him draw my whole shirt over my head and lie me down in the bright sunshine and just stare at me. The first time I'm shaking. I keep having the urge to cross my hands over my chest, to cover up my breasts, to hide. . . . But then he breathes, "Beautiful," and when his eyes meet mine I know that he really truly means it.[7]

This is Lena's sexual awakening. She realizes that the government and her parents have been lying to her. "That night, for the first time in my life, I stand in front of the bathroom mirror and don't see an in-between girl. For the first time . . . I believe what Alex said. I am beautiful."[8]

The dystopia in *Delirium* eerily resembles the Victorian morality prevalent in the late nineteenth and early twentieth centuries as well as the current sexual agenda of the conservative right in America. This prudishness and repression, promoted by the government as self-discipline and social responsibility, was and still is a major influence on what is marketed as sex education.

In Carrie Ryan's apocalyptic zombie novel *The Forest of Hands and Teeth*, Mary and other survivors of the Return live in what they have been told is the last remaining village in the world. Fences meant to keep the Unconsecrated out and the villagers safe surround the village. Beyond the fences lies a seemingly never-ending Forest of Hands and Teeth. The Sisterhood, a group of nuns led by Sister Tabitha, controls every aspect of village life. Their primary stated mission is procreation of the human species. Mary explains:

> In my village, an unmarried woman has three choices. She may live with her family; a man may speak for her, court her through the winter and marry her in the spring ceremonies; or she may join the Sisterhood. Our village has been isolated since soon after the Return and while we have grown strong and populous over the years, it is still imperative that every healthy young man and woman wed and breed if possible.[9]

"Marriage in our village is not about love, it is about commitment."[10]

As in *Delirium*, love and passion in *Forest* are viewed by authority as detriments to society. For example, when Sister Tabitha notices that Mary has feelings for Travis, she intervenes: "You think you want love, Mary. You think it is this beautiful gift that does nothing but fill you and make you whole. But you are wrong. Love can be cruel and ugly. It can become dark and cause the deepest pain."[11]

Mary and Lena, like many teenagers today, do not blindly accept what the authorities in their lives (parents, schools, political and religious leaders) promote as Truth, especially in matters of love and sex. Readers connect with them in the same way that we connect with Winston in *1984*. We admire the characters who set out to defy those who would have us conform.

Despite the lack of any graphic descriptions of sex, both *Delirium* and *The Forest of Hands and Teeth* allow teen readers to vicariously experience the emotions associated with love, the feelings that accompany a physical attraction to another human being. These relationships are also forming under the most extreme of circumstances. This is important because although adolescence may not be the zombie apocalypse, it can certainly feel that way. These stories allow readers to experience characters' responsible behaviors in the face of the dire circumstances that surround them.

For example, even though it is apparent throughout *Forest* that Mary and Travis love each other, Travis is promised to Mary's best friend Cass, and Travis's brother Harry has spoken for Mary. On one of the very few occasions when Mary and Travis are alone, readers can feel the passion between them while witnessing the responsibility and restraint that each, especially Travis, demonstrates.

> I lay my head on his shoulder and he turns to kiss my forehead. It's meant, I'm sure, as a tender gesture. To let me know that he's still here

for me. But the feel of his lips pounds in my body, throbbing every-where. . . . I am past desire. I need Travis with a fierceness I have never known. . . . There are too many layers of clothing between us and I am angry at all that separates us and that I can't consume him all at once, his whole being. For a moment I understand the craving of the Unconse-crated, the need for the flesh of a living soul. His hands slip through my hair and his lips are close, oh so close to mine. . . . We breathe each other, gasp for more air, for more of each other. And then his lips brush mine. . . . He takes my hands and then I feel his hesitation. . . . He pulls away from me, like ripping my own flesh from my body, and stands. [12]

Despite a never-ending onslaught of zombies, Ryan skillfully devel-ops the romance between Mary and Travis. The entire *Forest* trilogy—*The Dead-Tossed Waves* and *The Dark and Hollow Places* complete it—is a wonderfully horrific, DEFCON 5 dystopian apocalypse, and yet through Ryan's skillful use of tone, including her adept word choice—"craving," "flesh of a living soul," "ripping my own flesh from my body"—she is able to create romantic moods that are wedged amid the horror. The realistic portrayal of human desire within the chaos of the world is what connects teen readers.

DRUG-INDUCED SEXUAL APATHY: *THE GIVER*

The Giver—by Lois Lowry, winner of the Newbery Medal (1993) for distinguished contribution to American literature for children—is the most well-written YA dystopian novel of all time. The novel addresses sexual content yet contains no explicitly sexual scenes.

Jonas's community is founded on the belief that for everyone to achieve true happiness, all stimuli that cause emotion must be eliminat-ed to ensure that no one experiences pain, prejudice, injustice, or inse-curity. The community is controlled by the Elders, who enforce "same-ness" through a strict set of rules, regulations, and rituals. For example, community members must apply for spouses and are matched accord-ing to attributes. Those who fail to demonstrate the appropriate abilities are not given spouses. After three years of marriage, a couple can apply for children. Each family may receive one girl and one boy, given to them at a community ceremony. The babies are conceived by Birth-mothers, one of the "vocations" to which a woman in the community may be assigned by the Elders. The job is seen as vital (procreation) but not prestigious. Birthmothers are well fed and cared for, until they have borne three children. They then spend the remainder of their lives as laborers.

Past memories, positive and negative, are safely kept from the community by passage from the Giver to the Receiver—a community member who has been identified by the Elders as possessing special gifts or abilities. Unbeknownst to Jonas, he will soon be chosen as the community's new Receiver. The current Receiver, the soon-to-be Giver, will begin transferring to Jonas all the memories of humanity: memories of war, color, sex, love, music—memories that are pleasurable and memories that are painful.

Before his selection, Jonas—who, like all community members, is required to share his dreams with his parents—shares one in which he is trying to convince his friend Fiona to get into a tub of water with him. "I wanted her to take off her clothes and get into the tub," he explained quickly. "I wanted to bathe her. I had the sponge in my hand. But she wouldn't. She kept laughing and saying no." [13]

Jonas's father then asks him to describe the strongest feeling that he experienced in the dream. "The wanting," he said. "I knew that she wouldn't. And I think I knew that she *shouldn't*. But I wanted it so terribly. I could feel the wanting all through me." [14]

Later, Jonas's mother explains what he was experiencing:

> The feeling you described as the wanting? It was your first Stirrings. Father and I have been expecting it to happen to you. It happens to everyone. It happened to Father when he was your age. And it happened to me. . . . And very often," Mother added, "it begins with a dream." [15]

Jonas asks his mother about "the treatment." He has heard the Speaker, an electronic sound system, warn of the Stirrings: "ATTENTION. A REMINDER THAT STIRRINGS MUST BE REPORTED IN ORDER FOR TREATMENT TO TAKE PLACE." [16] His mother responds, "It's just the pills. You're ready for the pills, that's all. That's the treatment for Stirrings." [17]

Jonas enjoyed the feelings that the stirrings gave him, but soon the pills take effect, and the pleasures of the stirrings dissipate. It is not until after his first few meetings with the Giver that his entire belief system shifts. He begins to realize that depriving people of pleasurable and painful memories and choices to keep them from making poor decisions is a bad idea. He begins to understand that even though a world with love might be dangerous, it also might be worth the risk.

The Giver is introduced in classrooms as early as fifth grade and is currently taught in college classrooms as well. The power of the story lies in its many layers and the myriad themes and topical issues that it introduces. One of those themes is choice. We encourage teachers to consider focusing some student discussions on one of the biggest choices that the community is deprived of and one that Jonas eventually does not have to make because of his role as the Receiver: the Elders' decision to withhold factual information regarding the pleasures of sex.

DISEASE-INDUCED SEXUAL ABSTINENCE: *PEEPS, THE DARK AND HOLLOW PLACES*

In this type of dystopia, protagonists demonstrate impressive levels of restraint as a means to keep what remains of the existing healthy human population out of the hands of zombies, vampires, aliens, and the like. In Scott Westerfeld's scientifically detailed vampire masterpiece *Peeps*, the protagonists battle against ancient underground forces that carry highly infectious diseases and threaten to turn everyone into vampires. Here is what Westerfeld had to say about his creative process while creating *Peeps*:

> Some days you wake up, and you just have to write a vampire novel. I know, I know, there is no shortage of vampire novels already out there. If you search *Amazon* for "vampire" you get . . . opera-loving vampires, horny vampires, southern vampires, emotional vampires, bondage-loving vampires, and (of course) Canadian vampires who solve crimes. . . . The book had to be original, but also icky, scary, funny, tragic, and (ahem) not sucky. Besides getting a new take on the sunlight-impaired, my other big concern was that my vampires should actually make some sense as far as science goes. After consuming all there was to know . . . I came up with the four important features that any vampire novel (of mine) had to include: natural selection, sexual attraction, parasitic infection, and Elvis memorabilia. [18]

Peeps—an American Library Association Top Ten Book for young adults (2005)—stars Cal Thompson, a college student who until a year ago, had been more interested in hooking up with girls and partying than attending biology class. However, after a fateful encounter with a mysterious woman named Morgan, Cal is infected with a nasty parasite, and biology becomes his favorite subject. He unknowingly infects three girls through sexual intercourse, turning each of them into Peeps (vampires). Cal does not turn. However, he does acquire incredible hearing and an increased sense of smell, and he is exceedingly strong and fast. Cal explains:

> We're called carriers, because we have the disease without all the symp-
> toms. Although there is one extra symptom that we do have: The dis-
> ease makes us horny. All the time. The parasite doesn't want us carriers
> to go to waste, after all. We can still spread the disease to other humans.
> Like that of the maniacs, our saliva carries the parasite's spores. [19]

Cal begins hunting the girls down to prevent them from infecting others. Along the way, he demonstrates the same admirable levels of responsibility and restraint as the protagonists in the government-controlled dystopias. As a result of the parasite—which seems to produce effects similar to those of adolescence—his body constantly courses with lust, yet he soldiers on, understanding that he must stop the spread of the parasite.

In his search for Morgan, he meets Lace, her former roommate. Lace is attracted to Cal and is disappointed when she discovers that Cal is a carrier and has been hiding it from her.

> "What if you want to sleep with someone, Cal? You'd have to tell
> them."
>   "I can't sleep with anyone," I said.
>   "Jesus, Cal, even people with HIV have sex. They just wear a con-
> dom . . . "
>   "The parasites spores are viable even in saliva, and they're small
> enough to penetrate latex. Any kind of sex is dangerous, Lace." [20]

As Lace prepares to leave, Cal asks,

> "Why do you care if I'm sick?"
>   "Christ, Cal! Because I thought we had something." She shrugged.
> "The way you keep looking at me. From the first time we saw each
> other in that elevator."
>   "That's because . . . I *do* like you." I felt my throat swelling, my
> eyes stinging, but I was not going to cry. "But there's nothing I can do
> about it." [21]

In *The Dark and Hollow Places*, Carrie Ryan's last book in the *Forest of Hands and Teeth* trilogy, Annah encounters a sexual roadblock different from the one that Mary faced in *Forest*. Whereas Travis thwarts Mary's passionate advances because of his loyalty to his betrothed, Catcher is bitten by an Unconsecrated, and although he does not turn, he does becomes a carrier. Like Cal, Catcher is terrified that if he even kisses Annah, he will infect her. Annah acts on her passion, and it is Catcher who must help her keep that passion in check.

After being forced to evacuate what they believed was the last safe city on Earth, Annah, her sister, and Elias are held captive on an island, while Catcher, because of his immunity to the Unconsecrated and his ability to walk among them, is used as bait to collect supplies from the besieged city. After a particularly difficult and emotional journey, Catcher returns to the island and almost succumbs to Annah's passionate advances:

> "I can't lose you, Annah." His face hovers in front of me. "I won't lose you."
> And then his lips are on mine.
> It's the warmth I feel first. The pure heat of him when he opens his mouth as if to devour me. There's such urgency—such a hunger between us—born of a need to be something to someone. . . . I taste who he is and was and together we fall back onto the bed. I shove my hands into his hair, pulling him tighter—always tighter. We breathe each other. We are the other person in that moment—nothing distinct about us except the same desire. . . .
> He looks at me, *really* looks at me. "I'm terrified," he whispers. "Of us. Of hurting you." [22]

As the word *abstinence* in the subheading suggests, the books in this section do not contain any sexually explicit scenes. What they do offer in terms of meaningful context are the sexual thoughts, discussions, and actions of well-developed characters who are placed in situations that feel surprisingly like those that teen readers experience themselves.

SEX IN THE MIDST OF AN APOCALYPSE: *GRASSHOPPER JUNGLE*

In Andrew Smith's masterpiece *Grasshopper Jungle*, the protagonists are responsible—albeit accidentally—for the events that set the end of the world in motion. Austin Szerba, an aspiring historian in the fictional small town of Ealing, Iowa, narrates this account of a giant praying

mantis apocalypse. These six-foot-tall insects hatch from people who
have come in contact with a nasty ooze first developed in the 1960s.
They do two things: "they eat and they fuck."[23] *Grasshopper Jungle*
interweaves Austin's personal family history and his journey through
adolescence with these apocalyptic events. Readers also meet Austin's
girlfriend, Shann Collins, whom he loves and desperately wants to have
sex with, and Austin's gay best friend, Robby Brees, whom he also
loves and may have sexual feelings for as well. We also learn about
Austin's brother—hospitalized overseas due to a war injury—a (dead)
mad scientist, an underground bunker named Eden, and we are introduced to two furry lemur masks, a couple of film canisters, and a small
glass globe filled with a strange fluorescent liquid.

As Austin fights off giant insects that are almost indestructible, he
tries hard to make sense of sex, his family history, religion, relationships, and love. When he is alone with Shann, a simple touch sets his
hormones on fire. In this scene, he and Shann are hanging out at her
house:

> We sat beside each other on the staircase.
>   Our bare legs touched.
>   Shann had the perfect body, a Friday-after-school body that was
> mostly visible because she was barefoot and wore tight, cuffed shorts
> with a cantaloupe-colored halter-top. A boy could go insane, I thought,
> just being this close to Shann's uncovered shoulders, wheat hair, and
> heavy breasts.[24]

Austin sometimes thinks about what it would be like to be intimate
with Robby, too. But when he is with Robby, although he professes and
demonstrates his love, he never seems quite comfortable being alone
with him in a sexual way. For example, after being beat up for being
"queer," Austin and Robby sit on a rooftop above Grasshopper Jungle
and discuss what just happened. Robby asks Austin:

> "Do you realize that today we got beaten up for being queers?"
>   "I know."
>   "But you're not a queer," Robby offered.
>   "I don't think so."[25]

Later in the conversation, Robby says,

> "Well, if I'm going to get beat up for being queer, at least I'd like to
> know one time what it feels like to be kissed."

"Um, I guess you deserve that. You know. Everyone deserves to not feel alone."

"Can I kiss you, Austin?"

The air suddenly became unbreathably thin.

I thought about it. I shook my head.

"That would be too weird."

"Sorry."

"Don't be."[26]

Later in the conversation, Austin reconsiders:

I said, "I guess I would kiss you, Robby."

"Don't feel like you *have* to."

"I don't feel that way."

So Robby Brees, my best friend, and the guy who taught me how to dance so I could set into motion Shann Collins's falling in love with me, scooted around with his shoulders turned toward mine.

He was nervous.

I was terrified.

I watched him swallow a couple of times.

Then Robby placed his cigarette carefully down on the gravel beside his foot. He put his hand behind my neck and kissed me.

He kissed me the way I kiss Shann, but it felt different, intense, scary.[27]

Austin's feelings of uncertainty stem from his attempts to determine whether or not he is gay, as well as from his guilt, because he loves both Robby and Shann. When he is with Robby and his thoughts become sexual, he feels as though he is cheating on Shann. In Austin's fantasies, Robby becomes a "safer" sexual partner when he includes Shann as a third party. In this scene, Austin and Robby have stopped by to see Shann:

SHANNON KISSED ME on the lips at the door of her new old house. She kissed Robby on the lips, too.

Shann always kissed Robby on the mouth after she kissed me. It made me horny.

I wondered what she would say if I asked her to have a threesome with us in her new old, unfurnished bedroom.

I knew what Robby would say.

Duh.

I wondered if it made me homosexual to even think about having a threesome with Robby and Shann. And I hated knowing that it would be easier for me to ask Robby to do it than to ask my own girlfriend.

I felt myself turning red and starting to sweat uncomfortably in my
Animal Collective shirt.
And I realized that for a good three and a half minutes, I stood there
in the doorway to a big empty house that smelled like old people's skin,
thinking about three-ways involving my friends.
So I wondered if that meant I was gay. [28]

Austin's horniness, like that of the average adolescent male, appears
at the most inopportune moments. He is acutely aware of this phenome-
non, and like everything else in his life, he worries about it. After their
kiss on the roof above Grasshopper Jungle, Austin and Robby drive
home. Austin glances into Robby's backseat and ponders, "I wondered
if I would ever not be horny, or confused about my horniness, or
confused about why I got horny at stuff I wasn't supposed to get horny
at. As history as my judge, probably not." [29]

In addition to his numerous threesome fantasies, readers do witness
two intense sexual encounters between Austin and Shann. The first
occurs in a movie theater:

I slid my hand up inside the loose sweater Shann was wearing and
played with her perfect breasts. . . . I had never touched Shann's naked
breasts before. She liked it. I liked it more, I think. In fact, Shann
dropped her hand between my legs and rubbed me. Shann had never put
her hand there before. This caused a very sudden and accidental erup-
tion of Mount Austin Andrzej Szerba inside my jeans.
    I gasped and gulped.
    It happened exactly at the same moment where the dumb movie
went absolutely quiet.
    I was mortified. I nearly passed out. [30]

Afterward, Austin wrestles with what just happened. "Most of the way
home, I was trying to decide if what happened to me could technically
be considered *having* sex; if that was the first time I actually *had* sex
with someone else. I decided it was close enough . . . close enough to
be a forbidden subject in the library at Curtis Crane Lutheran Acade-
my." [31]

The second encounter takes place in an underground bunker that
Austin and Robby discover as the praying mantises begin to hatch and
multiply. By now, Austin understands that the best that he can hope for
is a life underground with his two best friends. Saving the world from
destruction does not seem possible (although they do give it a go).
Their desperation is evident in this scene:

Shann Collins and I threw off all our clothing. Naked, we fall down onto the floor together.

"Do you think this is the end of the world, Austin?"

"We'll be okay. We'll be okay."

Shann kissed me. She put her mouth everywhere on my body. It was electric.

But I could not stop myself from thinking about my brother, Eric, and the two prostitutes named Tiffany and Rhonda. . . . I thought about Robby in the clinic.

I thought about naming my balls.

Shann Collins helped me put my penis inside her vagina, and we had sexual intercourse right there on the floor of Eden's bowling alley, below a pair of shoes and a pink ball that had *Wanda Mae* embossed in gold on it.

Our sex was noisy and urgent and wet. I rubbed my kneecaps raw, scraping them on the rough carpeting at the shoe-changing station. I pushed Shann along her butt until her head and mine bumped against the rattling rack of bowling shoes.

I did not care about anything at that moment.[32]

The sex in *Grasshopper Jungle* is not limited to humans. If the giant praying mantises are going to take over the world, they will need to procreate. Austin's detailed description of this *bug sex* serves as a grim reminder to readers that sex has consequences:

Hungry Jack, whose real name was Charles R. Hoofard, but was now a massive green bug that looked like a praying mantis, and Travis Pope, who was also a massive green bug that looked like a praying mantis, were back in the alley at Grasshopper Jungle. They were fighting over mating privileges with Travis's wife, Eileen Pope, who was also a massive green bug that looked like a praying mantis.

It didn't matter. Travis had already inseminated her a dozen times that day, and now he was more hungry than horny. There was plenty of Eileen Pope to go around. . . .

Hungry Jack joined himself to Eileen Pope as she clamped four of her arms onto the dirty convertible sofa in Grasshopper Jungle and buzzed with contented, fizzling coos like a short-circuiting wall socket.[33]

Despite the premise, *Grasshopper Jungle* deals with sex in a realistic manner. Even as the world is coming to an end, the three teen protagonists' decisions are informed and motivated by love, passion, and even a mild sense of purpose amid the chaos. Austin, like other characters in apocalyptic circumstances, understands his responsibility to procreate if the human race is to survive, although this is possibly not the first thing on his mind in the movie theater or the bowling alley. The tone of these scenes, though descriptive, will most likely *not* elicit readers' sexual urges and desires, due to the awkward and at times even troubling nature of the circumstances. The relationship among Austin, Shann, and Robby—what is left of them as the world crumbles—is ultimately determined by their feelings and emotions for one another, not by the cataclysmic events that surround them.

Andrew Smith has created a brilliant narrative that accurately portrays the very real thoughts and concerns with which every adolescent male wrestles—sex, religion, politics, family history, biology, and so on—regardless of whether he is having sex, sitting in a movie theater, or participating in the end of the world. The novel is a metaphorical tale that uses apocalyptic events to comment on the trials and tribulations of adolescence. If *Grasshopper Jungle* were about the protagonists saving the world, then Earth's survival would depend on Austin and Robbie. But the book is not about saving the world. It is about Austin's quest to save himself before the world ends. As Smith explains, Austin

> is troubled by his awakening realization that the expectations placed on him by his school, community, church, and family of what it means to be a teenage boy don't match up with his own identity. . . . I knew from the beginning that I was going to destroy the world. It had to happen because becoming "adult," and coming to realizations about your identity (two important ideas from the book) are really events where worlds come to an end, aren't they?[34]

SEX AND ROMANCE IN DYSTOPIAN SERIES: *TWILIGHT, HUNGER GAMES, DIVERGENT, LEGEND*

A major trend in YAL is the dystopian romance. Typically written as trilogies (although several contain four or more installments), many dystopian romances have been criticized as being more romance than dystopia. Call them what you will, they are extremely popular. What may be most shocking to those who cringe every time they hear the words *YA* and *romance* together is that these books contain surprisingly little graphic sexual content. Instead, authors create sexual tone and mood by placing their characters in situations of extreme want and need, a task made easier when those characters are facing dire circumstances—that is, dystopian settings.

Stephenie Meyer's *Twilight Saga* is an example of a dystopia/romance whose plot is driven primarily by the *made for each other* love between Bella and Edward, with Jacob along for the ride as the third member of the love triangle. The setting, Forks, Washington, functions as a psychological dystopia for Bella. The circumstances of her arrival in Forks, the limitations placed on her as a result of her exclusive knowledge of the vampires and werewolves who also live here, and her frustration at not being able to be intimate with Edward make her life in Forks miserable. She describes the small town as a bleak and rainy place that boasts the most suicides per capita in the United States. Forks is also a dystopia for the vampires, as they are forced to live there in secrecy lest they incur the wrath of the Volturi, the governing vampires who create a hostile and unstable society amid the immortals. Conversely, everyone else who lives in Forks, oblivious to the existence of the vampires and werewolves, seems perfectly content.

The history of the vampires and werewolves in Forks and any descriptive background on the Volturi might place the *Twilight Saga* in the realm of pure dystopia, but Meyer devotes little time to their back stories. Instead, she focuses on the romantic growth and sexual tension between Bella and Edward and Jacob and Bella. In fact, the detailed myths associated with the vampires and werewolves are not explained until halfway into *New Moon* (book 2), and the Volturi are not fully revealed until *Breaking Dawn* (book 4).

In *Twilight* (book 1), Edward and Bella begin to explore their passion for each other. Edward tries to explain to Bella how difficult it is for him to control his feelings for her, likening it to a drug addiction. "There are other hungers. Hungers I don't even understand, that are foreign to me." Bella tells him, "I may understand *that* better than you think." Edward responds, "I'm not used to feeling so human. Is it always like this?"[35]

And then they kiss for the first time:

> His cold, marble lips pressed very softly against mine.
>   What neither of us was prepared for was my response. Blood boiled under my skin, burned in my lips. My breath came in a wild gasp. My fingers knotted in his hair, clutching him to me. My lips parted as I breathed in his heady scent.[36]

Bella and Edward kiss and hover around each other's necks and faces for most of *Twilight*, *New Moon*, and *Eclipse* (book 3). Similarly to Annah and Catcher's relationship in *The Dark and Hollow Places*,

their romance cannot progress to sex, because of the extreme consequences that will come crashing down on them. Edward tells Bella that
if they have sex he will *lose control* and hurt her, possibly even kill her.
He is also old-fashioned—he is, after all, a one-hundred-year-old virgin—and he wants to marry Bella before they have sex. In Edward's
eyes, sex before marriage would be a sin, and since he is already unsure
whether he even has a soul, he does not want to risk contributing to
Bella losing hers and therefore not going to heaven.

Enter Jacob, a werewolf, the mortal enemy of Edward and Bella's
best friend. After Edward repeatedly thwarts Jacob's efforts to see Bella alone, the two get some private moments in *Eclipse,* and Jacob takes
the opportunity to try to kiss her for the first time. After Jacob says that
his heart beats only for her, Bella provides this narration:

> He still had my chin—his fingers holding too tight, till it hurt—and I
> saw the resolve form abruptly in his eyes.
>
> "N—" I started to object, but it was too late.
>
> His lips crushed mine, stopping my protest. He kissed me angrily,
> roughly, his other hand gripping tight around the back of my neck,
> making escape impossible. I shoved against his chest with all my
> strength, but he didn't even seem to notice. His mouth was soft, despite
> the anger, his lips molding mine in a warm, unfamiliar way.
>
> I grabbed at his face, trying to push it away, failing again. . . . His
> lips forced mine open, and I could feel his hot breath in my mouth. . . . I
> let my hands drop to my side, and shut down. I . . . just waited for him to
> stop.
>
> It worked. The anger seemed to evaporate, and he pulled back to
> look at me. He pressed his lips softly to mine again. . . . I pretended I
> was a statue and waited.
>
> Finally, he let go of my face and leaned away.[37]

Bella does not appear to be a willing participant in this first kiss.
The tone of the scene feels less like a kiss and more like a sexual
assault—so much so that Internet fans of the *Twilight* books are quick
to correct anyone who refers to the scene as "Jacob and Bella kissing,"
pointing out that Bella is not into it at all. The second kiss is initiated by
Bella. She tells Jacob that she loves him—that she does not want him to
put himself in harm's way. But readers soon discover that despite what
she says, her heart beats for Edward. "I blurted out the words without
stopping to count the cost. 'Will you kiss me Jacob?' His eyes widened
in surprise, then narrowed suspiciously. 'You're bluffing.' 'Kiss me
Jacob. Kiss me and then come back.'"[38]

Jacob moves in, and Bella's description of the kiss, even more so than the first time, feels more like a sexual assault than a romantic moment.

> I knew he would take advantage of the situation. . . . I held very still, my eyes closed . . . as his hands caught my face and his lips found mine with an eagerness that was not far from violence. I could feel his anger as his mouth discovered my passive resistance. One hand moved to the nape of my neck, twisting into a fist around the roots of my hair. The other hand grabbed roughly at my shoulder, shaking me, then dragging me to him. His hand continued down my arm, finding my wrist and pulling my arm up around his neck. . . . All the while his lips, disconcertingly soft and warm, tried to force a response out of mine. . . . His lips gave up on mine for a moment, but I knew he was nowhere close to finished. His mouth followed the line of my jaw, and explored the length of my neck. He freed my hair, reaching for my other arm to draw it around his neck like the first. Then both of his arms were constricted around my waist, and his lips found my ear.[39]

Bella tries to fight back, but Jacob misreads her resistance as passion:

> With a wild gasp, he brought his mouth back to mine, his fingers clutching frantically against the skin at my waist. . . . My brain disconnected from my body, and I was kissing him back. Against all reason, my lips were moving with his in strange, confusing ways they'd never moved before—because I didn't have to be careful with Jacob, and he certainly wasn't being careful with me. . . . Why wasn't I stopping this? Worse than that, why couldn't I find in myself even the desire to *want* to stop?[40]

Despite the violent tone and Bella's resistance in this scene, she finally realizes that she has been lying to herself—that she really does love Jacob, although maybe not enough, and the love triangle is officially on.

Eventually, Team Edward triumphs over Team Jacob, and in *Breaking Dawn* Bella and Edward get married. Bella is still human, so their first sexual experience is a cautious one, neither of them wanting to see Bella seriously injured. "His arms wrapped around me, holding me against him, summer and winter. It felt like every nerve ending in my body was a live wire. 'Forever,' he agreed, and then pulled us gently into deeper water."[41]

The scene is brief and not explicit, but the aftermath of their first sexual encounter leaves Edward concerned:

> "Look, Bella!" he almost growled. He took my hand—very gingerly—and stretched my arm out. "Look at *that*."
>   This time, I saw what he meant.
>   Under the dusting of feathers, large purplish bruises were beginning to blossom across the pale skin of my arm. [42]

Bella feels that the sex was worth the consequences, but Edward is inconsolable. Bella wants more. She even barters with Edward for sex. He has decided that he will never have sex with her again, but Bella says that she will stay human longer—something that she knows Edward wants to hear—if he agrees to sleep with her. He tells her that blackmail won't work. However, after Bella falls asleep and has a sex-filled dream, she awakes upset because she cannot have sex with Edward—then this occurs:

> I couldn't tell if he was moved by the tears trembling in my voice, or if he was unprepared to deal with the suddenness of my attack, or if his need was simply as unbearable in that moment as my own. But, whatever the reason, he pulled my lips back to his, surrendering with a groan. And we began where my dream left off. [43]

Bella quickly becomes pregnant following this second sexual encounter. The baby develops at superhuman speed and makes it impossible for Bella to eat anything because the fetus wants blood. Bella decides that she will sacrifice herself for her unborn child. Edward is devastated, as is Jacob. Jacob blames Edward for killing Bella, and Edward blames himself. Edward is devastated over the fact that he succumbed to his sexual desires, even though he knew that he would—and did—hurt her.

After Edward turns Bella into a vampire, her thirst for sex is unquenchable:

> He pulled my face to his with a sudden fierceness, a low moan in his throat. The sound sent the electric current running through my body into a near-frenzy, like I couldn't get close to him fast enough. I heard the fabric tearing under our hands and I was glad my clothes, at least, were already destroyed. It was too late for his. It felt almost rude to ignore the pretty white bed, but we just weren't going to make it that far. This second honeymoon wasn't like our first. [44]

They have sex all night, and Bella's thoughts focus on how much she had been missing before becoming a vampire, due to Edward holding back:

> I was never going to get tired, and neither was he. We didn't have to catch our breath or rest or eat or even use the bathroom; we had no more mundane human needs. He had the most beautiful, perfect body in the world and I had him all to myself, and it didn't feel like I was ever going to find a point where I would think, *Now I've had enough for one day*. I was always going to want more. [45]

Their daughter Renéesme is Bella's only distraction, the one thing that pulls her back to the present and reminds her that there is more to life than having sex.

In many of the early YA books that we explored—*Two for the Town*, *A Girl Like Me*, *Mr. and Mrs. Bo Jo Jones* and others—both male and female characters suffer dire consequences as a result of engaging in promiscuous sexual activity, most typically premarital sex. The consequences that Edward and Bella suffer are not caused by promiscuity but rather because each chooses to engage in an intimate relationship with someone who is different. What are the consequences for having sex in the world of *Twilight*? Bella dies in childbirth after extreme suffering—broken bones and internal bleeding—so Edward must bring her back to life, but the only way that he can do this is by changing her into a vampire. Restoring her life results in the loss of her ability to experience many of the common human experiences, such as growing old together, maintaining contact with her friends and parents, sleeping, and enjoying food that is not blood. However, according to Edward, her desire and passion for sex may continue to burn for a decade or more.

Breaking Dawn concludes with a foiled rebellion against the dystopian society created by the Volturi, a society in which Bella now lives. The continued threat of the Volturi serves as a reminder that Edward and Bella must live cautious lives as vampires.

We believe that a true dystopian novel should contain well-defined dystopian settings and circumstances and that both must play primary roles in the decision-making processes of the characters. The dystopian conditions may serve as a catalyst for romance, but it is the conditions, not the romance, that drive the plot. We consider *Twilight* primarily a romance because, despite the dystopian setting, romance drives the plot. Bella and Edward's love moves the story forward, not the presence of the Volturi. Look no further than the avalanche of book reviews and fan fiction spawned from the series. Romance, not dystopia, is the predominant topic of discussion. In contrast, we consider *The Hunger Games*, *Legend*, and *Divergent* series to be primarily dystopian, because romance in these series does not overshadow the dystopian structure of the stories.

In *The Hunger Games*, by Suzanne Collins, a love triangle exists (Katniss, Peta, and Gale), but it is created and manipulated by the Capitol and the Games. Katniss does express an interest in Gale, but once the Games begin, survival overshadows romance. The only scene in *The Hunger Games* (book 1) that resembles a romantic encounter— Katniss and Peta kissing as she nurses him to health on the river bank— is instigated by Katniss to trick the viewers into believing that they are in love to receive gifts to aid in their survival:

> Impulsively, I lean forward and kiss him, stopping his words. This is probably overdue anyway since he's right, we are supposed to be madly in love. It's the first time I've ever kissed a boy, which should make some sort of impression I guess, but all I can register is how unnaturally hot his lips are from the fever. . . . If I want to keep Peta alive, I've got to give the audience something more to care about. Star-crossed lovers desperate to get home together. Two hearts beating as one. Romance. Never having been in love, this is going to be a real trick. [46]

The doomed romances in both *Twilight* and *The Hunger Games* invite comparisons to one of Shakespeare's romantic tragedies, with Meyer even referring to Edward and Bella as *star-crossed lovers*. What we cannot imagine is *Twilight* without the kissing, the passion, and the romance. Conversely, *The Hunger Games*, although strengthened by the ill-fated love triangle, would survive without any romance.

In *Divergent*, by Veronica Roth, Tris and Four's mutual attraction is significant but secondary to the dystopian plot line. Beatrice (Tris) Prior lives in a futuristic version of Chicago where teens are assigned to one of five distinct factions. Each faction represents a trait: Dauntless/ bravery, Erudite/knowledge, Abnegation/self-sacrifice, Amity/friendship, and Candor/truth. Tris was raised in an Abnegation family. When she turns sixteen, she decides to join Dauntless, because she does not view herself as all that selfless and because she tested as a Divergent: someone who does not really fit in anywhere.

Several of Tris's Dauntless simulations place her in situations in which she is forced to face her inner fears and then quickly get them under control. These are no ordinary fear simulations. Tris is held at gunpoint and told to kill her parents. She is burned at the stake, but because she is a Divergent, she realizes that she is experiencing simulations, and this allows her to manipulate the scenarios to her advantage.

Following yet another *kill her parents* simulation, Tris notices that Four is observing her, and she tells him that she knows that the simulations are not real. She soon realizes that he is not going to tell anyone. They stare longingly at each other for a few seconds, and as Tris leaves the simulation area, she thinks, "I shouldn't be so easily distracted by him. I shouldn't be able to think about anything but initiation. The simulations should disturb me more; they should break my mind, as they have been doing to most of the other initiates. . . . Is it being Divergent that makes me steady, or is it something else?"[47]

The remainder of the series progresses in similar fashion. Four and Tris continue to explore their romance, but what moves the plot is their continuous attempts to overthrow various levels of government control. Eventually, the rebellion triumphs, and Chicagoans are free to live as they choose. As in *The Hunger Games*, there is some kissing and sexual tension but no depiction of actual sex.

The setting for Marie Lu's *Legend* series is the dystopia of Los Angeles in the not-so-distant future. Day and June, both fifteen years old, alternate as narrators. They are instantly attracted to each other, but unfortunately, the militaristic nature of the society in which they live prevents them from ever acting on their romance, except for some occasional passionate kissing. Day is a futuristic Robin Hood and the government's most sought-after criminal. June was born into a prominent family in the wealthiest district and is likely to progress through the government ranks. Day and June are doomed from the beginning, but like all the romances described in these dystopias, they pursue the relationship despite the odds.

In *Prodigy* (book 2), Day and June's physical interactions are limited by the introduction of ancillary characters into the story. We learn that Day has been spending time with a girl whom he knew before he met June. She is in love with him, but Day sees her as a little sister and has no romantic interest in her. June is promised to the new government leader's son. He is good-looking, and she agrees to spend time with him to play spy for the other side. In the process, she begins to really like the guy, and she becomes conflicted. Should she live a lavish lifestyle with a hot guy who worships her or live on the run with the most wanted criminal in their society—a guy who is not very nice to her and, by the way, killed her brother. Guess whom she chooses?

In *Champion* (book 3), Day and June, now seventeen, finally have sex. The scene contains little description of the physical act, focusing instead on June's emotions during sex. Day is also emotionally raw, due to his concern over his younger brother, who is dying. Day asks June if she loves him, and she admits that she does but understands that no good can come of the love between the prodigy and the legend. June moves in to kiss Day, and the kiss continues through June's apartment until they fall on her bed:

> I fall into another kiss, running my hands through his hair, letting him know that I'm okay. He gradually relaxes. I suck in my breath as he moves against me. His eyes are so bright that I feel like I could drown in them. He kisses my cheeks tucking a strand of my hair behind my ear as he goes and I slide my arms around his back and pull him closer. No matter what happens in the future, no matter where our paths take us, this moment will be ours.[48]

June's description of her long-anticipated sexual union with Day is filled with emotion. As June narrates, she interprets Day's emotions and actions. She depicts him as feeling tortured by the thoughts that consume him—his belief that he is not good enough for her, that she does not really love him. The scene ends with both of them falling asleep. When Day awakes (he is now narrating), he finds June lying next to him naked. Realizing that he will no longer be able to hide his emotions, he accepts that he is doomed to love her forever. He leaves in the middle of the night, understanding that when June awakes, she will be without him.

FINAL THOUGHTS ON DYSTOPIAN SEX

One of the significant challenges that adolescents face is the attempt to integrate what they believed themselves to be as children with their newly discovered sexual desires and visions of their future selves. Dystopian YAL is popular because these stories create worlds that challenge the protagonists to question the status quo. The actions of well-developed characters within these dystopias enable teen readers to reflect on their own circumstances and consider how they would respond. One necessary trait that all protagonists in YA dystopias possess is rebellion. They fight to correct what they perceive to be unjust, whether it is a government that forbids sex or an invasion of vampires or zombies who spread disease. Historically, adolescent sexual activity has been discouraged and promoted as inappropriate, typically through government channels, so it is no surprise that teen readers connect to stories in which the heroes pursue what they have been told they cannot have or do not deserve. We urge teachers to include discussions of sex when reading these and other YA dystopias. They provide a perfect mix of science fiction, fantasy, reality, and romance—just like high school.

NOTES

1. Tvtropes.org, "Utopia," http://tvtropes.org/pmwiki/pmwiki.php/Main/Utopia.

2. M. Keith Booker, *Dystopian Literature: A Theory and Research Guide* (Westport, CT: Greenwood Press, 1994), 3.

3. George Orwell, *1984* (New York: New American Library, 1961), 65.

4. Lauren Oliver, *Delirium* (New York: HarperCollins, 2011), 147.

5. Oliver, *Delirium*, 2.

6. Oliver, *Delirium*, 133.

7. Oliver, *Delirium*, 261.

8. Oliver, *Delirium*, 261.

9. Carrie Ryan, *The Forest of Hands and Teeth* (New York: Delacorte Press, 2009), 24–25.

10. Ryan, *The Forest*, 4.

11. Ryan, *The Forest*, 68.

12. Ryan, *The Forest*, 182.

13. Lois Lowry, *The Giver* (New York: Houghton Mifflin, 1993), 36.

14. Lowry, *The Giver*, 36.

15. Lowry, *The Giver*, 37.

16. Lowry, *The Giver*, 37.

17. Lowry, *The Giver*, 38.

18. Scott Westerfeld.com, *Peeps*, http://scottwesterfeld.com/books/peeps/.

19. Scott Westerfeld, *Peeps* (New York: Razorbill, 2005), 22–23.

20. Westerfeld, *Peeps*, 227.

21. Westerfeld, *Peeps*, 228.

22. Carrie Ryan, *The Dark and Hollow Places* (New York: Random House, 2011), 265–66.

23. Andrew Smith, *Grasshopper Jungle* (New York: Dutton, 2014), 135.

24. Smith, *Grasshopper*, 29.

25. Smith, *Grasshopper*, 45.

26. Smith, *Grasshopper*, 45.

27. Smith, *Grasshopper*, 45–46.

28. Smith, *Grasshopper*, 23.

29. Smith, *Grasshopper*, 19.

30. Smith *Grasshopper*, 105–6.

31. Smith, *Grasshopper*, 108.

32. Smith, *Grasshopper*, 316–17.

33. Smith, *Grasshopper*, 192.

34. Andrew Smith, interview by Bryan Gillis, June 2014, http://www.alan-ya.org/page/alan-picks-june-2014.

35. Stephenie Meyer, *Twilight* (New York: Little Brown, 2005), 278.

36. Meyer, *Twilight*, 282.

37. Stephenie Meyer, *Eclipse* (New York: Little Brown, 2007), 330–31.

38. Meyer, *Eclipse*, 525.

39. Meyer, *Eclipse*, 526.

40. Meyer, *Eclipse*, 528.

41. Meyer, *Breaking Dawn* (New York: Little Brown, 2008), 85.

42. Meyer, *Breaking Dawn*, 89.

43. Meyer, *Breaking Dawn*, 107–8.

44. Meyer, *Breaking Dawn*, 481–82.

45. Meyer, *Breaking Dawn*, 282–83.

46. Suzanne Collins, *Hunger Games* (New York: Scholastic, 2008), 260–61.

47. Veronica Roth, *Divergent* (New York: HarperCollins, 2011), 265–66.

48. Marie Lu, *Champion* (New York: G. P. Putnam's Sons, 2013), 187.

Chapter Six

Sexual Content in Young Adult Romance

The Romance Writers of America categorize romance novels as contemporary, erotic, historical, inspirational, paranormal, short contemporary, and young adult. According to the organization, a young adult romance must possess the following characteristics: a book marketed to young adults, a plot driven by a love story in which the primary focus is the romantic relationship between two adolescents, and a resolution that is emotionally satisfying and optimistic.[1] When we were creating a roadmap for this book, we understood that a romance chapter would be imperative. Our experience with YA romance at that time was limited and also biased by what we thought we knew about the adult romance genre. Therefore, we assumed that most of the YA titles would be replete with ridiculously long monologues extolling the virtues of love and would, of course, contain massive amounts of gratuitous sex. Instead, we were pleasantly surprised to discover that quality YA romance novels celebrate relationships—pursuing them, running from them, and figuring them out, often in awkward and uncomfortable ways.

Some of the selections in this chapter do contain explicit descriptions of sex; some lead readers to imagine *off camera* sexual encounters; and others simply allow readers to consider the possibilities of sex. In each, the sexual content advances the plot, develops characters, and represents the emotional aspects of sex in a realistic manner.

YA author Tanya Stone provides what we feel is the appropriate function of sexual content in realistic YAL:

> Any scene that does not advance a story line or deepen character development is arguably gratuitous. . . . Exploring sex and sexuality in YA literature is worthwhile; exploiting it is not. . . . I would not be compelled to write a YA character—male or female—who jumped into bed without a care in the world and did not either experience some kind of transformation or trigger growth in another character. It's not because I think it would be immoral or dangerous or wrong to write a character like that, but because I write realistic fiction and I don't believe that reflects reality. Sex is complicated enough for adults, let alone for teens having their first experiences. It makes sense that YA characters reflect that complexity. Good books come from the heart, not from analyzing the market and intentionally attempting to fill in the missing blanks. [2]

Before delving into the two most prevalent contemporary subgenres of YA romance—paranormal and realistic—here is a very brief history of the romance novel.

HISTORY OF THE ROMANCE NOVEL

Medieval romances first appeared in French literature in the twelfth century. Whereas the epics of that period reflected heroics, the romances were lighter in tone and told tales of chivalry: adventures in which "knights, kings, or distressed ladies, motivated by love, religious faith, or the mere desire for adventure, are the chief figures."[3] A major literary evolution occurred during the Victorian era, as female writers began writing romances, replacing male heroes with females. The stories penned by such authors as Jane Austen (*Pride and Prejudice*, 1813), Emily Brontë (*Wuthering Heights*, 1847), and Charlotte Brontë (*Jane Eyre*, 1847) were extremely popular but not taken seriously.[4] Today, these same romantic novels are assigned reading in high school classrooms across the country and are considered classics.

In 1942, *Seventeenth Summer*, by Maureen Daly, was published. The novel is the journalistic account of seventeen-year-old Angie Morrow and her summer romance with Jack. Daly's first and only book is considered by some experts to be the earliest example of the young adult romance novel, although Daly herself stated in 1994 that the book was not originally marketed to young adults. The success of *Seventeenth Summer* and the emergence of a new youth culture in the late

1930s and early 1940s prompted marketers to begin publishing books that were more appealing to teens.[5] A number of romances followed, attempting to capitalize on the success of *Seventeenth Summer*. *Going on Sixteen* (Betty Cavanna, 1946), *Practically Seventeen* (Rosamund du Jardin, 1949), *And Both Were Young* (Madeline L'Engle 1949), and *Fifteen* (Beverly Cleary, 1956) were a few of the titles that younger teens eagerly read.[6] Michael Cart had this to say about the 1940s romances: "These books were set in a *Saturday Evening Post* world of white faces and white picket fences surrounding small-town, middle-class lives where the worst thing that could happen would be a misunderstanding that threatened to leave someone dateless for the junior prom."[7]

The arrival of the problem novel in the late 1960s and its growth in popularity throughout the 1970s may be one reason that interest in lighter romances diminished during this time. When romance did appear in YA fiction, it often took a backseat to the coming-of-age issues prominently featured.[8] The 1980s brought a renewed interest in romance novels, due in part to marketing tactics that placed paperback romance novels at the checkout counters of every grocery and drug store.[9] YA historian Patty Campbell explains:

> Previous purchasers of YA books had been teachers, parents, and librarians, but now, with this new market, more hardcover YA titles were translated into paperback. With the advent of the indoor shopping mall as a teen hangout, the stage was set for a wider marketing plan. Gambling that teens were tired of the gritty reality of the problem novel, and perhaps frightened by AIDS, publishers in the eighties began to bring out sweet, clean, and conventional paperback romance series, like *Wildfire*, *Sweet Dreams*, *Young Love*, *First Love*, *Wishing Star*, *Caprice*, and *Sweet Valley High*. They were an instant sensation with young girls, who bought them by the armload. The enormous significance of this move was that these were *original* paperbacks, not reprints.[10]

The *Sweet Valley High* series became so successful that in 1985, Bantam published a super edition entitled *Perfect Summer*, which became the first YA novel to appear on the *New York Times* bestseller list. In September 1989, *Brokenhearted* (*Sweet Valley High* 58) was number 3 on *Publisher's Weekly* young adult bestseller list. By the end of that same year, 34 million *Sweet Valley High* books were in print, in fifteen languages.[11]

By the 1990s, due to a tremendous increase in popularity, YAL expanded into several subgenres in addition to the problem novel. As American teens became more knowledgeable—thanks to the influence of television, movies, and the Internet—the sweet romances of the 1980s became less popular and were replaced by series romances such as *Gossip Girl* and *The A-List*. These romances are commonly issued under a single name, are sequentially numbered, and carry predetermined publisher word counts and basic content guidelines. The stories focus on "current pop culture fixations—teen obsessions with lifestyles of the rich and famous, extravagant vacations, expensive cars, hot club scenes, and toned bodies and sex."[12] The following is the tagline for the *A-List* series:

> Seventeen-year-old blueblood Anna Percy leaves Manhattan to spend the second half of her senior year with her father in Los Angeles. Upon enrolling at Beverly Hills High School and brushing shoulders with the rich and powerful, Anna finds herself caught up in the whirlwind world of Hollywood's most beautiful and glamorous people. Welcome to the A-List.[13]

Harlequin—established in 1949 in Canada by Jack Palmer, the head of the *Ladies Home Journal*—has long been synonymous with romance. Initially, *Harlequin* sold romance novels for twenty-five cents each, but it has now grown into a powerhouse that publishes nearly 110 titles per month in thirty-four languages and 110 international markets.[14] *Harlequin* has ten imprints, including *Harlequin Teen*, whose target audience is teenage girls between the ages of thirteen and eighteen. When the *Harlequin Teen* imprint first launched, senior editor Natashya Wilson provided some guidelines for the series: "We do not have specific guidelines about sexual and language content. . . . The majority of our list is relatively clean, as in sex and swear-word free. You'll find the content of our titles very much in line with many other popular single-title YA releases in the market today."[15]

For many, the mention of a *Harlequin* romance brings forth images of longhaired, bare-chested men, each standing behind a beautiful woman with windblown hair. Readers who indulge in these stories are guaranteed their fair share of sexually explicit content. *Harlequin Teen* breaks from this mold by promoting romance and relationships over sex. Not that the stories are void of sexual content. Wilson states, "If a story does include sex, it must be a natural part of plot and character development, not gratuitous, and not described in graphic detail."[16]

One of the more popular Harlequin Teen series is *Kimani Tru*. The novels are written by black authors (male and female) and feature black characters. According to the Harlequin website, "Harlequin Kimani Romance stories feature sophisticated, soulful, and sensual African-American and multicultural heroes and heroines who develop fulfilling relationships as they lead lives full of drama, glamour, and passion."[17] *Indigo Summer* (2007), the first book in the series, debuted at number 7 on the *Essence* bestsellers list and appeared on the American Library Association's 2008–2010 lists of Quick Picks for Reluctant Young Adult Readers.[18]

PARANORMAL ROMANCE

Paranormal romance is defined by settings and themes that stem from urban or traditional fantasy, science fiction, or horror and feature such characters as vampires, werewolves, faeries, wizards, witches, ghosts, magical creatures, and telekinetic beings. Authors of paranormal romances are free to create any world that they can imagine, provided that it remains internally consistent. They can then populate that world with humans and mythical creatures alike. Of course, the story must revolve around a romance, typically between a human and a nonhuman. The protagonist is most often a strong female.

Intertwined, by Gena Showalter (2009)

Gena Showalter is the author of fifty-five adult and young adult romance novels. Her work has appeared in *Cosmopolitan* and *Seventeen* magazines, and her books have made numerous appearances on the *New York Times* and *USA Today* bestseller lists. Showalter's *Intertwined* series (*Intertwined, Unraveled, Twisted,* and a fourth book in production) is published by Harlequin Teen and features Aden, a teenager who has four souls trapped inside his body: each of them telling him to do different things. One night, he wanders into a graveyard, fights with some zombies, meets Mary Ann (who has the ability to repel the paranormal), and falls in love with her. Later, he meets and also falls in love with Victoria, a vampire princess. Love triangle established! The romance between Aden and Mary Ann becomes complicated thanks to Aden's love for the irresistible Victoria. The series continues to explore the complications between these relationships.

The sexual content in *Intertwined* is not explicit, and most of the physical contact is described in past tense. Nevertheless, Showalter's descriptions create a fair amount of sexual tension for readers—or what the characters refer to as "heat." In the following scene, Aden arrives to pick up Mary Ann, and as she lingers at the door, staring at Aden, she recalls their previous kiss:

> He smiled his bad boy smile, half wicked, half *really wicked.* "Hey."
>
> "Hey." Yep. Sexy. He had dark hair and light green eyes. He was tall, with the body of a dedicated, can't-be-sacked football player having an affair with weights. His shoulders were broad, his stomach roped. Tragically, she couldn't see those mouth-watering ropes under his black T-shirt. His jeans bagged a little on his strong legs, and he wore boots caked with dirt.
>
> Wait. Had she just given him a total body scan? Yep. Cheeks heating, she brought her gaze back to his face. Clearly, he was trying not to laugh.
>
> "Do you approve?" he asked.
>
> The heat intensified. "Yes. But I wasn't done," she added. He wasn't beautiful in a male model kind of way, but he was ruggedly appealing, with a slightly crooked nose—probably from being broken so many times—and a strong jaw. And she had once kissed him, right on those gorgeous lips.
>
> When will we kiss again?
>
> She was ready. More than ready. That was the most fun her tongue had ever had. [19]

The romantic relationships in *Intertwined* feel genuine, despite the paranormal events that take place throughout. Adolescent readers will relate to the awkwardness and lust that are synonymous with being a sixteen-year-old in love. And as we continue to discover, sexual content in YAL can be just as effective at painting a picture when it is more suggestive than explicit.

Wings, by Aprilynne Pike (2008)

Aprilynne Pike is an award-winning young adult author whose *Wings* series has been a constant presence on the *New York Times* bestseller lists. *Wings*, unlike *Intertwined*, is marketed primarily to middle schoolers. When asked about the sexual content in the series, Pike said, "It's almost non-existent. These are middle school kisses, not high school kisses." [20] *Wings* does feature a love triangle, reminiscent of

Twilight, but it is described as "milder than *Twilight*."[21] *Wings* is the story of Laurel, a seemingly ordinary girl who begins to notice a pimple on her back that eventually blooms into a flower. She soon discovers that she is a faerie who has taken the form of an evolved plant. Laurel is sent to live among humans so that she can protect them from evil trolls. Laurel has a human love interest named David and a sexy faerie guardian named Tamani. Laurel finds herself inextricably drawn to Tamani, and he complicates matters by insistently pursuing her.

In this scene, Laurel asks Tamani how it is possible for faeries to have sex since they are plants:

"How do you . . . we . . . you know, faeries pollinate?"

"The male produces pollen on his hands and when two faeries decide to pollinate, the male reaches into the female's blossom and lets the pollen mix. It's a somewhat delicate process."

"Doesn't sound very romantic."

"There's nothing romantic about it at all." Tamani replied, a confident smile spreading across his face. "That's what sex is for."

"You still . . . ?" She let the question hang.

"Sure."

"But faeries don't get pregnant?"

"Never." Tamani winked. "Pollination is for reproduction—sex is just for fun."[22]

Tamani's explanation of the act of reproduction—*the male reaches into the female's blossom and lets the pollen mix*—is a wonderfully creative, albeit thinly veiled, description of human coitus. More intriguing, however, is the distinction that Tamani makes between reproduction (pollination) and sex. Pollination serves a purpose, he explains, but sex is reserved for romance and fun. We like this message, although we admit that lacking the ability to become pregnant is a rather convenient way to sidestep the safe-sex conversation.

Shiver, by Maggie Stiefvater (2009)

Shiver is Maggie Stiefvater's debut novel and the first book in the *Shiver* series (*Linger*, *Forever*, and *Sinner*). An American Library Association Best Book for Young Adults, *Shiver* is the story of seventeen-year-old Grace, who, as a nine-year-old girl, was saved from a wolf attack by another wolf. Each winter, when the wolves return to the forest behind her house, Grace watches them, especially the wolf with the yellow eyes that saved her. Grace's wolf seems to always be watching her, almost as if he is longing for her. After a wolf kills a local teen, the town assembles a hunting party in an attempt to eradicate them. Grace runs into the woods to try to stop the hunters, and when she returns home, a wounded boy lies on her back porch. After one look at his yellow eyes, she realizes that this is her wolf in human form.

Once Grace meets Sam in human form, the story is narrated from alternating points of view, and their romance quickly heats up. Each winter, Sam transforms from human to wolf, but because wolves can change into human form only a limited number of times, his time with Grace is running out. The intensity of their relationship increases as Grace desperately tries to find a cure for Sam's wolfness so that they can be together in human form forever.

In this scene, toward the end of the first book, Grace and Sam find themselves alone in Grace's bedroom. Winter is upon them, and Grace is trying to keep Sam warm, to trick his body, just long enough to find a cure. Narrated from Sam's point of view, the scene begins with Sam telling Grace that he wants to go to bed. He immediately regrets asking because he knows how strong his desire is for her.

> "Why are you so careful with me, Sam Roth?"
>
> I tried to tell her the truth. "I—it's—I'm not an animal."
>
> "I'm not afraid of you," she said. . . .
>
> As if reading my thoughts, she said, "Can you tell me it's only the wolf in you that wants to kiss me?"
>
> All of me wanted to kiss her hard enough to make me disappear. I braced my arms on either side of her head, the door giving a creak as I leaned against it, and I pressed my mouth against hers. She kissed me back, lips hot, tongue flicking against my teeth, hands still behind her, body still pressed against the door. Everything in me buzzed, electric, wanting to close the few inches of space between us.
>
> She kissed me harder, breath huffing into my mouth, and bit my lower lip. Oh, hell, that was amazing. I growled before I could stop myself, but before I could even think to feel embarrassed, Grace had pulled her hands out from behind her and looped them around my neck, pulling me to her.
>
> "That was so sexy," she said, voice uneven.
>
> More kissing and touching, and then:
>
> "Oh, God, Grace," I gasped. "You—you greatly overestimate my self-control."
>
> "I'm not looking for self-control."
>
> My hands were inside her shirt, palms pressed on her back, fingers spread on her sides; I didn't even remember how they got there. "I—I don't want to do anything you'll regret."

Grace's back curved against my fingers as if my touch brought her to life. "Then don't stop."

Clumsily, we backed onto her bed, part of me thinking we should be quiet in case her parents came home. But she helped me tug my shirt over my head and ran a hand down my chest, and I groaned, forgetting everything but her fingers on my skin. . . .

She let me push her gently down on the pillows and I braced my arms on either side of her, straddling her in my jeans.

"Are you sure?" I asked.

Her eyes were bright and excited. She nodded.

I slid down to kiss her belly; it felt so right, so natural, like I'd done it a thousand times before . . .

Grace pulled the blankets up over us and we kicked off our clothes beneath them. As we pressed our bodies against each other, I shrugged off my skin with a growl, giving in, neither wolf nor man, just Sam.[23]

Stiefvater's description of Grace and Sam's first sexual encounter is beautifully and tastefully written. Not only does the scene ring true emotionally, but the author also uses the couple's intimacy to further establish Grace as a strong female character who is on equal footing with her physically powerful boyfriend/wolf. Stiefvater explains her approach to creating her complex characters and rich stories: "I navigate readers' emotions like a small ship through a rocky strait. If I have not gotten inside your brain and moved emotional furniture around during the course of my novel, I feel I've failed."[24]

Authors of YA paranormal romances often place their protagonists in settings and situations in which they are responsible for saving entire worlds. These stories typically deal with problems and issues that fall far outside the realm of possibility, thus creating scenarios in which the adolescent protagonists are better equipped to handle the problems than the adults are—adults who are often unaware that paranormal activities are occurring. As a result, readers may view characters in teen paranormal romances as being more adultlike because of the extreme situations in which they are placed.

REALISTIC ROMANCE

All subgenres of YAL can contain romance threads, but a true YA romance follows the basic conventions outlined by the Romance Writers of America—specifically, a plot driven by a love story and a romantic relationship between two adolescents as the primary focus. A realis-

tic romance tackles additional elements, those present in the YA problem novel, although most often they are presented in a less serious
light. And although most do end somewhat optimistically, most do not
simply end as happily-ever-afters. The following four novels contain
scenes that range from subtle to explicit descriptions of sex. In each,
however, the scenes serve to advance the plot, develop characters, and/
or portray the emotional aspects of sex in a realistic manner.

Annie on My Mind, by Nancy Garden (1982)

Annie on My Mind is narrated by seventeen-year-old Liza Winthrop,
student body president at an exclusive prep school. Annie Kenyon, also
seventeen, attends public high school and lives with her Italian immi-
grant family in a blue-collar area of town. Liza and Annie first meet at
the Metropolitan Art Museum in New York, where they discover that
they have a love of art in common. They are instantly attracted to each
other, and their friendship soon deepens. Both of them begin to realize
that their attraction is sexual as well as spiritual. In this scene, Liza
recalls the first time they kissed:

> I remember we were both watching the sun slowly go down over one
> end of the beach, making the sky to the west pink and yellow . . .
>   Without thinking, I put my arm across her shoulders to warm her,
> and then before either of us knew what was happening, our arms were
> around each other and Annie's soft and gentle mouth was kissing
> mine. [25]

Liza immediately struggles with her sexual attraction to another
female.

> It was like a war inside me: I couldn't even recognize all of the sides.
> There was one that said, "No, this is wrong, you know it's wrong and
> bad and sinful," and there was another that said, "Nothing has ever felt
> so right and natural and true and good," and another said it was happen-
> ing too fast. [26]

Although Annie appears more aware of her sexuality, "I—I've
thought sometimes, even before I met you, I mean, that I might be
gay,"[27] neither she nor Liza wants anyone to know about their relationship. For months they kiss, touch, and then pull away, both too shy to
talk about what was or was not happening. One evening, their discussion deepens after Liza realizes that she loves Annie and that she is

"probably gay": "I went downstairs to Dad's encyclopedia and looked up HOMOSEXUALITY, but that didn't tell me much about any of the things I felt. What struck me most, though, was that, in that whole long article, the word 'love' wasn't used even once. That made me mad; it was as if whoever wrote the article didn't know that gay people actually love each other."[28] Annie tells Liza that encyclopedias are not good for that sort of thing, and she gives Liza a book entitled *Patience and Sarah*, by Isabelle Miller.[29]

Liza and Annie get their first opportunity for real intimacy after Liza is asked to house-sit and feed the cats of two female teachers who will be away on spring vacation (spoiler alert: the two teachers are gay, but no one at the school knows). When spring break arrives, Liza and Annie finally get some alone time. Liza recalls their first intimate encounter at the home of the two teachers:

> I remember so much about that first time with Annie that I am numb with it, and breathless. I can feel Annie's hands touching me again, gently, as if she were afraid I might break; I can feel her softness under my hands. . . . I can close my eyes and feel every motion of Annie's body and my own—clumsy and shy—but that isn't the important part. The important part is the wonder of the closeness and the unbearable ultimate realization that we are two people, not one—and also the wonder of that: even though we *are* two people, we can be almost like one, and at the same time delight in each other's uniqueness.[30]

Unfortunately, the relationship is exposed, rather dramatically, when Ms. Baxter, another teacher at Liza's school, shows up at the home of the two teachers, looking for Liza. She and a friend of Liza put two and two together after Liza answers the door barefoot, wearing a "not-very-well-buttoned shirt."[31]

> "I was afraid for a moment that I would find young men up there," Ms. Baxter whispered, actually trembling as she put a maternal arm around Sally, "but what I did find—oh, dear heaven—is far, far worse—though I should have known," she moaned . . . "I almost wish I had found young men," she said. "Sodom and Gomorrah are all around us, Sally."[32]

The consequences rain down immediately. The principal/overlord of Liza's school, Ms. Poindexter, dismisses the two gay teachers and threatens Liza with expulsion. She is reinstated by the board of trustees, but she undergoes quite a bit of emotional stress during the process.

Ultimately, after working through their own issues, Liza's parents support her. Annie goes to Berkeley; Liza goes to MIT; and after months of silence, they resume contact. Readers are left with the hope that their relationship may be resurrected.

Annie on My Mind is notable for being the first YA novel to portray lesbians in a positive light. They were not cured or killed, although they certainly were persecuted. As a result, Garden's book has remained controversial in some parts of the country. In fact, it has appeared on lists of most frequently banned books for the past three decades and—we can't make this stuff up—was publicly burned in Kansas City in 1993.[33]

In November 2013, in one of the last public appearances before her death, Nancy Garden discussed why she wrote *Annie on My Mind*. "I grew up a lesbian in the 1950's and there were no books to read about being gay. I wanted to write a book about two young women in love who end up happily-ever-after."[34]

Eleanor and Park, by Rainbow Rowell (2013)

Eleanor and Park is the story of two teenagers who meet one day on a school bus in Omaha, Nebraska, in 1986. Park is biracial, his mother Korean and his father white. He is the only Asian student in his school, but despite the racist attitudes that emanate from the town and from the times, Park is accepted by the other, more popular kids due to his family's deep roots in their lower-middle-class neighborhood. Not so for Eleanor, the new kid in town. She is a "big girl" with bright red hair. She immediately becomes the target of the popular kids, who refer to her as "Big Red." Park notices Eleanor as she walks down the aisle looking for a seat. Once he realizes that no one is obliging, he reluctantly scoots over. They avoid speaking to each other. Eleanor thinks that Park is a stupid Asian kid. Park thinks that Eleanor is weird. Park finally breaks the ice by loaning his comics to her. Soon he shares his music and more of his comics, and they begin to make a connection.

Eleanor's family is poor, and as the story unfolds, readers gain a better understanding of how poverty and abuse interact to make Eleanor's home situation unbearable. For example, she and her siblings share one room, and they buy their clothes at the thrift store. Eleanor's stepfather, Ritchie, is a drunken tyrant. Eleanor, her mother, and her siblings walk on eggshells as a result of Ritchie's violent behavior. The story opens with Eleanor returning to her family a year after Ritchie kicked her out. Before her return, she had been living with various relatives and acquaintances.

Eventually, Park introduces Eleanor to his family, and as they begin to realize how terrible her home life is, they embrace her. Eleanor keeps Park a secret from her family. She begins spending time at Park's house in the evenings, telling her family that she is hanging out with one of the girls from school. Eventually, her brothers and sisters find out. When Ritchie finds out, everything falls apart.

Eleanor and Park is not a typical romance. The story is told through the dual narratives of the protagonists. This enables readers to gain unique insights into the minds of both protagonists. These insights, the thoughts of Eleanor and Park, are what makes this story so brilliant and beautiful. Rowell does not include what most readers would consider sexually explicit descriptions, but what she does describe is intense with an capital *I*. In a *New York Times* book review, John Green, author of *Looking for Alaska* and *The Fault in Our Stars*, remarked,

> I have never seen anything quite like *Eleanor & Park*. Rainbow Rowell's first novel for young adults is a beautiful, haunting love story—but I have seen those. It's set in 1986, and God knows I've seen that. There's bullying, sibling rivalry, salvation through music and comics, a monstrous stepparent—and I know, we've seen all this stuff. But you've never seen *Eleanor & Park*. Its observational precision and richness make for very special reading. . . . The hand-holding, by the way, is intense. . . . Evocative sensual descriptions are everywhere in this novel, but they always feel true to the characters.[35]

Here are a few examples of Rowell's intense hand-holding descriptions, with the characters' names listed before their thoughts:

Park: Holding Eleanor's hand was like holding a butterfly. Or a heartbeat. Like holding something complete, and completely alive. As soon as he touched her, he wondered how he'd gone this long without doing it. He rubbed his thumb through her palm and up her fingers, and was aware of every breath.[36]

Eleanor: Disintegrated . . . if you've ever wondered what that feels like, it's a lot like melting—but more violent. Even in a million different pieces, Eleanor could feel his thumb exploring her palm.[37]

Park: Jesus. Was it possible to rape someone's hand? . . . He sat down next to her and let his hands hang between his knees . . . which meant she really had to reach for his wrist, to pull his hand into hers. She wrapped her fingers around his and touched his palm with her thumb. Her fingers were trembling.[38]

Here, Park describes their first kiss:

> He laid his thumb on her lips to see if she'd pull away. She didn't. He leaned closer. He wanted to close his eyes, but he didn't trust her not to leave him standing there.
>
> When his lips were almost touching hers, she shook her head. Her nose rubbed against his.
>
> "I've never done this before," she said.
>
> "S'okay," he said.
>
> "It's not, it's going to be terrible."
>
> He shook his head. "It's not."
>
> She shook her head a little more. Just a little. "You're going to regret this," she said.
>
> That made him laugh, so he had to wait a second before he kissed her.
>
> It wasn't terrible. Eleanor's lips were soft and warm, and he could feel her pulse in her cheek. . . . He pulled away before he wanted to. He hadn't done this enough to know how to breathe. . . .
>
> "Come here," he said. "I want to show you something."
>
> She laughed. He lifted her chin.
>
> The second time was even less terrible.[39]

Eleanor and Park consummate their relationship in the backseat of Park's car. Arriving home after their tryst, Park cannot sleep and recalls what just happened:

> That night, before they'd climbed back into the front seat of the Impala, he'd taken off all of Eleanor's layers and even unpinned her bra——then layed her down on the blue upholstery. She's looked like a vision there, a mermaid. Cool white in the darkness, the freckles gathered on her shoulders and cheeks like cream rising to the top.
>
> The sight of her. Still glowed on the inside of his eyelids.
>
> It was going to be constant torture now that he knew what she was like under her clothes.[40]

For us, *Eleanor and Park* was a reminder of the days when holding someone's hand was special, because the person whose hand you were holding was special. Rowell's debut is a shining example of what a realistic romance should be. We do not want to give away the ending, but we do believe that love will conquer all.

Anatomy of a Boyfriend, by Daria Snadowsky (2007)

Seventeen-year-old high school senior Dominique Baylor wants to be a doctor. "Dom" is a student at a small private school where her mom teaches, and when she is not studying medical books, she is busy filling out college applications. Dom has limited sexual experience with boys, but fortunately, her best friend, Amy, dates regularly and has engaged in some "everything but intercourse" activities.

With Amy's help and encouragement, Dom meets Wes, a cute boy who is on the track team. They converse first by e-mail (it is 2007), and when they do start hanging out, Dom finds Wes to be shy and sweet, so much so that he does not attempt to pursue her romantically or physically. Once they do connect physically and emotionally, thanks in large part to Dom's persistence, the remainder of the story revolves around the two protagonists' sexual explorations—alone and with each other.

Anatomy of a Boyfriend contains sexually explicit scenes. Many reviewers have compared it to Blume's *Forever* in that it deals honestly with sex through the eyes of a girl who is somewhat insecure but also curious and in love. As we have discussed throughout the book and as Tanya Stone points out in her article, sexual content in YAL can be an effective learning tool for teens when it is not used gratuitously—simply for the purpose of arousing the reader. Authors avoid this by making the sexual interaction between characters, often first-time experiences, awkward, uncomfortable, and sometimes even painful, as in Kathy (*Forever*) thinking about her mother as she is having an orgasm—"I came right before Michael and as I did I made noises, just like my mother"[41]—or Jody (*It's Ok If You Don't Love Me*) describing sex with Lyle by comparing it to a line from her grade school sex book: "The father puts his penis in the mother's vagina."[42] In *Anatomy*, there is some awkwardness and some pain. What really keeps Snadowsky's explicit descriptions of sex from becoming gratuitous or erotic, however, is the clinical manner in which Dom (the aspiring doctor) describes them. The scenes serve as accurate descriptions for curious readers without feeling sexually charged.

The following are a few selected scenes that provide a feel for the way in which the sexual content is presented—to begin, Dom's first foray into masturbation:

> I start lightly stroking my breasts with my fingertips until I feel my nipples harden. Then I move my hand down my torso and slowly tickle the area below my belly button. . . . I can even feel my undies start to get wet. . . .
>
> In my human anatomy class, we learned the clitoris has eight thousand nerve fibers, at least twice as many as a penis. That deserves a little experimentation. [43]

The first time that they engage in intimate touch, in Wes's car, Dom teaches the inexperienced Wes how to undo her bra. She then reaches under his shirt to feel his bare chest and stomach for the first time and thinks, "I don't think I'll ever enjoy reading *Gray's Anatomy* or playing Operation again, now that I get to handle a live specimen."[44]

Finally, Dom's grandparent's condo becomes available, and readers are treated to a seven-page description of their first real sexual encounter, following prom. Dom's proclivity for anatomical description kicks into gear:

> Even by the dim blue moonlight filtering in through the glass balcony doors, I can recognize the features of his penis from my anatomy books. The shaft, the head, the urethral opening—it's definitely all there. Only it looks so much more alive and urgent than any photograph could ever capture. I lean forward over Wes's torso so I can study it head-on. Then I notice it bobbing up and down slightly with his heartbeat, as if it's waving me on. [45]

The anatomy lesson continues: The "consistency" of his balls reminds her of "a baby bird, or squishy nectarine skin, scattered with hair,"[46] and she refers to his scrotum as his "personal sperm generator."[47] Ultimately on this night, Dom settles for giving Wes a hand job. After ten minutes, while complaining to herself of sore arms and shoulders, she thinks,

> "Hand job" is such a misnomer for this full-body routine. It's like I'm a one-man band.
>
> Soon a few drops of something hot leak onto my fingers. Wes's breathing is getting heavier too. . . .
>
> "Tighter. Ah, Aah, Dom. Dom—"

I feel a stiffening of his penis in my hands as the tip expels a thick, creamy liquid. . . . I discover the warm, white goo cascading down my knuckles serves as a great lubricant, so I stroke even faster.
"Dom . . . you can stop . . . Stop now!"[48]

Later in the story, Wes leaves for college. When he returns for Thanksgiving, Dom, desperate to please, decides to try oral for the first time:

I close my eyes and take the head into my mouth. I'm afraid I'm going to bite him accidentally, so I keep my lips tightly pursed over my teeth. I get only half of his penis inside before I feel like I'm going to gag. So I continue to suck just the top half of it and bob my head up and down slightly. The more I do it, the more I'm able to fit in my mouth. Unfortunately, the condom does not taste like any strawberry made by nature—imagine sucking on a rubber band dipped in Kool-Aid. I don't know why they call it *blow* job either, because I'm not really blowing anything, but it *is* a job. My neck and shoulders are sore from bending over, and I barely have sensation left in my jaw by the time he comes.[49]

Many of the sex scenes in *Anatomy of a Boyfriend* begin with passionate kissing but end with much less passionate clinical descriptions. The novel leaves the reader questioning how much of the couple's desire to have sex is driven by love and how much is motivated by lust and curiosity. Wes is portrayed as an extremely nice guy, but he is also sexually naive, and we are led to believe that he, as well as Dom, may be confusing sex for love, which we find a refreshing twist on the *all guys care about is sex* trope.

Snadowsky's debut novel is an honest portrayal of an adolescent girl's sexual awakening, and like *Forever*—the book is dedicated to Judy Blume—it contains well-developed characters and realistic dialogue. Snadowsky does not shy away from portraying sex in an honest and open way, but she does so accurately and tastefully.

The Infinite Moment of Us, by Lauren Myracle (2013)

The Infinite Moment of Us is the story of Charlie Parker and Wren Gray, two graduating high school seniors who are both entering into their first serious relationship. Charlie is a foster kid who has experienced a lifetime of unstable homes and bad parents. Finally, he is adopted by a kind and supportive family. Charlie's new little brother is in a wheelchair as a result of abuse suffered at the hands of his biological father, and he is often bullied at school. This has caused Charlie to feel as though he needs to act as his brother's protector. Conversely, Wren Gray has led a traditional upper-middle-class life, complete with overprotective parents who attempt to dictate her every decision. Her goal throughout grade school and high school has been to please her parents. As her senior year comes to an end, however, she is forced to decide whether to make a life choice that will please her father or one that will make her happy. After unexpectedly running into Wren at the hospital where she volunteers, Charlie is faced with having to carry on a conversation with her. Until now, he has loved Wren from afar, too shy to approach her, believing that she was way out of his league. After they get to know each other, Charlie finds the nerve to ask Wren on a date, and their romance begins to thrive.

Wren and Charlie are from opposite sides of the tracks. This is always a good recipe for romance. Wren now has someone who will encourage and support her, and Charlie has someone in his life (unlike his last girlfriend) who has his best interests at heart and makes him feel loved. Both are experiencing the fear of leaving home and the worry of disappointing their families. Of course, there are problems with their relationship along the way. Wren struggles with the amount of time that Charlie devotes to his family, and even though she is aware that she is being selfish, she cannot always help feeling jealous. Some of this jealousy is indeed warranted because on more than one occasion, Charlie uses the family-time excuse to spend time with his ex-girlfriend, Starrla, who continually runs back to him whenever she is in need of an emotional crutch. Charlie's intentions are noble, but any time spent with Starrla has a negative effect on his relationship with Wren.

The Infinite Moment of Us is a true realistic romance. The plot is driven by an all-consuming, heartbreaking, life-changing first love, while issues such as bullying, foster care, emotional damage, and destructive parenting styles make cameo appearances. The story, like *Eleanor and Park*, is told from both characters' points of view, offering readers insight into the minds of the male and female protagonists. The following scenes provide a brief portrait of the sexual content presented.

Charlie and Wren have several heavy-petting sessions in the back of Wren's Prius. Here, Charlie wonders why Wren has not taken it any further:

She had yet to touch his dick, for example.

Was she shy? Nervous? Worried he wouldn't like it? He would love it. Christ. . . .

"God, you drive me crazy," he said. He kissed her neck. Ran his hand over the curve of her breast, and then down along her side. Down farther, pulling her close. She was wearing a skirt today, and he found the hem and slipped his hand underneath. Her thigh. Her ass. Silk panties with soft lace around the edges.

He ran his fingers below the lace, and Wren made a small sound . . . his cock strained against his jeans. He pulled back slightly and used his forearm to push her legs apart. He slid his hand beneath her panties again and found the spot he was looking for—heat and wetness and skin softer than any silk or lace—and slipped two fingers inside her.

"Oh," Wren said. She was breathing hard. Charlie drew away from their kiss, but kept on with his fingers, watching her. Her eyes were closed. Her lips were parted. She lifted her hips, and when Charlie leaned in and kissed her again, the universe opened up and swallowed him whole, and Charlie brought Wren with him. This, the two of them together, was how it should be.[50]

To spend some alone time, Charlie and Wren begin going to a park at night and pitching an army blanket in what Wren describes as a secluded ditch. In these selections, excerpted from an eight-page description, Wren describes her first intercourse with Charlie:

He dipped his fingers under the lace, sliding the fabric of the bra of her breast and anchoring it beneath, so that it pushed her flesh higher. . . . "I like this better," he murmured, bowing his head and sucking first one nipple and then the other. . . .

Oh my God, she thought, and she moved beneath his touch, following his hands with her body.

He fiddled with her bra. It took him a moment to work the clasp, and she smiled as she kissed him.

She was wet.

She was scared, but she wanted him inside her.[51]

Several minutes later:

Her heart pounded, and she hooked her thumbs beneath the band at the top of his boxers. . . . She bit her lip and used her fingers to pull the waistband up and over him. She tugged them to his knees and didn't know what to do next.

But okay. Wow. She bent and took him in her mouth before she realized what she was doing. And then . . .

Really wow, and really strange. Not bad, but really, really strange.
He moaned, and Wren moved up and down. [52]

And then:

Wren lifted her legs higher. She pressed against him and found his
mouth with hers. His dick was hard against her but not yet in her. How
was he going to . . . ? Was she supposed to . . . was there something he
was supposed to do? With his knee, he spread her legs. She gasped. She
clung to his shoulders, and the night sky was above her and around
her. . . . Warmth between her legs. Pressure. Slippery, hard, soft—but it
didn't go in, or it didn't feel as though it did.

"Charlie? I don't—"

He pushed harder, and she widened her legs. She didn't know what
she was doing, but she was willing to try.

Charlie did something with his fingers—she wasn't sure what—and
her body acted on its own. She arched her spine and pressed the back of
her head into the blanket. She smelled the earth, and she smelled Charlie, who thrust into her. She cried out at a sharp sudden pain, and
Charlie stilled.

"Are you okay?" he asked, bearing his weight on his forearms.

"I'm fine," she said, wanting to be. But *ow*. He was sweaty and she
was sweaty, and the pain took her out of the moment, and was it gross
that she was all sweaty? [53]

We love that Wren and Charlie's lovemaking scenes have been
written with such positive energy. Not all of the sex scenes, however,
will leave readers feeling encouraged. Here, Charlie recalls the first
time that he had sex with Starrla, who he now realizes does not care for
him as Wren does:

As for sex. Well. They were fourteen the first time they "fucked," and
afterward, Charlie tried to tell her how pretty she was. In his mind, back
then, she was. Objectively, she still was, beneath her black eyeliner and
vampy outfits. But that first time, tangled together in Starrla's bed,
Charlie came fast and hard and then collapsed on top of her.

She laughed and shoved his torso. "You're crushing me," she said.
"Get off."

He rolled sideways, dazed and spent and thankful, so thankful. He
was also worried that he'd hurt her. "Sorry," he said. "You okay?"

She looked at him as if he were nuts. Then a knowing look altered
her features. She smirked and said, "Is this you being tender? In case
you haven't noticed, I don't do tender." [54]

Myracle's sex scenes are explicit—some may even say provocative—and although the protagonists are eighteen, the young adult label will incense potential censors. So, what responsibilities do YAL authors have when it comes to writing adolescent sex scenes? One study on the portrayal of sex in YAL concluded that they should include more information about contraception and the dangers of unprotected sex:

> References to the consequences of sex were rare. The few instances where consequences were noted were emotional in nature and unwanted pregnancy, abortion, and disease were never mentioned. In addition, portrayals of sexual intercourse rarely mentioned safe sexual practices, and discussion among characters of such practices was also nonexistent. Consistent with social cognitive theory, this lack of consequence and discussion of potential risks associated with sexual intercourse may remove perceived barriers or concerns among adolescents that would otherwise encourage them to think more carefully or cautiously about sexual behavior.[55]

We view instances of the "emotional" consequences of sex as a positive quality of YAL and argue that realistic portrayals of these emotions are far more important to include in a fictional story than facts about birth control and STDs: facts that can be provided by a doctor and a parent or accessed on the Internet. Furthermore, an author's inclusion of a "safe sexual practices" discussion for the sole purpose of demonstrating responsible behavior on the part of fictional characters seems like a sure way to alienate teen readers who will undoubtedly see it as a public service announcement. YAL should never function as an information manual.

Roberta Seelinger Trites, in *Disturbing the Universe: Power and Repression in Young Adult Literature*, emphasizes this point: "Adolescent literature is often an ideological tool used to curb teenagers' libido as it is some sort of depiction of what adolescents' sexuality actually is. . . . Some YA novels seem more preoccupied with influencing how adolescent readers will behave when they are not reading than describing human sexuality honestly."[56] It is this honesty that draws readers in and keeps them reading. A lack of honesty, particularly emotional honesty, is what has led to the failure of school sex education programs across the country. As we discuss in chapter 1, the primary developmental task of adolescence is identity development. Sex education classes, whether based on clinical or abstinence models, do not provide adequate opportunities for teens to develop into mature and healthy sexual beings.

Romance novels that contain physically and emotionally descriptive scenes allow teen readers to contextualize the physical descriptions of sex. This provides them "with a vocabulary of intimacy they can use to make sense of their own sexual and romantic feelings."[57] It is this union of the physical, the emotional, and the romantic that makes the sexual content in YAL romance so valuable to its adolescent readers. "Teens should see sex as both an emotional and a physical experience, and one that is special and unique. To do otherwise is to trivialize it. In the fiction they read, teens should see that sex is a serious business."[58]

Finally, to those potential censors who consider these books pornographic, we would like to remind them that for any material to be considered pornographic, it must be proven that the intention or purpose of the material in question is solely to arouse, with no concern for aesthetic or emotional feelings. We rest our case.

NOTES

1. Romance Writers of America, "RITA Awards," http://www.rwa.org/p/cm/ld/fid=532.
2. Tanya Stone, "Now and Forever: The Power of Sex in Young Adult Literature," *VOYA* (February 2006): 464–65.
3. William Harmon and Hugh Holman, *A Handbook to Literature*, 10th ed. (New York: Pearson, 2006), 315.
4. Pam Cole, *Young Adult Literature in the 21st Century* (New York: McGraw-Hill, 2009), 164.
5. Michael Cart, *Young Adult Literature: From Romance to Realism* (Chicago: American Library Association, 2011), 11.
6. Cole, *21st Century*, 164.
7. Michael Cart, in Cole, *21st Century*, 164.
8. Cole, *21st Century*, 164.
9. Cole, *21st Century*, 165.
10. Patty Campbell, "Trends in Young Adult Literature," in Cole, *21st Century*, 69.
11. Mary M. Huntwork, "Why Girls Flock to Sweet Valley High," *School Library Journal* 36, no. 3 (1990): 137–40.
12. Cole, *21st Century*, 167.
13. Alloy Entertainment, *The A-List*, http://alloyentertainment.com/books/the-a-list/.
14. Harlequin, "About Harlequin," http://www.harlequin.com/articlepage.html?articleId=36&chapter=0.
15. Carlie Webber, "Natashya Wilson of Halequin Teen," interview, August 2009, http://librarillyblonde.blogspot.com/2009/08/guest-post-natashya-wilson-of-harlequin.html.
16. Webber, "Natashya Wilson."
17. Harlequin, *Kimani TRU*, http://www.harlequin.com/store.html?cid=482.
18. "About Monica McKayhan," http://www.monicamckayhan.com/about.html.

19. Gena Showalter, *Intertwined* (New York: Harlequin Teen, 2009), 147.

20. Joanne Simpson, e-mail interview with Aprilynne Pike, March 25, 2014.

21. Common Sense Media, review of *Wings*, by Aprilynne Pike, https://www.commonsensemedia.org/book-reviews/wings.

22. Aprilynne Pike, *Wings* (New York: Harper Teen, 2008), 115.

23. Maggie Stiefvater, *Shiver* (New York: Scholastic, 2009), 291–94.

24. Maggie Stiefvater, "I Navigate Readers' Emotions like a Small Ship through a Rocky Strait," *Guardian*, October 8, 2013, http://www.theguardian.com/books/2013/oct/08/maggie-stiefvater-music-teen-fiction-mood.

25. Nancy Garden, *Annie on my Mind* (New York: Square Fish, 2007), 92.

26. Garden, *Annie*, 93.

27. Garden, *Annie*, 94.

28. Garden, *Annie*, 143.

29. Set in the nineteenth century, Isabel Miller's novel tells of the romance between Patience White, an educated painter, and Sarah Dowling, a cross-dressing farmer. Their relationship is not viewed favorably by the puritanical New England farming community where they live.

30. Garden, *Annie*, 146.

31. Garden, *Annie*, 164.

32. Garden, *Annie*, 166–67.

33. Nancy Garden.com, http://www.nancygarden.com/books/teens.html.

34. Bryan Gillis, conversation with Nancy Garden, National Council of Teachers of English conference, November 24, 2013.

35. John Green, "Two against the World," *New York Times*, March 8, 2013, http://www.nytimes.com/2013/03/10/books/review/eleanor-park-by-rainbow-rowell.html?_r=0.

36. Rainbow Rowell, *Eleanor and Park* (New York: St. Martin's Press, 2013), 71.

37. Rowell, *Eleanor*, 72.

38. Rowell, *Eleanor*, 74.

39. Rowell, *Eleanor*, 166–67.

40. Rowell, *Eleanor*, 284.

41. Judy Blume, *Forever* (New York: Simon Pulse, 2003), 130.

42. Norma Klein, *It's OK If You Don't Love Me* (New York: Fawcett Juniper, 1977), 132.

43. Daria Snadowsky, *Anatomy of a Boyfriend* (New York: Delacorte, 2007), 23.

44. Snadowsky, *Anatomy*, 102.

45. Snadowsky, *Anatomy*, 113.

46. Snadowsky, *Anatomy*, 113.

47. Snadowsky, *Anatomy*, 114.

48. Snadowsky, *Anatomy*, 116.

49. Snadowsky, *Anatomy*, 189.

50. Lauren Myracle, *The Infinite Moment of Us* (New York: Amulet, 2013), 147.

51. Myracle, *The Infinite Moment*, 240.

52. Myracle, *The Infinite Moment*, 241.

53. Myracle, *The Infinite Moment*, 242–43.

54. Myracle, *The Infinite Moment*, 205–6.

55. Mark Callister et al., "A Content Analysis of the Prevalence and Portrayal of Sexual Activity in Adolescent Literature," *Journal of Sex Research* 49, no. 5 (2012): 483.

56. Roberta Seelinger Trites, *Disturbing the Universe: Power and Repression in Young Adult Literature* (Iowa City: University of Iowa Press, 2000), 85.

57. Amy Pattee, "The Secret Source: Sexually Explicit Young Adult Literature as an Information Source," *Young Adult Library Services* (winter 2006): 34.

58. Ed Sullivan, "Going All the Way: First Time Sexual Experiences of Teens in Fiction," *VOYA* 26, no. 6 (2004): 463.

Chapter Seven

Sexual Content in Realistic Contemporary Young Adult Fiction

The terms *realistic* and *contemporary*, when paired with young adult fiction, are often misinterpreted as synonyms. Realistic YAL tackles issues that are currently relevant to teens. A YA novel that deals with a character's struggle following the loss of a loved one, for example, will always be classified as realistic, but will it always be considered contemporary? First, let us develop a working definition for *contemporary*.

"A story that takes place in the present and possesses characteristics of the present time" would seem to provide an adequate description. However, this definition invites another question: When does the setting (time) of a story cease to be contemporary and instead become historical? Today's sixteen-year-olds were born in 1998 and became teenagers in 2011. Does this suggest that only books with settings from the past three years should be considered contemporary, thus ruling out most of the YA canon? Not necessarily.

Time limitations may not be as critical an indicator of being in the present as the cultural references that a book contains. Cultural references that fall outside an adolescent reader's limited experiential range may be perceived as more historical than contemporary. If a scene revolves around a character's ability to access a pay phone, for example, teen readers may be forced to build contextual background, with many having never used or even seen one. This sort of reference could disqualify a novel as contemporary. Of course, there are always exceptions.

Nick and Norah's Infinite Playlist and *Eleanor and Park* are two examples of realistic and relatable stories that clearly reference past decades, but they do so primarily through musical references. For us, the musical references alone do not lessen the relevancy or the contemporary feel of these stories, but we are adults who love to read YAL. Other popular titles, such as *The Catcher in the Rye* and *The Outsiders*, are now considered historical fiction, but readers still flock to these stories, continuing to find them relevant. We surmise that the perception of contemporary and relevancy will depend largely on each reader's unique response to each piece of literature based on his or her past and present experiences.

Definitions and speculations aside, the selections in this chapter all represent extraordinary examples of how the most accomplished authors use sexual content in their work to develop the complexities of character, progress and enrich a story, and create verisimilitude.

UNREQUITED LOVE

manicpixiedreamgirl, by Tom Leveen (2013)

Tyler Darcy has been infatuated—his friends would say obsessed—with Rebecca (Becky) Webb since his freshman year in high school. Now a junior, he still cannot seem to muster the courage to talk to her. Tyler has a steady girlfriend named Sydney. The problem is that Tyler's feelings for Sydney are not as strong as Sydney's feelings for Tyler. As a result, Sydney's patience for some of Tyler's behavior goes far beyond that of the typical girlfriend. For example, she is aware of Tyler's infatuation with Becky yet gallantly endures his attempts to learn more about Becky and, at times, even helps him gain information.

When Tyler does finally create an opportunity to interact with Becky—he joins the drama club—he becomes discouraged because he begins to see and hear things that do not mesh with the perfect image of her that he has created in his mind. Becky has been damaged in some way, and Tyler decides that he must save her from herself, but because he is unable to act on his feelings for her, he writes a story instead, a story of the relationship between him and Becky that he is too afraid to live. He enters the story in a writing contest, and when he is notified that, not only did he win, but that the story is to be published in a notable literary magazine, he worries that Becky will read it and immediately recognize herself as the protagonist. This poses a huge problem for Tyler because the Becky character whom he has created is based on the girl that Tyler imagines Becky to be: the Becky that he has constructed from his observations of her from afar.

In *manicpixiedreamgirl*, Tom Leveen tells a finely crafted story of the measures that a teenage boy is willing to take to keep his vision of his dream girl alive.[1] As we experience, through Tyler, the realization that Becky is not the person whom he imagined her to be, our hearts break with him. As he continues to try to get more intimate with Becky, we begin to understand just how much he really cares for her—worships her, really. Conversely, Becky's responses to Tyler's attempts at intimacy reveal that the secrets that she hides affect her ability to be intimate with anyone. In the following two passages, Tyler shares his thoughts on how his relationship with Becky has progressed since he joined the drama club:

> After her hug last summer, the way was paved for Becky and me to make more physical contact. It wasn't a lot by your usual standards. . . . But I was allowed to hug her now, and that was awesome.
>
> We grew closer as friends during that show. But only as friends. Which hurt in many ways. I sometimes just thought about coming out with it, telling her how I felt and what I wanted, but I couldn't. What I wanted amounted to little more than a kiss. To just feel her lips one time. And not on my forehead.[2]

Tyler's spirits are lifted when Becky invites him to her house. He has been there before, has even sat in her bedroom as they rehearsed lines for the play and talked about school. This time is different, though. At Becky's request, Tyler brings ice cream. They sit on her bed and talk. Tyler listens as Becky speaks of her parents' lack of interest in her life. Then Becky begins to undress:

> Becky lifts her shirt up and over her head, tossing it toward her shoes. Her hands reach behind her back to undo her black bra. . . .
>
> "One rule," she says as I try not to let my mouth hang open. "You ever tell anyone about this, it'll never happen again. Got it?" . . .
>
> She's not smiling, not being sexy, and not kidding. I hardly recognize her voice.
>
> Mechanically, I slide off the bed to one side and pull my shirt off. I step on the heels of my shoes and strip out of them. Seeing this, Becky continues to undress in front of me, pulling her jeans down, kicking them into a denim puddle at her feet.

I follow her lead, taking my jeans off. I stop, thumbs hooked into the waistband of my boxers, when she slides her underwear down. . . . My hands quake at my hips, and tremors vibrate my legs. My breath comes out in tiny, silent gasps. I pull my boxers off as Becky climbs back onto her bed and rolls to one side, opening the drawer in her night table. . . .

. . . My entire body is shaking now, as if in the throes of frostbite. I crawl my way between her, above her, elbows locked.

I lower my head toward hers, looking straight into her eyes, so deep I can see my own reflection. For the first time, I see little flecks of gold and amber in her irises. . . . So beautiful.

Becky blinks up at me. "Why are you looking at me like that?"

The volume in her voice startles me. Not yelling, but speaking in an everyday tone of voice, not all whispery and soft like Sydney does. Did. "Like what?" It's impossible to keep from panting.

"No, I mean . . . at all?"

Not knowing what else to do, how to answer, I bend my head down to, at long last, kiss Becky Webb.

She twists away.

"What—what're you doing?" she says.

. . . "Kissing you."

"Why?"

Why? I almost say it right back to her. Why? Why else? Isn't it obvious? How can I possibly make it more clear that not only is my single biggest dream in life coming true, but that she is at the center of it?

Becky tilts her head against the pillow. The frown on her face slowly relaxes away, replaced by something else. I don't know what . . .

"Wait," Becky says.

. . . She says it so softly that it's almost mouthed rather than spoken. And once again—I almost scream.

"Just—don't kiss me," she says, not meeting my eyes. "Okay?" . . .

Part of me screams in agony, *Go! Just do it, what are you waiting for, you idiot, go go go!*

Becky's gaze is still turned away from me, her eyes open, absently studying her desk chair. Like she's doing math homework in her head.

"You're beautiful," I say. It just sort of pops out.

One of Becky's eyes twitches. The corners of her mouth turn down, and her lower lip trembles ever so slightly as she looks back at me.

"What?" Becky says.

I stare into her eyes so hard that soon all I can see is the blackness of her pupils. I fall into them. . . . "I love you."

Becky's head twists to one side again, but she keeps her eyes on me, lids narrowing to near slits. She slides to a sitting position, making me shuffle backward. She points shamelessly to my groin.

"*That's* not love," she says. "So you don't get to say that. Not you, you fucking asshole, don't you say that to me, don't . . ."

Her eyes squeeze tight, breaking our gaze. A soft hiccup escapes her throat. . . .

Unthinking now, I scramble off the bed and pull up my boxers. I grab the royal-purple robe from the hook in the bathroom and take it over to her, draping it over her hunched form. Then I sit beside her, crossing my own legs too, and pull her against my body as tightly as I can.[3]

manicpixiedreamgirl is a realistic look at first love through the eyes of an extremely likeable and relatable teenage male protagonist. Leveen's effective use of believable teen dialogue and actions to develop rich characterizations enables readers to make sense (as Tyler does) of life, love, and sex. For example, in the previous scene, Tyler's emotional growth is triggered by his interactions with Becky. Ultimately, Becky's reasons for sex become clear to Tyler and lead to the realization that for him, sex and love go together. His actions demonstrate that he is unwilling to compromise that belief. Scenes like this—not preachy narrators or thinly disguised public service messages—ring true for adolescent readers.

Leveen explains how he decides what to include in a sex scene:

When I encounter a "sex scene" in one of my novels, my responsibility goes beyond telling a good story. Certainly, contemporary YA doesn't have to be about or include sex. My characters and settings, though, which many people have termed "edgy," do talk about it, think about, and sometimes even have it. Pretending it doesn't happen, or that teens aren't talking and thinking about it, has caused more problems than trying to keep it quiet. I don't find it necessary, nor desirable, to write a sexual scene that is designed to be explicit or scintillating; everyone knows where they can find that kind of material. What I attempt to do is be honest about the emotional and social aspects of any sexual act.

Every YA author I know takes sex in their novels very seriously, and believes that caution—at the *very least*—is always best for adolescents considering taking steps toward any sexual act. I won't guilt a reader (or character) for having sexual thoughts, words, desires, or actions, but I won't hesitate to take them to the days, weeks, and years after, to see what kind of effect it had on them. Sex *is* a big deal, to both adults and adolescents. Pretending it's *not* makes no sense, and can in fact be dangerous, on physical, emotional, and social levels most teens aren't equipped yet to deal with.

"Explicit" can have many meanings. Most people probably take it to mean graphic, visually charged, or in some way meant to excite. If I'm going to use any explicit language or imagery, such as is found in *manicpixiedreamgirl*, then it is my goal to make it *emotionally* explicit more than simply graphic. There is so much more going on between Becky and Tyler in the final bedroom scene than a physical act, and that's true of all physical acts—hugs, kisses, punches, slaps, or even a *lack* of touching. I want to get into the characters' and readers' heads, confront what is really at stake rather than get people *turned on*. I'd rather a reader get excited by how the characters treat each other.[4]

Openly Straight, by Bill Konigsberg (2013)

Rafe Goldberg came out as gay in eighth grade. Boulder, Colorado, seemed like the most accepting, diverse, and socially conscious place in the world to make such a move so early in life, and that turned out to be true, which is precisely why Rafe has decided to move to a preparatory boarding school in New England for his junior year. Everyone has become so accepting that Rafe begins to wonder if being gay is the only thing that defines him. His mother is president of the local chapter of Parents, Families and Friends of Lesbians and Gays (Pflag), and he was once featured in a local newspaper article entitled "Gay High School Student Speaks Out." Rafe feels as though he is losing his identity. He says of his decision to leave, "As of tomorrow, I was going to have new skin, and that skin could look like anything, would feel different than anything I knew yet. And that made me feel a little bit like I was about to be born. Again. But hopefully not Born Again."[5] His plan? To tell no one at his new school that he is gay. He rationalizes that he is not really lying; he just wants people to see him as Rafe, not gay Rafe.

Once he arrives at his new school, Rafe experiences what it feels like to hang out with the boys, free from any judgments that might accompany physical activities, like pickup football games or using a communal shower. He makes friends with people who like him for his personality and his athletic ability, not because he is gay. He even joins the soccer team. This is when Rafe's life becomes complicated. He develops a crush on his teammate, Ben, and when Ben's roommate is forced to leave school, Rafe is invited to move in, which further intensifies their relationship.

As a result of Konigsberg's excellent first-person narration, readers experience Rafe's rollercoaster of emotions right along with him. Here, he tries to define his relationship with Ben:

In public, we toned the intensity of our friendship down, knowing that Steve and his posse would not quite get our strange but unusual bond. But in private, we threw away most of our barriers, and that was more than fine with me.

Sex was not on the menu. I hadn't found the line yet where things would be "too much" for Ben, but I had a feeling we were pretty close to it. For all my fantasies about Ben—and I'd had a lot of them—I couldn't really picture any of them coming true. So many nights, after lights out, I snuck off to the bathroom and "took care of business," hoping to God no one would come in and utilize the bathroom in a way that would ruin the mood.[6]

The two become closer, and as Thanksgiving approaches, Rafe invites Ben to come home with him to Boulder. Since Rafe has yet to tell his parents about his plan to keep his sexuality a secret, he now must ask his parents to play along. In this scene, it is Thanksgiving night, the boys are in Rafe's bedroom:

I got into my bed and Ben lingered. I patted the space next to me, and he came and lay down. The bed creaked from his added weight. My heart felt so full, like it could burst. Like I could.

"Would your parents freak out if they walked in?"

I shook my head. "Please. My dad just about married us off already."

"Yeah, what's up with that? I would think any parent would not want their kid to be, you know. And ever since we met, they've treated me like, I don't know. A son-in-law. It's odd."

"Tell me about it," I said. "My mom told me when I was fourteen that she wanted me to be gay."

"Therapy much?" he said, laughing, and I laughed too. I left out the small fact that I'd just told her I *was* gay.

"If I told my parents I was gay, they would probably throw me out of the house," Ben said.

"Wow," I said. I imagined that happening, and how I would be there for him. It would be me and Ben, against the world. The fantasy made me tingle with excitement.[7]

Soon after, things heat up:

"Thanks for bringing me here," Ben said softly. . . . "I wish my family were like them."

"You can take 'em," I said.

"I swear to God, I wish I really was gay, I'd totally marry you."

I had had enough wine to do what I wouldn't have done otherwise. I rolled over onto my side and faced Ben, looking deep into his soulful, kind eyes. "I can't figure out any way to get closer to you, and I feel it. Like I want to get closer. It's not sex I want, it's just . . ."

I kissed him then, on the lips, keeping my lips there until he kissed back. And he did, he kissed back, and we opened our lips slightly and then wider, and our mouths were two Os pressing together, and I could taste his tongue because it was so close to mine. Ben breathed into my mouth. It felt like I'd shot to the moon, this pulsing, rushing roller coaster from below that overtook my body, and I shook.

He pulled back. "Wow," he said. "That was, that was different."

I was wet. I could feel it in my pajama bottoms. "Yeah," I said, breathless.

"Did you like it?"

"Did you?" I asked.

"It was—it was okay. Your lips are different than a girl's. It was sort of alien."

"Totally," I said.

"Did you get, you know, hard?" he asked.

"Did you?"

He looked down, so I did too, and he was definitely tenting the front of his sweatpants.

"I guess so," he said.

"Thank God," I said, relieved. "I did more than that."

He looked down at the wet stain forming on my pajama bottoms. Then he looked back up at me, his eyes wide. I felt as if my heart were in my throat.

"That'll happen," Ben said, but his voice was a little shaky, and I knew he was scared. I was too.[8]

In *Openly Straight*, Rafe and Ben are both attempting to discover their true sexual identities. This sex scene is an effective illustration of the change that occurs in Rafe and Ben's relationship, achieved through Konigsberg's skillful use of tone to portray Ben's uncertainty. Ultimately, Rafe realizes that being openly straight is just as difficult as being openly gay.

Konigsberg explains how he decides when to include a sex scene and what to include when he does:

> When I'm deciding where to draw the line when it comes to sexual content, I focus on one question: what would be gained by showing the intimate behavior? I am only interested in sexual content in YA books that illuminates character. Does something happen in the scene that changes a character? Does something happen that shows character? Are

there other ways to illuminate that without lifting the veil on the bedroom? Because if there is another way, all things being equal, I'd probably nix the sex scene. This scene in Rafe's bedroom simply has to be shown. There is a shift in how both characters feel based on the action and we learn something about both boys. This would not be the same if I simply "told" the reader what happened. While I don't consider myself by any means a prude, I am simply uninterested in reading or writing sex scenes about teenagers that could be considered gratuitous. That's just not how I like to do things.[9]

WHEN SEX GOES WRONG: LESSONS LEARNED

Thirteen Reasons Why, by Jay Asher (2007)

Thirteen Reasons Why is told from the alternating viewpoints of Clay Jensen and Hannah Baker. Clay comes home one day to find a box filled with seven cassette tapes filled with Hannah's voice recordings, each of the thirteen sides meant for a specific person and each one containing one of the reasons that she perceived led to her committing suicide. Clay is not the first or the last person who will receive the tapes, but as we listen and follow along with him (Hannah has also left behind a map so that each participant can visit the places where events in her downward spiral occurred), we learn not only about Hannah but much about Clay.

Thirteen Reasons Why is a masterpiece of plot development. Despite our knowing from the outset that Hannah has already killed herself, her posthumous taped narration, paired with Clay's commentary in the form of thoughts and memories, keeps readers riveted, as our need to know why she took her life builds to a fever pitch. Furthermore, because Clay and Hannah are both unreliable narrators, we are forced to look deeper than the narration if we hope to draw any reasonable conclusions. There are no monumental defining moments here, just a succession of seemingly minor incidents that snowball and become unmanageable for Hannah.

First, Justin Foley, Hannah's first kiss, tells his friends that they did more than kiss. Next, Alex Standall, in an attempt to get back at his ex-girlfriend, creates a "Hot or Not" list and votes Hannah "Best Ass of the Freshman Class." Alex's ex, Jessica Davis, is placed on the "Not" list, and she then begins spreading and amplifying the same rumors that Justin started. From there, the snowball grows and picks up speed.

The most shocking, heart-wrenching, controversial, and necessary
scene in *Thirteen Reasons Why* is so well known to lovers and critics of
the book that it is simply referred to as "the hot tub scene." Readers are
already familiar with Bryce Walker (reason 12) as a guy who is skilled
at misrepresenting his intentions to get what he wants from women,
typically sex. When Hannah takes a walk after a party, she spies Bryce
and Courtney (reason 5) in a backyard hot tub. Bryce calls for her to
join them and Courtney quickly excuses herself. At this point in the
story, Hannah's spirits have deteriorated, and she seems to be searching
for that one final reason that will allow her to simply give up. She strips
to her underwear and gets into the hot tub (italics are used in the book
to indicate Hannah's narration):

> *Everyone knows who you are, Bryce. Everyone knows what you do. But
> I, for the record, did nothing to stop you.*
>
> *You asked if I had fun at the party. Courtney whispered that I
> wasn't at the party. But you didn't seem to care. Instead, your fingers
> touched the outside of my thigh. . . .*
>
> *Your whole hand was back. And when I didn't stop you, you slid
> your hand across my belly. Your thumb touched the bottom of my bra
> and your pinky touched the top of my underwear.*
>
> *I turned my head sideways, away from you. And I know I didn't
> smile.*
>
> *. . . I felt a shift in the water and opened my eyes for one brief
> second.*
>
> *Courtney was walking away.*
>
> *"Remember when you were a freshman?" you asked.*
>
> *Your fingers made their way under my bra. . . . Testing the boundar-
> ies, I guess. . . . "Weren't you on that list?" you said. "Best ass in the
> freshman class."*
>
> *Bryce, you had to see my jaw clench. You had to see my tears. Does
> that kind of shit turn you on?*
>
> *"It's true," you said.*
>
> *And then, just like that, I let go. My shoulders went limp. My legs
> fell apart. I knew exactly what I was doing.*
>
> *Not once had I given in to the reputation you'd all set for me. . . .*
>
> *. . . Until Bryce.*
>
> *. . . I was not attracted to you, Bryce. Ever. In fact, you disgusted
> me.*
>
> *You were touching me . . . but I was using you. I needed you, so I
> could let go of myself, completely.*
>
> *For everyone listening, let me be clear. I did not say no or push his
> hand away. All I did was turn my head, clench my teeth, and fight back
> tears. And he saw that. He even told me to relax.*

> *. . . But in the end, I never told you to get away . . . and you didn't.*
>
> *Your pinky made its way under the top of my panties and rolled back and forth, from hip to hip. Then another finger slipped below, pushing your pinky further down, brushing it through my hair.*
>
> *And that's all you needed, Bryce. You started kissing my shoulder, my neck, sliding your fingers in and out. And then you kept going. You didn't stop there. I'm sorry. Is this getting too graphic for some of you? Too bad.* [10]

Asher has said that he and his editors considered removing or at least toning down this scene, but they all agreed that the scene as written was necessary to accurately portray the moment that Hannah gives up hope. [11] This scene provides some incredible opportunities for thought-provoking discussions. In the young adult literature classes that we teach, for example, many students will argue that the scene portrays a sexual assault, while others contend that Hannah, regardless of her unreliability as a narrator, engages in consensual sex, because she does nothing to stop Bryce's advances.

We consider *Thirteen Reasons Why* to be contemporary and relevant; therefore, an explanation why cassette tapes were used in the story seems important to share. In a supplement at the end of the book entitled "Thirteen Reasons Why (Between the Lines)—13 Questions for Jay Asher," the author responds to the question "So why cassette tapes? You do realize they're extremely outdated."

> With technology changing so fast, it's impossible for a present-day novel to stay current if your characters use the most up-to-date material. So rather than have Hannah post her reasons online—in which case, the terminology could change overnight and the characters in the book wouldn't know it—I used an even older form of recording and made the characters acknowledge it. When something is out-of-date but the characters know it, the book is suddenly up-to-date.

After reading *Thirteen Reasons Why*, many of our students comment that no amount of public service announcements or teen suicide prevention websites could match the impact of reading this story of a girl who felt that she was left with no options. Our students and millions of readers from around the world have shared lessons that they have learned from *Thirteen Reasons Why*, including being responsible for our own actions, the meaning of friendship, treating others with kindness, and understanding the implications of our actions on others. Not bad for a story that contains a hot tub scene and a suicide.

Sex and Violence, by Carrie Mesrobian (2013)

Evan Carter is a slender, athletic, good-looking guy. Hooking up with girls has always come easily for him. Evan's mom died when he was young, and ever since, he has been forced to move all over the country so that his dad can stay employed. Constantly being the new kid at every school he attends, combined with his father's lack of emotional connection to his son, has helped Evan develop some very specific coping skills. He is proficient at identifying females who are willing to have sex with him, females who will not subsequently expect or desire a long-term emotional commitment. Evan explains his modus operandi:

> But it wasn't just being new and shiny that made me successful with chicks. The selection of the target was also important. . . . It wasn't that I had high standards or anything. I just looked for Girls Who Would Say Yes. Not yes to giving me phone numbers or hanging out. . . . Yes to getting naked—or at least naked enough. Yes to sex. Because I didn't live anywhere for too long and didn't have time to mess around going on a million dates or whatever. I've got a profile of the Girl Who Would Say Yes.[12]

The first several pages of *Sex and Violence* portray Evan as a somewhat unlikeable predator. However, Evan is about to meet Collette Holmander and—in what turns out to be a cruel twist of fate—he completely misreads her intentions. What Evan believes is a visit to his dorm to assess his interest in one of Collette's friends turns into something quite different:

> When I came out of the Connison gang shower, Collette Holmander was waiting for me. She was standing in the hallway, her long red hair splashing down her black jacket and white shirt, her red knee socks on her pretty legs beneath her little black skirt. Even though Remington Chase was a vaguely religious boarding school, the girls' uniforms were unreasonably sexy—practically porn fantasies.[13]

She then follows Evan into his room:

> Collette kicked the door shut, grabbed my towel and shower kit, and dropped them to the floor. She was so close to me that my whole body popped up in goose bumps, which was embarrassing enough, but things got worse below the belt . . .
> "Collette . . ." I started, not sure what to say.
> Then she rose on tiptoes and kissed me.

So. All right. This was the first thing about Southern boarding school that I could recommend. Alone in my room, with a cute girl who had nice boobs and made all the moves. . . . She was wrapped around me, my hands on her ass over her skirt, her boobs smushed against my chest and her hair everywhere in a big awesome mess. I thought about the box of condoms stashed in a duffel bag in my closet. . . . I wondered if I could get Collette's clothes off in time. [14]

The next day, at Collette's request, she and Evan again rendezvous in Evan's dorm, during chapel:

I locked the door and Collette flopped against me on my unmade bed and we made out until her shirt was off and I was so hard I was almost sick to my stomach. But before I could test the idea of where she was on the sex thing (I usually started with just this basic hand motion toward the belly-button area and then just a little lower toward the edge of the panties, as if to acknowledge they were there, as Girls Who Said No were always touchy about things going in that direction), Collette just shoved her (ringless) hand down my pants and jerked me off. [15]

Evan's life changes dramatically when Collette's ex-boyfriend, Patrick, who happens to be Evan's roommate, discovers that Evan is stealing intimate moments with Collette. He and a friend (both having been previously and accurately described by Evan as "douchebags") attack Evan as he is getting out of the shower:

"Carter," Tate said. . . . "Why you gotta fuck around with what doesn't belong to you?"

"This is for firecrotch," Patrick said, reaching forward and grabbing my head, his hands in my hair, slamming my face against a shower door and then Tate kicked me in the stomach and I fell on the orange industrial tile and spit up a blob of blood and the last things I remembered were Patrick Ramsey calling me a fucking fag and Tate Kerrigan laughing when my nose broke open under his fist. [16]

Evan is rushed to the hospital with a ruptured spleen, a broken nose, and several other external and internal injuries. Readers discover later that Collette did not escape unharmed, ending up in the hospital as well.

Soon after, Evan and his father move to Marchant Falls, where Evan's dad grew up. Initially, Evan dislikes it there, and to complicate matters, he is struggling with emotional issues—he worries about showing any interest in a female for fear that some current or former boyfriend will beat him up, and he bathes in the lake because the shower in his new house (cabin) does not have a lock. As the story progresses, Evan has several epiphanies that are influenced by and take shape as a result of the letters that he writes to Collette—he never sends them—in which he tries to explain, rationalize, and apologize for what happened and through conversations he has with his counselor. His learning curve is slow but completely realistic.

Evan is initially characterized as a guy who rationalizes much of his sexual behavior. He attempts to validate himself as a way to increase his self-confidence by seducing girls—never in his bed (until Collette) and never fully unclothed. Evan views sex—and this attitude does not magically disappear after the assault—as a way to forget about the outside world for a while, as a way to disconnect. Fear and the recollection of the assault are not enough to control the coping mechanisms that he has worked so hard to put into place. As we delve deeper into Evan's psyche, we begin to realize that Evan may be attracted to damaged women, women who have more in common with him than he wants to recognize.

The sex scenes in *Sex and Violence* help to paint a picture of a young man who is trying to make sense of his world. Evan is characterized as respectful and caring in most situations, but when it comes to relationships, especially ones with the opposite sex, he has learned that intimacy can be harmful; therefore, he is unable to make any meaningful connections between sex and love. We suggest that you read the book to find out if he ultimately makes a move in the right direction.

ONE AMAZING NOVEL ABOUT SEXUAL EXPERIENCES FROM MULTIPLE PERSPECTIVES

Doing It, by Melvin Burgess (2004)

Doing It is told from third-person limited narrations of several British teenagers, all of whom are trying to navigate the slippery slope of adolescent sexual desire. The alternating viewpoints help readers experience the physical and emotional effects of sex from perspectives both female and male.

Dino, popular and handsome, is desperately trying to win the affection of Jackie, the prettiest girl in school, who, as the story begins, wants nothing to do with him. After becoming aware of a physical attraction to Dino, Jackie then struggles with how far she should allow the relationship to go. Dino's two best friends, Jonathon and Ben, have their own sexual issues. Jonathon finds himself physically and emotionally attracted to Deborah, but because she is overweight, he worries that his friends will judge him. Deborah, however, is extremely confident and has no issues with "snogging" Jonathon in public. Ben has been coerced into a controlling affair with his attractive drama teacher, a relationship that he at first embraces but later finds smothering and downright scary.

Burgess opens with a chapter that serves to introduce Dino, Ben, and Jonathon. The opening lines of the book provide some keen insight into what teenage boys talk about when the girls are not around. The conversation involves a game of *would you rather*, and Jonathon has given his friends the choice of "shagging" either Jenny Gibson, the ugliest girl in school, or a homeless woman who begs change on the corner near the bakery. Ben considers the homeless woman. "Can I shag her from behind?" Jonathon responds, "No, from the front. With the lights on. Snogging and everything. And you have to do oral sex on her, too. . . . Oral sex until she comes."[17]

As crass and insensitive as this opening may sound, it serves to establish the boys' lack of sexual experience and maturity. In addition, the images of engaging in sex with a homeless woman or the ugliest girl in school create an unsettling, discomforting tone for the reader. Awkward and uncomfortable sex scenes continue throughout, thus further reinforcing the vulnerabilities and insecurities of the characters.

Dino is determined to lose his virginity, primarily to confirm that he is the stud that his peers perceive him to be, and he has finally convinced Jackie to oblige him. Their plan is to have sex at the weekend party he is throwing while his parents are out of town. The party soon gets out of hand, and Dino gets so caught up in the party vibe that when he finally realizes that Jackie has been ready and waiting, he misses his opportunity. She finds vomit in the bed where their rendezvous was to take place and leaves abruptly.

Fortunately for Dino, just as he is lamenting her departure, he finds another girl sleeping in the corner of the bedroom, apparently passed out. The girl, who tells Dino her name is Siobhan, asks him if he minds if she stays the night, and Dino immediately begins to devise a plan to try to sleep with her. "He frowned. She knew what he wanted all right! There she was with her party dress up round her knickers. . . . He said, 'You can stay the night . . . so long as you sleep with me.'"[18] He then moves her toward his bed.

"You don't mind?"

She shrugged, and he thought to himself it would be truer to say she didn't care. . . . He kissed her again to stop her mouth in case she complained. Then he pulled her pink dress over her head and there she was, with her knickers hardly covering her bush and her little titties out. Dino said, "Oh, oh, oh."

He pushed her gently to the bed, and she got in. He took his trousers off and got in after her. . . . He peeled her knickers off and she lifted her legs to help him. And then . . .

Dino began to lose it.

She was lying there; she felt all chilly under his hands as if she'd just come out of the fridge and he was trying to spread her on his bread. He kissed her again, hard, to try to stop his erection from collapsing. . . . He rubbed his pubis on hers, but as his fear of failure grew so his knob got softer and softer and now at last it was nothing but a felty slug hanging off him.[19]

Each time Dino attempts to act on his physical desires, whether it be with Siobhan—we later learn this is not her real name and that she is using Dino to get something she wants—or with Jackie, whom he believes to be his true love, some mishap inevitably prevents him from following through. If we were searching for a message, it might be that Dino's lack of sexual success is somehow related to his misguided motivations for pursuing his desires. Once he finally decides to break things off with Jackie, we are given hope that Dino may be able to make at least a superficial connection between the joy of sex and a meaningful relationship.

Ben is about to experience every teenage boy's fantasy—having sex with his hot drama teacher. In this scene, Miss Young first makes her intentions known after suggesting that she and Ben stop by her house for coffee after picking up some supplies for the play:

"Sorry, but I've been wanting to do this for a long time. Ever since I showed you my knickers," she added. Then she leaned down and gave him a dirty big snog. Ben responded with his tongue and she almost fell on top of him, running her hands over his face and up under his sweat-shirt. Blinded by a sudden rush of hormones, he put his hand on her hip, then let it slide down to the side of her bum. She pulled up her blouse, and Ben slid his hand up and cupped a breast. He thought he was going to faint with lust and had to sit up. . . . Her hand caressed his thigh and stroked the bulge in his school trousers. Ben heard himself muttering "Jesus," three times, one after the other. . . . She unzipped him. Mad with lust but terrified by authority, Ben suddenly froze up and couldn't think what to do next, but that didn't seem to bother her.[20]

Ben is both excited and frightened by Miss Young. She gropes him behind the curtains at play practice, performing oral sex on him while he watches through the curtains to make sure that no one surprises them. She assigns him detention so that she can spend time with him after school, and she invites him to her house for long sessions of intercourse in which she acts out her fantasies on him. Over time, Ben becomes increasingly disenchanted with the arrangement, feeling that he has little to no control over what is happening. When Miss Young tells him that she loves him during one of their sessions, he finally realizes that he has to get out.

The sex scenes between Ben and Miss Young are graphic but not sensual or erotic. This is due to Burgess's expert juxtaposition of Ben's thoughts with his physical descriptions of sex. For example, Ben wonders if he will ever be able to talk to anyone about his situation. He promised Miss Young that he will not tell anyone, and he has kept his word. But the more that he thinks about it, the more he begins to feel as though he has been preyed on. In the middle of one of their sexual encounters, he thinks, "It's what people do with little kids, isn't it? 'This is our secret, just you and me; you must never tell or awful things will happen.'"[21]

Jonathon cannot seem to keep from becoming sexually aroused whenever he is with Deborah, who, despite being a little overweight, is extremely likeable and confident. Deborah enjoys kissing and touching Jonathon in places that make it impossible for him to not become aroused. As the story progresses, Jonathon tries to make sense of the disconnect between caring for someone and having sex with that person. He likes the feelings that he experiences when he spends time with Deborah, and he likes sex, at least the limited amount of it that he has had, but he cannot seem to put the two together. Here he struggles to understand why girls even engage in sex:

> Sex is . . . well, it's so rude, isn't it? You wouldn't think girls would like sex. . . . Doing sex with a girl, it's a bit like putting a frog down their backs or scaring them with dead mice or throwing worms at them. They're such sensible, grown-up sorts of people. And yet apparently even the nice ones like you sticking the rudest thing you have on your whole body up the exact, rudest part of their body that they have![22]

One of the defining characteristics of young adult literature—and adolescence—is the search for self. Throughout this journey toward adulthood, teenagers will experience losses of control, as well as repeated attempts to regain measures of that control. In each sex scene in *Doing It*—and there are too many to cite here—Burgess expertly illustrates the dichotomy between losing and gaining control of one's life. He accomplishes this by creating verisimilitude, or the semblance of truth. As readers identify and correlate characteristics in the story with those from their own experiences, believable connections between fictional worlds and the real world are established. And although these story characteristics or pieces may be similar to readers' previous experiences, they are new enough to encourage a reassessment of existing perspectives—in this case, on life, love, and sex.

Creating these types of reading experiences for adolescents is crucial if we hope to prepare critical thinkers who will be capable of intelligent and independent decision making. Let us be clear. Critical thinkers are not developed by reading fiction that is filled with unrealistically good and bad characters whose narration feels preachy. These types of stories are known as fairy tales, and although many teens still enjoy reading them, the adolescents of today are not gleaning life lessons from fairy godmothers or wicked witches. *Doing It* is no fairy tale; it is realistic contemporary fiction that accurately portrays teenage experiences—peer pressure, life at home, and, yes, the innermost thoughts of hormonal adolescents—in ways that allow readers to personalize and internalize their own life lessons.

SEX AND THE SHORT STORY

Losing It, edited by Keith Gray (2013)

Losing It is a collection of ten short stories written by an international superstar cast of YA authors, including A. S. King, Melvin Burgess, Keith Gray, Patrick Ness, Anne Fine, Sophie McKenzie, Bali Rai, Jenny Valentine, Mary Hooper, and Andrew Smith.[23] The *It* in the title refers to each protagonist's virginity. A promotional tag line for the book captures the theme of the collection best: *Everything you wanted to know about virginity but your parents were too embarrassed to tell you.* This collection could easily function as a textbook for a sex education course in the public schools if the goal of the class were to enlighten adolescents about the physical, moral, social, and emotional aspects of sex. The following are several select story summaries and a few accompanying scenes that we found particularly scintillating.

In "The Age of Consent," a seventy-year-old grandmother named Dora recalls—at the dinner table—her first sexual experience. While the parents are appalled, the two teen girls are fascinated. At one point in the conversation, the grandmother asks, "What do they teach you about sex at school?" and one of the girls responds, "Mechanics . . . they teach you mechanics." "Ooh, mechanics," Dora said. "I like those. I had a couple of mechanics when I worked at the factory."[24]

Melvin Burgess returns to his theme of teen boys getting involved with older women in "Chat Up Lines." Brian is fifteen and Samantha is seventeen, but this does not stop Brian from "chatting up" Sam, which leads to an almost immediate connection between the unlikely pair. Brian, however, neglects to tell Sam that he is two years younger than she: a detail that he tries to rationalize as not at all important, even though deep down he knows that it will most likely kill any chance that he may have at getting physical with her. In this scene, Sam makes the first move, to Brian's shock and delight:

> It was on her doorstep to start with—just a bit of a hug and a kiss. She pressed up closer against me than she needed to. Then she slipped me a little bit of tongue and I slipped her a bit back and suddenly there it was, full frontal snogging. With a seventeen-year-old.
> How cool am I?
> "Mmm," she said. "That's too good to stop." She grabbed my hand and pulled me round the side of the house so we could "say goodnight properly."
> Yeah. You heard. She said, "Say goodnight properly."
> And we did . . . I slid my hand onto her boob, and she gave me this lovely little muffled groan, but I wasn't too clear what that meant because she had her tongue down my throat. Then I slid my hand under her top and tried to wriggle under her bra, but she pulled and twisted a bit and said, "Not here, not here."
> Yeah. You heard. She said, "Not here." Translate that, if you like.[25]

Sam invites Brian to come to her house the following afternoon. Soon after Brian arrives, Sam asks,

> "We're going upstairs. Do you mind?"
> Language left me. I was speechless. She led me upstairs to her bedroom. She asked about condoms, but I hadn't come supplied . . .

"Boys," she said. But she had some. So then we, then we, then
we . . .
       I was always scared that when it came down to it, it wouldn't work.
That things just wouldn't stand up under pressure. But they did. . . .
Naked. In bed. With Samantha Harding. You could have your dick
chopped up and made into a sandwich for the bears, and it would still
work.
       It was about the best day of my life by about ten thousand miles. [26]

Brian finally does admit his age to Samantha, and she promptly dumps
him. He is ostracized at school and grows apart from his closest friend,
a girl named Drew. But in true Burgess style, the story ends with this
wonderful reflection:

> I hate it that she [Drew] thinks of me like that. I hate it that she's grown
> up and left me behind, when what was supposed to happen was, we
> were going to grow up together.
>   But.
>   You know what?
>   But wow.
>   It was still worth it. [27]

   In Keith Gray's "Scoring," a soccer player is forced to choose between heeding his coach's advice or giving into what could be a once-
in-a-lifetime opportunity. The coach's pep talk the night before the big
game leaves no doubt in Jase's mind what is expected of him:

> "You know in the old days players were even banned from seeing their
> wives the night before a match? You lads heard that story? Footballers
> need a bit of aggression when they're on the pitch, when they're fight-
> ing for the ball. Storing it all up, keeping it all in, makes you aggres-
> sive." He winked. "Yes, lads, no sex tonight is what I'm talking
> about. . . . That includes with yourselves." [28]

Jase wavers on his decision to the very end. When he arrives at his
girlfriend's house, she leans around the front door wearing the school's
football shirt. He sees it as a sign. He decides that he will forego sex on
this day and focus on the game—that is, until . . .

> She stepped out all the way from behind the door. She wasn't wearing
> anything on her lower half except for a pair of thin black panties. Her
> legs were so long and so smooth and so gorgeous. I blinked twice. My

grin went a bit lopsided, my arms held out there like an idiot. She was really being no help at all. [29]

In Andrew Smith's "Green Screen," Spencer Chapman, fifteen years old and the self-proclaimed "dorkiest kid in tenth grade," is paired with the beautiful "reformed slut" Laurel Weinstein for an English class project on *Lord of the Flies*. Lauren, a seventeen-year-old senior, is repeating tenth-grade English to graduate. While working on the project with Laurel, the extremely reserved Spencer stumbles over his words and worries that his mother will find out that his after-school hours are being spent at a girl's house.

Smith's characters are always so wonderfully detailed and quirky, and Laurel is no exception. Her idea for the *Lord of the Flies* project involves creating a calendar—she has her own photo studio complete with a green screen at home—and Spencer is going to be the model for each month's scene. Laurel has previous experience with calendar creation, as she is almost finished with her current project, "Babies with Guns."

As the story progresses, these two mismatched characters grow closer and closer. Spencer tries—with little success—not to think about Laurel in a sexual way, and Laurel continues to test Spencer's reserved nature with each month's calendar shoot. In this scene, Spencer tells readers what he has endured so far:

> The shirt was only the beginning. Laurel Weinstein opened the book to chapter 3 to prove her point. Of course, after the shirt removal, I knew this was inevitable. In chapter 3—the scene we were shooting—the character Jack is walking along the beach, hunting pigs, spear in hand, and he's dressed in nothing but his underwear and a knife belt.
>
> The argument did not go well for me. Here are some of the highlights:
>
> "I have a knife belt for you."
>
> "I don't care. I'm not going to take my pants off." I'll be honest. I thought it would be fun to take my pants off in front of Laurel Weinstein.
>
> "Don't be such a prude."
>
> " . . . Haven't you ever been in your underwear in front of a girl? It's no big deal, *the Spencer*."
>
> "I've never been in my underwear in front of *anyone* except for my doctor and Coach Warner." [30]

Ultimately, Laurel takes a more hands-on approach:

Laurel kept her hand behind my neck. Our eyes were open, and we stared directly at each other as she pulled my face to hers and slid her tongue between my lips. Then she kissed my shoulders and collarbones and each one of my nipples while her hand caressed the front of my briefs.

She stood back and pulled off her sweatshirt. . . . We stood there, pressed together on the cool mat of Laurel Weinstein's green screen, and she looked into my face and said, "Do you want to fuck?"

I'll be honest: I did not think that she would say something like that, and I definitely did not think that we were actually getting ready to have sex. . . .

"I. Uh. I don't think that would be right, Laurel. I really care about you."

She said, "I know. It's weird. Because I really care about you too, *the Spencer.*"

"Then I guess the answer to your question is yes, I do want to."

"Good. Because I do too."

The final scene includes more description of this first encounter, and there were several more that day that readers only learn about when Spencer tells us:

I lost my virginity to Laurel Weinstein five times that day. (It's important to give an exact number.) In all honesty though, I suppose a guy can only lose his virginity once. That's the idea, right?—maybe the myth— because in reality anything and everything became possible on Laurel Weinstein's green screen, where we re-created ourselves as frequently as possible.[31]

Love and Sex: Ten Stories of Truth, edited by Michael Cart (2001)

In the foreword to *Love and Sex,* editor Michael Cart laments that there are (in 2001) "still too few works of fiction for young adults that deal artfully yet honestly with the complexities of human sexuality and how they affect 'life as it is lived.'"[32] Sadly, this statement rings true in 2014. This short story collection came about as a result of Cart's attempt to search for the "equation between sex and love in adolescent life."[33] The ten stories in *Love and Sex* are written by a cast of outstanding YA authors, including Laurie Halse Anderson, Angela Johnson, Joan Bauer, Chris Lynch, Garth Nix, and Sonya Sones. The collection addresses, in a truthful way, all the physical, emotional, moral, and cultural complexities of sex—"abstinence and obsession, heterosexuality and homosexuality, gender and transgender, confusion and certainty, fantasy and reality, hurt and healing."[34]

Sonya Sones's "Secret Shelf" introduces readers to Sophie, a four-teen-and-a-half-year-old girl who is obsessed with sex. Through a series of poems, Sophie tries to make sense of the "difference between love and lust."[35] The following excerpt is from "In My Dreams":

> I'm dreaming of him kissing me,
> of his lips sizzling
> all the cells in my body,
> of wishing he would remove
> every stitch of my clothes . . .
> I'm dreaming of my nipples rising up,
> yearning to know
> how his hands will feel
> when he cups his palms
> over the lace of my bra.

In the poem entitled "Secret Shelf," Sophie discovers "some of the dirtiest books"[36] that she has ever seen and then realizes,

> I'll never be able
> to think of my parents
> in quite the same way as I used to
> and that every time they go out
> and leave me alone in the house,
> I'll be racing right back up here
> to grab another one off the shelf.[37]

Sones explains that "Secret Shelf" is a small sampling of poems that would later become the book *What My Mother Doesn't Know*.[38] In the opening of *What My Mother Doesn't Know*, which was published in the same year as *Love and Sex* (2001), we meet Sophie, who tells us,

> My name is Sophie.
> This book is about me.
> It tells the heart-stoppingly riveting story
> of my first love.
> And also of my second.
> And, okay, my third love, too.
> It's not that I'm boy crazy.
> It's just that even though
> I'm almost fifteen
> I've been having sort of a hard time
> trying to figure out the difference
> between love and lust.[39]

In "The Acuteness of Desire," by Michael Lowenthal, Jesse tries to enter into a romance with the same logical approach that he utilizes to solve the math equations that he loves. Jesse has known of his attraction to Matt Thompson ever since Matt lost a strip poker game at a birthday party at the age of ten. The other boys teased Matt, calling him a "faggot" because of the "boner" that popped out when he was forced to remove his last article of clothing. Jesse had been avoiding the actual Matt ever since, but in the privacy of his room, he fantasized about Matt. When Matt shows up as the new kid in Jesse's math class, Jesse constructs a logical reason for Matt's appearance:

> Every consequence has an antecedent. And this was the consequence I'd been dreading all along, my inevitable punishment for buying a pack of Bicycles every week, inhaling the crisp new vinyl smell, and being able to picture exactly how Matt had looked when he lost the poker game . . . for keeping the eighth-grade yearbook under my bed and opening it to the page with his picture and studying it, then slamming the book closed with my dick over his smiling face, whipping it harder and harder until the pages stuck together . . . for thinking of him in the shower, on the way to school, during band . . . for wanting to do more than just think.[40]

Jesse gets his chance at love when Matt asks him to tutor. When Matt arrives at Jesse's house, Jesse wastes no time trying to determine whether Matt is interested in him:

> "Can I ask you something?"
> "Sure, what?" He stood over me, his book bag draped casually over his left shoulder.
> "Well, I know you are going to think this is goofy and stuff. But I wanted to ask if you think something is normal, or if it means I'm like, totally weird or something."[41]

After a bit of rambling, Jesse tells Matt what he is thinking:

> "Well, a while ago, I don't know, maybe a month? It was a day you were wearing shorts. You turned around to hand me a paper and—God, this sounds so dumb. . . . You turned around and I could see your dick; it was hanging out of your underwear. . . . I didn't think about it at all until a couple of nights ago when I was jacking off and suddenly it popped into my head. You know, the thought of your dick that day? I mean, I could picture it in my head. And I kept thinking about it, and . . . "

"So, um, what do you think?" I said. "I mean, do you think I'm a total queer?"

. . . "Nah," he said, stretching the syllable. "I think that's pretty normal. I don't think you should worry too much."[42]

After a little more discussion, the boys get physical:

I don't remember which of us moved first. Maybe both at the same time. My hand met the smooth curve of his forearm, and his met mine. . . . Matt let his body go limp so I could lift off his T-shirt. . . .

He slipped his hand under my shirt and whisked it up, a magician revealing the stuffed rabbit turned real. . . .

In seconds we had each other's pants off. . . . We just lay there a minute, getting used to the sheer fact of so much skin. . . .

Matt had one leg locked between mine, so that his dick was smushed between his stomach and my thigh. As his hand jerked up and down on me, his hips humped with the same rhythm. He began murmuring under his breath, the way people talk in their sleep. "Oh my God. This is the best when it's flattened and . . . shit . . . it feels like . . . it hurts but . . . "

Matt cried one last word, something like "now" or "no," and I felt a pool of warmth seeping on my thigh. *Acute*, I sang to myself. *Hyperboloid!* And then I came, letting Matt's hand catch it all.

"Wow," Matt said.[43]

In the weeks that follow his encounter with Matt, Jesse is ignored, shunned, told in no uncertain terms to leave Matt alone. Lowenthal explains that he was inspired to write the story because he "wished there were guidelines to follow—some mathematical formula"[44] when it comes to love. He goes on to say, "For gay people things are especially confounding, because society doesn't even hand us the right textbook."[45]

"Watcher," by Angela Johnson, begins with a definition of the word *obsession*: "a persistent disturbing preoccupation with an often unreasonable idea or feeling."[46] This definition, combined with the ominous one-word title, may lead readers to believe that they are in for a story with creepy overtones and an antagonist who is a stalker. Instead, "Watcher" is a rich and surprisingly complex tale—especially for a short story—of an extraordinarily caring and perceptive teenager who wants nothing more than to be in the presence of his girlfriend. The unreasonable idea or feeling that he is disturbingly preoccupied with? Love.

Johnson's protagonist—we never learn his name—is madly in love with Jacqueline, whom he calls Jacks. Here, he describes how they first met:

> She followed me. It all started with obsession, you see. I was in a jewelry store with my sister on the first floor, and Jacks was watching me from a railing on the second.
>
> She says there was something about me that moved her. She says it was the way I leaned my head to the side to talk to my sister.
>
> The second thing that got her was my hands. When I walked out of the shop, I held up a necklace my sister had bought to the light above us. The hands did it.
>
> And she had to know me.
>
> The way that Jacks talks about following me, you'd think she was some kind of stalker. She says maybe she was, but she says people are too strange not to take an interest in. Jacks was a watcher, and I would be one soon too. [47]

The narrator understands that Jacks is a troubled soul, and he recognizes that her *watching* is a coping mechanism. He tells us, "Even though Jacks is always surrounded by people, I think she's lonely. I think that's why she watches. She can get only so far out of her loneliness. . . . Since she lived on the top floor, she watched the world." [48]

The narrator is not interested in watching the world, however—only Jacks. Watching allows him to experience Jacks in new and different ways. He tells us,

> Most people who follow other people around secretly have been told to stay away from that person. It's not like that with me and Jacks.
>
> I follow her because I want her in all different ways. Not just walking along with each other or eating greasy fries at the Diner. I want to have her time when she thinks she's having it alone. . . . I want to be there when she sleeps, eats, and cries.
>
> I'm not a dangerous stalker. Watching Jacks (and she knows I do it) is passion. It's very safe sex, watching and wanting. [49]

He also watches her in his dreams. "Some days when I'm alone I dream that I can touch her, feel how the room changes when she walks through it. When Jacks walks toward me, I almost pass out sometimes. . . . She is my religious experience." [50]

When our narrator finally describes his first sexual encounter with Jacks, we know that it will be a "religious experience."

The first time Jacks and me made love, I don't think I breathed the whole time. It wasn't 'cause I thought we'd be caught or anything. . . . I held my breath because I knew I was going to die. . . .

I remember how her neck tasted as I ran my tongue slowly, so slowly, from the front of it to the back.

I remember when we were finally lying down on the big, soft couch, I thought I'd melt into her—and she into me.

It wasn't anything like what my running buddies—who claimed to have done it a hundred times—with a thousand girls—told me it would be.

There wasn't anyone else in the world but me and her. After a while I didn't know where her body stopped and mine started. I didn't know if I was doing it right. How would I know?

How would she know? . . .

It's okay that we didn't know anything, because it was okay to make it up as we went. [51]

Angela Johnson had this to say about "Watcher": "Obsession is a strong word but apt in situations of overwhelming want and overpowering attraction. Yet, in the end 'Watcher' is about a love between two young people that may not be conventional but is love, nonetheless." [52]

The short story can be a powerful medium for teaching literature and literary elements, due to its focus on a single idea; a single character, incident, or situation; and a single main plot that builds toward a unified conclusion. For years, short stories from such authors as Poe, Hawthorne, and Chekhov have been taught in classrooms across the country. Yet despite the classic short story's popularity, short stories written by young adult authors remain scarce. In fact, the first collection of YA short stories did not surface until the 1980s when a compilation of Robert Cormier's stories entitled *8 + 1* was published. Since then, only a handful of quality YA short stories collections have been published. A few prominent YA authors, such as Chris Crutcher, have put out collections of their own short stories (*Athletic Shorts*). As Don Gallo, editor of several YA short story collections, shared with us, "YA short stories just don't sell well." *Losing It* and *Love and Sex: Ten Stories of Truth* are two great examples of why we wish they did.

FINAL THOUGHTS ON SEX AND CONTEMPORARY YAL

In many ways, this was the most difficult chapter to write because of the number of amazing YA books that we had to exclude. The great news, however, is that realistic contemporary YAL is thriving. As is apparent from this small sampling, contemporary authors are not shying away from the subject of sex. It is our hope that for each story in this chapter, readers will make connections—with topics and issues, with settings, and with characters—that will in some small way lead toward enlightenment.

NOTES

1. Bryan Gillis, review of *manicpixiedreamgirl*, May 2013, http://www.alan-ya.org/page/alan-picks-may-2013.
2. Tom Leveen, *manicpixiedreamgirl* (New York: Random House, 2013), 211, 212.
3. Leveen, *manicpixiedreamgirl*, 220–26.
4. Bryan Gillis communicated with Tom Leveen via e-mail on August 15, 2014.
5. Bill Konigsberg, *Openly Straight* (New York: Arthur Levine, 2013), 4–5.
6. Konigsberg, *Openly Straight*, 196.
7. Konigsberg, *Openly Straight*, 241–42.
8. Konigsberg, *Openly Straight*, 242–43.
9. Bryan Gillis and Bill Konigsberg communicated via e-mail on August 10, 2014.
10. Jay Asher, *Thirteen Reasons Why* (New York: Razorbill, 2007), 263–65.
11. Bryan Gillis interviewed Jay Asher at the Kennesaw State University Literature Conference, March 2011.
12. Carrie Mesrobian, *Sex and Violence* (Minneapolis, MI: Carolholda Books, 2013), 9.
13. Mesrobian, *Sex and Violence*, 4.
14. Mesrobian, *Sex and Violence*, 5.
15. Mesrobian, *Sex and Violence*, 10.
16. Mesrobian, *Sex and Violence*, 18–19.
17. Melvin Burgess, *Doing It* (New York: Holt, 2003), 1–2.
18. Burgess, *Doing It*, 98.
19. Burgess, *Doing It*, 99–100.
20. Burgess, *Doing It*, 26–27.
21. Burgess, *Doing It*, 248.
22. Burgess, *Doing It*, 144.
23. The first publication of the collection in 2010 contained only eight stories. Stories by American authors Andrew Smith and A.S. King were added in 2013.
24. Jenny Valentine, "The Age of Consent," in *Losing It*, ed. Keith Gray (Minneapolis, MI: Carolrhoda Books, 2013), 35–36.
25. Melvin Burgess, "Chat Up Lines," in *Losing It*, 57–58.
26. Burgess, "Chat Up Lines," 60–61.
27. Burgess, "Chat Up Lines," 66.
28. Keith Gray, "Scoring," in *Losing It*, 7.
29. Gray, "Scoring," 14.
30. Andrew Smith, "Green Screen," in *Losing It*, 177–78.
31. Smith, "Green Screen," 181.
32. Michael Cart, ed., *Love and Sex: Ten Stories of Truth* (New York: Simon Pulse, 2003), ix.
33. Cart, *Love and Sex*, x.
34. Cart, *Love and Sex*, xi.

35. Sonya Sones, "About 'Secret Shelf,'" in *Love and Sex*, 86.

36. Sones, "About 'Secret Shelf,'" 76.

37. Sones, "About 'Secret Shelf,'" 77.

38. Sones, "About 'Secret Shelf,'" 86.

39. Sonya Sones, *What My Mother Doesn't Know*, http://www.sonyasones.com/books/whatmymother/a_syn_book.html.

40. Michael Lowenthal, "The Acuteness of Desire," in *Losing It*, 134.

41. Lowenthal, "Acuteness," 144.

42. Lowenthal, "Acuteness," 144–45.

43. Lowenthal, "Acuteness," 146–47.

44. Lowenthal, "Acuteness," 157.

45. Lowenthal, "Acuteness," 157.

46. Angela Johnson, "Watcher," in *Losing It*, 183.

47. Johnson, "Watcher," 183–84.

48. Johnson, "Watcher," 187.

49. Johnson, "Watcher," 190.

50. Johnson, "Watcher," 184.

51. Johnson, "Watcher," 187–88.

52. Johnson, "Watcher," 192.

Chapter Eight

The Censorship of Young Adult Fiction

Censorship is the control (removal, suppression, or restricted circulation) of literary, artistic, or educational material (images, ideas, and information) by individuals, special interest groups, or government leaders who find said material objectionable or dangerous. History is replete with examples of censorship being used to influence and control the mores and belief systems of entire societies. From the execution of Socrates in ancient Rome to China's recent banning of Hillary Clinton's newest book, *Hard Choices* (2014), censorship is alive and well.

How does an individual or group initiate an attempt to censor a book? The process begins with a challenge—an attempt to restrict or remove a specific text, based on the documented objections of a person or group. Challenges involve more than expressing a viewpoint; they are formal attempts to remove a text from a classroom, curriculum, or library for the purposes of restricting access to that text.[1] In 1986, the Intellectual Freedom Committee developed terminology and definitions for the various book and material challenges that librarians were facing for the first time, due to the increasingly controversial content being addressed in YAL:

Expression of concern: An inquiry that has judgmental overtones.
Oral complaint: An oral challenge to the presence and/or appropriateness of the material in question.

Written complaint: A formal written complaint filed with the institution (library, school, etc.), challenging the presence and/or appropriateness of specific material.

Public attack: A publicly disseminated statement challenging the value of the material, presented to the media and/or others outside the institutional organization to gain public support for further action.

Censorship: A change in the access status of material, based on the content of the work and made by a governing authority or its representatives. Such changes include exclusion, restriction, removal, or age/grade-level changes.[2] Censorship occurs when a challenge is successful.

From 1990 to 2009, a total of 5,099 materials challenges were reported to the American Library Association's Office of Intellectual Freedom. It estimates "that for every reported challenge, four or five remain unreported."[3] The top three reasons for challenges were (1) considered sexually explicit (1,577 challenges), (2) contained offensive language (1,291 challenges), and (3) unsuited to a specific age group (989 challenges). Other reasons listed were homosexuality, violence, drugs/alcohol/smoking, religious viewpoint, and political viewpoint.[4]

CANONICAL LITERATURE

Classic literature has taken its share of hits from censors, and as we discuss in chapter 3, teachers themselves do quite a bit of censoring of canonical texts. For example, many of the teachers whom we polled shared that they choose to ignore sexual content within classic texts (e.g., sexual puns in Shakespeare) for fear of rocking the parental boat. It is also possible that the complexity of language in these texts creates a barrier for a potential censor who may be merely skimming a text for specific content. YAL expert Pam Cole suggests that it may also be due to the modern parent belief that "if *Macbeth* or *The Miller's Tale* didn't damage their own moral fiber, then they're not likely to damage young minds today."[5] The following are several canonical texts that have appeared on American Library Association's annual list of challenged books:

The Great Gatsby, by F. Scott Fitzgerald—challenged at the Baptist College in Charleston, South Carolina (1987), because of "language and sexual references in the book."

To Kill a Mockingbird, by Harper Lee—challenged at the Brentwood, Tennessee, middle school (2006) because the book contains "profanity" and "adult themes such as sexual intercourse, rape, and incest." The complainants also contend that the book's use of racial slurs promotes "racial hatred, racial division, racial separation, and promotes white supremacy."

1984, by George Orwell—challenged in Jackson County, Florida (1981), because Orwell's novel is "pro-communist and contained explicit sexual matter."

Of Mice and Men, by John Steinbeck—banned from the George County, Mississippi, schools (2002) because of profanity; challenged in Normal, Illinois, community high schools (2003) because the book contains "racial slurs, profanity, violence, and does not represent traditional values."

The Lord of the Rings, by J.R.R. Tolkien—burned in Alamagordo, New Mexico (2001), outside Christ Community Church along with other Tolkien novels as satanic.[6]

YOUNG ADULT LITERATURE

YAL books are the clear leaders in number of challenges received for the past twenty-five years. A review of the American Library Association's top-ten most challenged books from 1990 to 2009 reveals that more than 60 percent of the titles were marketed to either children or young adults, including eight of the top ten books on the 2000–2009 list. More than 80 percent of the association's most challenged authors list from 2001 to 2012 is made up of authors who write primarily for children and young adults. This list includes such names as Lauren Myracle, Chris Crutcher, Ellen Hopkins, Sherman Alexie, Judy Blume, Phyllis Reynolds Naylor, Dav Pilkey, and Patricia Polacco. School classrooms and school libraries were the primary institutional sources of challenges, and parents were the number one initiator of these challenges, by a three-to-one margin over the next-closest competitor, listed as *other*.[7] What motivates parents to challenge books that their children are reading at school or checking out from the library?

First, YAL's origins are rooted in the *problem novel*: realistic fiction that "addresses personal and social issues across socioeconomic boundaries and within both traditional and nontraditional family structures."[8] Problem novels are the most accurate fictional windows for teens to experience a particular period's (often controversial) coming-of-age issues, such as pregnancy, sexuality, gender roles, social/racial injustice, and suicide. When these fictional windows are made available for adolescents to leap through, concerned parents—overwhelmed by a world in which their kids are able to access all forms of media by simply touching a button on their phone—may feel as though they have lost control of what their children watch and read. Challenging a book is a way to regain a measure of that control.

Second, many parents are motivated by the belief that controversial topics (e.g., sex) should be introduced and discussed only at home, if at all. Evidence of this can be found in the American Library Association's 2001–2013 most challenged books list, which reveals that the challenge reason most frequently paired with complaints about content is *unsuitable for age group*. Why? Sexually explicit content is typically identified as offensive because a parent or group of parents associates the content with a specific age range or group. The book is a problem for a potential censor not simply because his or her child is reading it but because it has been marketed and labeled as appropriate for a specific age group.

Publishers are tasked with the job of marketing books, and a significant part of that marketing involves the identification of an audience. Once a book has been marketed for young adults, for example, booksellers, teachers, librarians, and media specialists will order it and make classification decisions based largely on the way in which it was marketed. The book will reside in the young adult section of the local bookstore. Many bookstores will create displays for nearby schools advertising the book as *required reading* or *summer reading*. The book will live in the teen section of the public library, in the middle school and high school libraries, and on a classroom teacher's bookshelf. Once read, reviews for the book might appear on websites such as Goodreads, accessed by clicking on the appropriately labeled tab (e.g., *young adult genre*). This market saturation (some might argue oversaturation)—including movies such as *The Fault in Our Stars* and *The Hunger Games*, television series such as *Gossip Girl*, and online fan fiction from books such as *Twilight*—has loudly and clearly identified these books as *suitable* for young adults.

A recent (2014) example of a parent group challenge that resulted in a ban on a young adult book occurred in Idaho. The Meridian School District, prompted by local parents, voted to remove *The Absolutely True Diary of a Part-Time Indian*, by Sherman Alexie, from its high school supplemental reading list, where it has been in use since 2010. *Absolutely True Diary*, a National Book Award winner, is the fictional and semiautobiographical account of life on a reservation and the struggles that one teen faces in an effort to escape. A few of the reasons given for the removal of the book were unsuitable for age, sexually explicit content, offensive language, and anti-Christian. The sexually explicit content complaint is directed at a reference to masturbation.

Soon after the ban went into effect, local teens started a petition to reinstate the book, collecting 350 signatures. In a show of support, Rediscovered Books, a local bookstore, initiated a campaign to raise money to purchase a copy of the book for each student who signed the petition. The bookstore collected $3,400, and all but twenty books were distributed at an evening event—but not before parents called police in an attempt to shut down the giveaway. Police say that they were called by "someone concerned about teenagers picking up a copy of the book without having a parent's permission."[9] The police arrived and then let the book giveaway proceed as planned. When Alexie's publisher was made aware of the incident, it sent the bookstore an additional 350 free copies.

A perceived loss of parental control, combined with the belief that certain subject matter should be introduced only at home, is further magnified by society's perception of the school and its personnel as surrogate parents.[10] When a book is challenged for unsuitable content, the author, the librarian, the teacher, and even the principal are often perceived as guilty by association. Creation and/or ownership of this book is seen as a personal endorsement of the viewpoints, lifestyles, and actions of the characters represented. These individuals are viewed as complicit in the intent to corrupt or harm, not one child, but all children within a given environment, because the book in question was made available to an unsuitable age group.

A recent example clearly illustrates this point. In July 2013, Dr. Richard Swier authored an article for the Education Action Group Foundation on its EAGnews.org website entitled "Poll: Florida Middle School Students Reading Child Pornography: Principal Finds Child Porn Age Appropriate."[11] The book in question was *Speak*, by Laurie Halse Anderson. The article—which repeatedly used the names of the school, principal, and teacher—states in part,

> Parents at [school name omitted] in Sarasota, Florida became outraged
> when they learned their children were reading the child pornography

book *Speak* by Laurie Halse Anderson. *Speak* is about a 13-year old
being raped.

One of the parents submitted a complaint to the [name omitted]
School Board to have the book removed from the [name omitted] reading list. The book is used in a "gifted language arts class" taught by
[name omitted]. It is the language used in the book that the parents
object to.

Speak promotes "group rate abortions" on page 30. Other examples
of bad behaviors in the book are: "Student steals late passes" (theft)—
page 26, "sleep with the football team on Saturday night and be reincar-
nated as virginal goddesses on Monday" (promiscuity)—page 29; "slit
my throat" (child suicide)—page 32, and "the crowd bumping and
grinding the horny Hornet heinies" (group sex)—page 141.[12]

One parent commented, "The teacher [name omitted] is using the book
to push an agenda. It is child pornography, nothing more and nothing
less. It does not belong in our public schools. We are have [sic] our
youngest reading child porn sanctioned by a teacher. What message
does that send? That is plain wrong!"[13]

A school curriculum council ruled in favor of the book. The principal stated,

We feel this book should remain as an end of 8th grade book selection,
with an alternate selection provided. It provides our students with a
guided approach to think about some of the choices that will face many
of them within ten weeks of 8th grade graduation, as they move into
high school and are socializing with much older, more mature high
school students.[14]

The author's response to the ruling was to note that "the council members at the school level were all teachers or administrators at the school.
A member of the panel was [name omitted] the only teacher in the
school using the book."[15] What is most shocking about this article is
the fact that the teacher's name was not only listed but linked to a
profile on an education website.

Challenges such as this are concerning for several reasons. First,
note that the author refers to *Speak* as pornography, summarizes the
entire book as being "about a 13-year old being raped,"[16] which is
grossly inaccurate, and then proceeds to use words such as "promote"
to persuade readers into believing that the selected words and
phrases—taken out of context and many presented as inner thoughts or
jokes (the book is called *Speak* for a reason!)—somehow represent

pornography. Second, qualified teachers, making decisions based on expert knowledge of their students' curricular needs, are being vilified in the media by groups who clearly have agendas that are in no way related to education. The Education Action Group Foundation, for example, has strong connections to Fox News and consistently aligns itself with the Christian conservative right.

Most important, a successful challenge results in "a change in the access status of material, based on the content of the work."[17] This change restricts access, not only to the child or children of the parents who made the challenge, but also to a much larger group of people. As Chris Crutcher, winner of the National Council of Teachers of English Intellectual Freedom Award and the National Coalition Against Censorship Intellectual Freedom Award, so eloquently states, "I have no problem with a parent or a student saying a book is offensive and that teen being allowed to read an agreed-upon substitute. I do have a problem, however, with that parent being allowed to say what is good for all kids or being treated as an equal with a trained educator."[18]

Most young adult authors whom we have spoken to do not write with the intent to upset potential censors. An author's responsibility is to convey the small truth of the story, and if that writer worries about placating censors, he or she cheats the story. "Censors either do not understand this fundamental tenet of good writing or have other agendas that they care more about than story."[19]

The following are books marketed for children and young adults from the 2001–2013 top-ten most challenged lists that contain sexual content and unsuitable-for-age complaints, along with any other objections.

Children's Literature

> *And Tango Makes Three*, by Justin Richardson and Peter Parnell—antifamily, homosexuality, unsuited to age group
>
> *The Color of Earth* (series), by Kim Dong Hwa—nudity, sex education, sexually explicit, unsuited to age group
>
> *In the Night Kitchen*, by Maurice Sendak—nudity, offensive language, sexually explicit
>
> *Uncle Bobby's Wedding*, by Sarah S. Brannen—homosexuality, unsuited to age group

Young Adult Literature

The Absolutely True Diary of a Part-Time Indian, by Sherman Alexie—offensive language, racism, sex education, sexually explicit, religious viewpoint, violence, unsuited to age group

Alice (series), by Phyllis Reynolds Naylor—homosexuality, sexually explicit, unsuited to age group

The Chocolate War, by Robert Cormier—offensive language, sexually explicit, violence, religious viewpoint, unsuited to age group

The Earth, My Butt, and Other Big Round Things, by Carolyn Mackler—antifamily, offensive language, sexually explicit, unsuited to age group

Flashcards of My Life, by Charise Mericle Harper—sexually explicit, unsuited to age group

It's Perfectly Normal: Changing Bodies, Growing Up, Sex, and Sexual Health, by Robie H. Harris—abortion, homosexuality, nudity, religious viewpoint, sex education, unsuited to age group

Gossip Girl (series), by Cecily Von Ziegesar—homosexuality, sexually explicit, offensive language, unsuited to age group

The Hunger Games, by Suzanne Collins—sexually explicit, violence, antiethnic, anti-family, insensitivity, offensive language, occult/satanic, unsuited to age group

Looking for Alaska, by John Green—drugs/alcohol/smoking, offensive language, sexually explicit, unsuited to age group

Lush, by Natasha Friend—drugs, offensive language, sexually explicit, unsuited to age group

My Sister's Keeper, by Jodi Picoult—homosexuality, offensive language, religious viewpoint, sexism, sexually explicit, violence, unsuited to age group

The Perks of Being a Wallflower, by Stephen Chbosky—drugs/alcohol/smoking, homosexuality, sexually explicit, unsuited to age group

Thirteen Reasons Why, by Jay Asher—drugs/alcohol/smoking, sexually explicit, suicide, unsuited to age group

ttyl; ttfn; l8r, g8r (series), by Lauren Myracle—drugs, nudity, offensive language, sexually explicit, religious viewpoint, unsuited to age group

Twilight (series), by Stephenie Meyer—religious viewpoint, sexually explicit, unsuited to age group

What My Mother Doesn't Know, by Sonya Sones—nudity, sexism, offensive language, sexually explicit, unsuited to age group[20]

LIBRARIES AND CENSORSHIP

School and public libraries experience fewer challenges than classrooms because patrons are given the opportunity to choose the books that they read. The American Library Association states,

> We affirm the responsibility and the right of all parents and guardians to guide their own children's use of the library and its resources and services. Librarians and library governing bodies cannot assume the role of parents or the functions of parental authority in the private relationship between parent and child. Librarians and governing bodies should maintain that only parents and guardians have the right and the responsibility to determine their children's—and only their children's—access to library resources. Parents and guardians who do not want their children to have access to specific library services, materials, or facilities should so advise their children. [21]

Mary Jo Heller and Aarene Storms are public teen service librarians who host a book talk program "for middle and high school students, teachers, parents, public library patrons, and librarians about sexual content in books written for teen readers."[22] Their program is entitled *Sex in the Library*. The content of their presentation includes selection policies and mission statements of school and public libraries, including comparisons of the books available in a public library that may not be available in a school library. More interesting, however, are their presentation and reviews of the "hottest titles with sexual content written for teen readers."

In their book *Sex in the Library: A Guide to Sexual Content in Teen Literature*, the authors discuss the concept of "*in loco parentis*—the responsibility of teachers and school librarians to act 'in place of a parent' regarding the safety and education of students."[23] They are quick to point out that public libraries do not have this philosophy, because it would contradict the public library mission, which guarantees "free, open, and equal access to ideas and information to all members of the community."[24] Both authors fully support the idea that parents should take an active role in monitoring what their children read, but they are clear that this monitoring is not the role of the public librarian. Teachers, however, do not have this luxury.

PROTECTING AND DEFENDING AGAINST CHALLENGES

School boards are legally responsible for the curriculum in most districts in the United States. This responsibility is then delegated to school officials, who are charged with setting school policy. These policies include procedures designed to protect and defend against censorship. For example, school districts create committees that determine the appropriateness of materials, based on qualities such as relevance to grade-level curriculum, presence of obscenity and/or vulgarity, and appropriateness to students' age, sophistication, and grade level. The approved materials list generated from a committee such as this serves to protect teachers in that the district will support the use of the material in case of a challenge, provided that the teacher can prove that the material's use in an educational context supports the curriculum.

All non-school-owned materials used by teachers must also support the curriculum for the course being taught and be appropriate for the targeted audience. It is always the responsibility of the teacher to preview any supplemental materials. Of course, some very powerful educational tools can be found in the world of young adult literature. Unfortunately, it is possible that at least a few of these titles will not be found on a school district's approved list, because they will contain what is perceived as objectionable content. And, of course, the presence of a title on that list does not prevent it from being challenged. The following are some suggestions for teachers on how to avoid the wrath of the censor.

First, offer choices when assigning books that contain content that parents may perceive as objectionable. By providing classroom book options, students and parents will both feel more empowered. In contrast, providing one book option as a reaction to a parent's complaint will often be interpreted as a punishment, especially from the student's perspective. When faced with a complaint, remember that, oftentimes, it can be defused if a teacher or administrator views the complaint as a way to solve one child's access to what a parent considers objectionable. This is accomplished by offering choices.

Second, keep documentation that speaks to the quality and significance of the books that students are reading. State and national book awards, positive reviews from reputable sources, and examples of lesson plans posted to well-known educational sites that use the book are a few ways that these books can be supported.

Third, provide parents and students with recommended rather than required reading lists. In an introductory syllabus and letter home to parents, include an invitation to visit your room, where they can view a wonderful book collection where their children have the opportunity to check out books for their personal reading pleasure. Ask students to summarize and review the books that they read. Make these reviews available for students and parents (after revisions and editing, of course).

Finally, be prepared to defend a book choice with support from the approved curriculum. YAL can be a powerful tool for engaging students in discussions about a number of issues, but these discussions alone will not be enough to defend against a determined censor. Teachers must be able to support a challenged book with specific standards and objectives from the curriculum. For example, a defense of *Thirteen Reasons Why*, by Jay Asher, may not withstand a defense that rests on a discussion of suicide, but by providing evidence that dual or multiple narration in fiction is being taught—and by offering other choices of books that feature multiple narrators—chances are good that the book will remain in the classroom.

We staunchly support the rights and responsibilities of parents to make decisions regarding what their children are reading in school and at the library. Whether a teacher assigns a book or offers it as a choice, we encourage parents to make educated decisions about the book and its suitability for *their* children, by reading the entire book and taking into consideration its educational connection to the curriculum. We do not believe that parents should *ever* be allowed to make decisions regarding what other parents' children read. As we have stated, the absence of any type of effective sex education in schools (at home as well) creates a desperate need for literature that deals honestly and openly with sexual information that teens want and deserve to possess. Only when we make this literature available will our society be able to address the disconnect between the transmission and reception of sexual information and the accurate transference of that information to sexual behavior.

Perhaps this story from Patty Campbell offers the best reflection of the current state of our lack of sexual openness:

> A few months ago there was this impassioned discussion on the listserv childlit about a note that was sent home from school to alert parents that the movie *Schindler's List* would be shown in class but assuring them

that the sexual references would be edited out. What peculiar priorities and attitudes this reflects! Exposure to sex is perceived as more disturbing than exposure to the greatest horror of the twentieth century. Could there be a clearer statement of the sex negativity in our society? [25]

NOTES

1. American Library Association, "Banned and Challenged Books," http://www.ala.org/bbooks.

2. American Library Association, "Banned and Challenged Books."

3. American Library Association, "Frequently Challenged Books of the 21st Century," http://www.ala.org/bbooks/frequentlychallengedbooks/top10.

4. American Library Association, "Frequently Challenged Books," http://www.ala.org/bbooks/frequentlychallengedbooks.

5. Pam B. Cole, *Young Adult Literature in the 21st Century* (New York: McGraw-Hill, 2009), 71.

6. American Library Association, "Banned and/or Challenged Books from the Radcliffe Publishing Course Top 100 Novels of the 20th Century," http://www.ala.org/bbooks/frequentlychallengedbooks/classics/reasons.

7. American Library Association, "Challenges to Library Materials," http://www.ala.org/bbooks/challengedmaterials.

8. Cole, *Young Adult Literature*, 98.

9. Alex Moore, "Parents Call Cops on Teen for Giving Away Banned Book; It Backfires Predictably," *Death and Taxes*, April 28, 2014. http://www.deathandtaxesmag.com/219767/parents-call-cops-on-teen-for-giving-away-banned-book-it-backfires-predictably/.

10. Alleen Nilsen et al., *Literature for Today's Young Adults* (New York, Pearson, 2013), 399.

11. Richard Swier, "Poll: Florida Middle School Students Reading Child Pornography," http://watchdogwire.com/florida/2013/07/02/florida-middle-school-students-reading-child-pornography/.

12. Swier, "Poll."

13. Swier, "Poll."

14. Swier, "Poll."

15. Swier, "Poll."

16. Swier, "Poll."

17. American Library Association, "Challenges to Library Materials."

18. Bryan Gillis and Pam B. Cole, *Chris Crutcher: A Stotan for Young Adults* (Lanham, MD: Scarecrow, 2012), 48.

19. Gillis and Cole, *Chris Crutcher*, 51.

20. American Library Association, "Frequently Challenged Books of the 21st Century."

21. American Library Association, "Advocacy, Legislation, and Issues," http://www.ala.org/advocacy.

22. Mary Jo Heller and Aarene Storms, *Sex in the Library* (Bowie, MD: VOYA, 2009), ix.

23. Heller and Storms, *Sex in the Library*, 15.

24. Heller and Storms, *Sex in the Library*, 15.

25. Patty Campbell, *Campbell's Scoop: Reflections on Young Adult Literature* (Lanham, MD: Scarecrow, 2010), 130.

Bibliography

NOVELS AND SHORT STORIES CITED

Asher, Jay. *Thirteen Reasons Why*. New York: Razorbill, 2007.

Austen, Jane. *Pride and Prejudice*.

Blume, Judy. *Forever*. New York: Simon Pulse, 2003.

———. *Then Again, Maybe I Won't*. New York: Yearling, 1986.

Brontë, Charlotte. *Jane Eyre*. Project Gutenberg. http://www.gutenberg.org/files/1260/1260-h/1260-h.htm.

Brontë, Emily. *Wuthering Heights*. Project Gutenberg. http://www.gutenberg.org/files/768/768-h/768-h.htm.

Burgess, Melvin. *Doing It*. New York: Holt, 2003.

Cart, Michael, ed. *Love & Sex: Ten Stories of Truth*. New York: Simon Pulse, 2003.

Cavanna, Betty. *Going on Sixteen*. New York: Scholastic, 1973.

Cleary, Beverly. *Fifteen*. 1956. New York: HarperCollins, 2007.

Cohn, Rachel, and David Levithan. *Nick and Norah's Infinite Playlist*. New York: Knopf, 2006.

Collins, Suzanne. *Hunger Games*. New York: Scholastic, 2008.

Cormier, Robert. *8 + 1: Stories by Robert Cormier*. New York: Pantheon, 1980.

Crutcher, Chris. *Athletic Shorts*. New York: Greenwillow, 1989.

Daly, Maureen. *Seventeenth Summer*. New York: Simon Pulse, 2002.

Donovan, John. *I'll Get There, It Better Be Worth the Trip*. Woodbury, MN: Flux, 2010.

Drexler, Rosalyn. *I Am the Beautiful Stranger*. New York: Dell, 1965.

du Jardin, Rosamund. *Practically Seventeen*. Philadelphia: Lippincott, 1949.

Emery, Anne. *Free Not to Love*. Philadelphia: Westminster Press, 1975.

Eyerly, Jeanette. *Bonnie Jo, Go Home*. Philadelphia: Lippincott, 1972.

———. *A Girl Like Me*. New York: Berkley Highland, 1966.

Felsen, Henry Gregor. *Two and the Town*. New York: Pennant, 1952.

Gray, Keith, ed. *Losing It*. Minneapolis, MN: Carolrhoda Books, 2013.

Halevy, Julie. *The Young Lovers*. New York: Dell, 1955.

Head, Ann. *Mr. and Mrs. Bo Jo Jones*. New York: Signet, 1968.

Hinton, S. E. *The Outsiders*. New York: Viking, 1967.

Hunter, Evan. *The Blackboard Jungle*. New York: Simon & Schuster, 1999.

———. *Last Summer*. New York: Doubleday, 1968.
Huxley, Aldous. *Brave New World*. New York: Everyman's Library, 2013.
Klein, Norma. *Beginner's Love*. New York: Dutton, 1983.
———. *It's OK If You Don't Love Me*. New York: Fawcett Juniper, 1977.
Konigsberg, Bill. *Openly Straight*. New York: Levine, 2013.
L'Engle, Madeline. *And Both Were Young*. New York: Farrar, Straus and Giroux, 1949.
Leveen, Tom. *manicpixiedreamgirl*. New York: Random House, 2013.
Lipsyte, Robert. *The Contender*. New York: Harper & Row, 1967.
Lowry, Lois. *The Giver*. New York: Houghton Mifflin, 1993.
Lu, Marie. *Champion*. New York: Putnam, 2011.
———. *Prodigy*. New York: Putnam, 2013.
McKayhan, Monica. *Indigo Summer (Kimini Tru)*. New York: Harlequin Kimani, 2007.
Mesrobian, Carrie. *Sex and Violence*. Minneapolis, MN: Carolrhoda Books, 2013.
Meyer, Stephenie. *Breaking Dawn*. New York: Little Brown, 2008.
———. *Eclipse*. New York: Little Brown, 2007.
———. *New Moon*. New York: Little Brown, 2006.
———. *Twilight*. New York: Little Brown, 2005.
Myracle, Lauren. *The Infinite Moment of Us*. New York: Amulet, 2013.
Naylor, Phyllis Reynolds. *Achingly Alice*. New York: Atheneum, 2012.
———. *The Agony of Alice*. New York: Atheneum 2011.
———. *Alice in April*. New York: Atheneum, 2011.
———. *Alice the Brave*. New York: Atheneum, 2011.
———. *Alice In-Between*. New York: Atheneum, 2011.
———. *Alice in Blunderland*. New York: Atheneum, 2012.
———. *Alice in Lace*. New York: Atheneum, 2011.
———. *Alice in Rapture*. New York: Atheneum, 2011.
———. *Alice on Her Way*. New York: Atheneum, 2005.
———. *Alice on the Outside*. New York: Atheneum, 2012.
———. *All but Alice*. New York: Atheneum, 2011.
———. *Dangerously Alice*. New York: Atheneum 2007.
———. *The Grooming of Alice*. New York: Atheneum, 2012.
———. *Intensely Alice*. New York: Simon Pulse, 2010.
———. *Lovingly Alice*. New York: Atheneum, 2012.
———. *Now I'll Tell You Everything*. New York: Atheneum 2014.
———. *Outrageously Alice*. New York: Atheneum, 1997.
———. *Reluctantly Alice, Sort Of*. New York: Atheneum, 2011.
———. *Starting with Alice*. New York: Atheneum, 2012.
Oliver, Lauren. *Delirium*. New York: HarperCollins, 2011.
Orwell, George. *1984*. New York: New American Library, 1961.
Pascal, Francine. *Brokenhearted*. New York: Bantam, 1989.
———. *Perfect Summer*. New York: Sweet Valley, 1985.
Peck, Richard. *Are You in the House Alone?* New York: Viking, 1976.
Pike, Aprilynne. *Wings*. New York: Harper Teen, 2008.
Rand, Ayn. *Anthem*. Project Gutenberg. http://www.gutenberg.org/files/1250/1250-h/1250-h.htm.
Roth, Veronica. *Divergent*. New York: HarperCollins, 2011.
Rowell, Rainbow. *Eleanor and Park*. New York: St. Martin's Press, 2013.
Ryan, Carrie. *The Dark and Hollow Places*. New York: Random House, 2011.
———. *The Dead-Tossed Waves*. New York: Delacorte Press, 2010.
———. *The Forest of Hands and Teeth*. New York: Delacorte Press, 2009.
Salinger, J. D. *The Catcher in the Rye*. New York: Little Brown, 1991.
Showalter, Gena. *Intertwined*. New York: Harlequin Teen, 2009.
Smith, Andrew. *Grasshopper Jungle*. New York: Dutton, 2014.

Snadowsky, Daria. *Anatomy of a Boyfriend.* New York: Delacorte, 2007.
Sones, Sonya. *What My Mother Doesn't Know.* New York: Simon and Schuster, 2001.
Stiefvater, Maggie. *Forever.* New York: Scholastic, 2011.
———. *Linger.* New York: Scholastic, 2010.
———. *Shiver.* New York: Scholastic, 2009.
———. *Sinner.* New York: Scholastic, 2014.
Westerfeld, Scott. *Peeps.* New York: Razorbill, 2005.
Zindel, Paul. *My Darling, My Hamburger.* New York: Harper Crest, 1969.

OTHER WORKS CITED

ALAN. http://www.alan-ya.org/.
Alexander, Catherine M. S., and Stanley Wells, eds. *Shakespeare and Sexuality.* New York: Cambridge University Press, 2001.
Alloy Entertainment. "The A-List." http://alloyentertainment.com/books/the-a-list/.
American Library Association. "Advocacy, Legislation, and Issues." http://www.ala.org/advocacy.
———. "Banned and Challenged Books." http://www.ala.org/bbooks/.
———. "Banned and/or Challenged Books from the Radcliffe Publishing Course Top 100 Novels of the 20th Century." http://www.ala.org/bbooks/frequentlychallenged-books/classics/reasons.
———. "Challenges to Library Materials." http://www.ala.org/bbooks/challengedmate-rials.
———. "Frequently Challenged Books." http://www.ala.org/bbooks/frequentlychallen-gedbooks.
———. "Frequently Challenged Books of the 21st Century." http://www.ala.org/bbooks/frequentlychallengedbooks/top10.
Arnett, Jeffrey J. "Emerging Adulthood: A Theory of Development from the Late Teens through the Twenties." *American Psychologist* 55, no. 5 (2000): 469–80.
———. "G. Stanley Hall's Adolescence: Brilliance and Nonsense." *History of Psychology* 9, no. 13 (2006): 186–97.
Booker, Keith M. *Dystopian Literature: A Theory and Research Guide.* Westport, CT: Greenwood Press, 1994.
Brandt, Allan M. *No Magic Bullet: A Social History of Venereal Disease in the United States since 1880.* New York: Oxford University Press, 1987.
Braun-Courville, Debra K., and Mary Rojas. "Exposure to Sexually Explicit Web Sites and Adolescent Sexual Attitudes and Behaviors." *Journal of Adolescent Health* 45, no. 2 (2009): 156–62.
Bristow, Nancy K. "Commission on Training Camp Activities." In *Encyclopedia of War and American Society,* edited by Peter Karsten. Thousand Oaks, CA: Sage, 2005.
Brown, Jane D., and Kelly L. L'Engle. "X-Rated: Sexual Attitudes and Behaviors Associated with U.S. Early Adolescents' Exposure to Sexually Explicit Media." *Communication Research* 36 (2009): 129–51.
California Department of Education. "Comprehensive Sexual Health and HIV/AIDS Instruction." http://www.cde.ca.gov/ls/he/se/faq.asp.
Callister, Mark, Sarah M. Coyne, Lesa A. Stern, Laura Stockdale, Malinda J. Miller, and Brian M. Wells. "A Content Analysis of the Prevalence and Portrayal of Sexual Activity in Adolescent Literature." *Journal of Sex Research* 49, no. 5. (2012): 477–86.
Campbell, Patty. *Campbell's Scoop: Reflections on Young Adult Literature.* Lanham, MD: Scarecrow, 2010.

————. *Sex Guides: Books and Films about Sexuality for Young Adults.* New York: Garland, 1986.

Cart, Michael. *Young Adult Literature: From Romance to Realism.* Chicago: American Library Association, 2011.

Cart, Michael, and Christine A. Jenkins. *The Heart Has Its Reasons: Young Adult Literature with Gay/Lesbian/Queer Content, 1969–2004.* Lanham, MD: Scarecrow, 2006.

Cole, Pam B. *Young Adult Literature in the 21st Century.* New York: McGraw-Hill, 2010.

Common Sense Media. Review of *Wings*, by Aprilynne Pike. https://www.commonsensemedia.org/book-reviews/wings.

Conrad, Barnaby. *101 Best Sex Scenes Ever Written: An Erotic Romp through Literature for Writers and Readers.* Fresno, CA: Quill Driver, 2011.

Cooper, Al, and Eric Griffin-Shelley. "The Internet: The New Sexual Revolution." In *Sex and the Internet: A Guidebook for Clinicians*, edited by Al Cooper. New York: Brunner-Routledge, 2002.

Cornell University Legal Information Institute. "Griswold vs. Connecticut." http://www.law.cornell.edu/supct/html/historics/USSC_CR_0381_0479_ZO.html.

Cross, Tracy L., and Andrea Dawn Frazier. "Guiding the Psychosocial Development of Gifted Students Attending Specialized Residential STEM Schools." *Roeper Review* 32 (2010): 32–41.

Daniels, Cindy Lou. "Literary Theory and Young Adult Literature: The Open Frontier in Literary Studies." *ALAN Review* (winter 2006): 78–82.

Drexler, Rosalyn. *I Am the Beautiful Stranger: Paintings from the '60's.* New York: Pace Wildenstein, 2007.

Dube, Eric, and Ritch C. Savin-Williams. "Sexual Identity Development among Ethnic Sexual-Minority Male Youths." *Developmental Psychology* 35 (1999): 1389–98.

Dumas, Tara M., Wendy E. Ellis, and David A. Wolfe. "Identity Development as a Buffer of Adolescent Risk Behaviors in the Context of Peer Group Pressure and Control." *Journal of Adolescence* 35, no. 4. (2012): 917–27.

Edwards, Margaret. *The Fair Garden and the Swarm of Beasts: The Library and the Young Adult.* Reprint. Chicago: American Library Association, 1994.

Erikson, Erik H. *Childhood and Society.* 2nd ed. New York: Norton, 1963.

Ferguson, David. "Oklahoma School District Giving Up on Abstinence-Only Education." http://www.rawstory.com/rs/2013/09/04/oklahoma-school-district-giving-up-on-abstinence-only-education.

Flood, Michael. "Exposure to Pornography among Youth in Australia." *Journal of Sociology* 43 (2007): 45–60.

Gillis, Bryan. "Interview with Andrew Smith." June 2014, http://www.alan-ya.org/page/alan-picks-june-2014.

Gillis, Bryan, and Pam B. Cole. *Chris Crutcher: A Stotan for Young Adults.* Lanham, MD: Scarecrow, 2012.

Green, John. "Two against the World." *New York Times.* March 8, 2013. http://www.nytimes.com/2013/03/10/books/review/eleanor-park-by-rainbow-rowell.html?_r=0.

Grotevant, Harold D. "Adolescent Development in Family Contexts." In *Handbook of Child Psychology: Social, Emotional, and Personality Development*, edited by N. Eisenberg, 3:1097–1149. New York: Wiley, 1998.

Grotevant, Harold D., and Catherine R. Cooper. "Patterns of Interaction in Family Relationships and the Development of Identity Exploration in Adolescence." *Child Development* 56 (1985): 415–28.

Harlequin. "About Harlequin." http://www.harlequin.com/articlepage.html?articleId=36&chapter=0.

———. "Kimani TRU." http://www.harlequin.com/store.html?cid=482.

Harmon, William, and Hugh Holman. *A Handbook to Literature*. 10th ed. New York: Pearson, 2006.

Heller, Mary Jo, and Aarene Storms. *Sex in the Library*. Bowie, MD: VOYA, 2009.

Hertz, Sarah K., and Donald R. Gallo. *From Hinton to Hamlet: Building Bridges between Young Adult Literature and the Classics*. 2nd ed. Westport, CT: Greenwood Press, 2005.

Homer. *The Odyssey*. 1900. Public domain.

Hubler, Angela E. "Beyond the Image: Adolescent Girls, Reading, and Social Reality." *NWSA Journal* 12, no. 1 (2000): 84–99.

Huntwork, Mary M. "Why Girls Flock to Sweet Valley High." *School Library Journal* 36, no. 3 (1990): 137–40.

James, Henry. *Notes on Novelists*. New York: Charles Scribner's Sons, 1914.

Kaywell, Joan. *Adolescent Literature as a Complement to the Classics: Addressing Critical Issues in Today's Classroom*. Lanham, MD: Rowman & Littlefield, 2010.

Keniston, Kenneth. *Youth and Dissent: The Rise of a New Opposition*. New York: Harcourt Brace Jovanovich, 1971.

Kiernan, Pauline. *Filthy Shakespeare: Shakespeare's Most Outrageous Sexual Puns*. New York: Gotham, 2008.

Kirkus Reviews. Review of *Are You in the House Alone*. https://www.kirkusreviews.com/book-reviews/richard-peck/are-you-in-the-house-alone/.

———. Review of *Beginner's Love*. https://www.kirkusreviews.com/book-reviews/norma-klein-16/beginners-love/.

———. Review of *I Am the Beautiful Stranger*. https://www.kirkusreviews.com/book-reviews/rosalyn-drexler-4/i-am-the-beautiful-stranger/.

———. Review of *The Young Lovers*. https://www.kirkusreviews.com/book-reviews/julian-halevy/the-young-lovers/.

Klein, Rebecca. "Tulsa Schools to Include Sex Education in Regular Curriculum for the First Time." *Huffington Post*. September 4, 2013. http://www.huffingtonpost.com/2013/09/04/tulsa-sex-education_n_3867876.html?utm_hp_ref=politics.

Lambdin, Laura C. *Chaucer's Pilgrims: An Historical Guide to the Pilgrims in "The Canterbury Tales."* Westport, CT: Greenwood, 1999.

Leaper, Campbell, and Christia Spears Brown. "Perceived Experiences with Sexism among Adolescent Girls." *Child Development* 79, no. 3 (2008): 685–704.

Lee, Elizabeth. "Victorian Theories of Sex and Sexuality. http://www.victorianweb.org/gender/sextheory.html.

LeVay, Simon. *Queer Science: The Use and Abuse of Research into Homosexuality*. Cambridge, MA: American Psychological Association, 1996.

Leyland, Eric. *The Public Library and the Adolescent*. London: Grafton, 1937.

Literature Network. "Inferno." http://www.online-literature.com/dante/inferno/.

Lo, Ven-hwei, and Ran Wei. "Exposure to Internet Pornography and Taiwanese Adolescents' Sexual Attitudes and Behavior." *Journal of Broadcasting & Electronic Media* 49 (2005): 221–37.

Machiavelli, Nicolo. *The Prince*. Translated by W. K. Marriott. http://www.gutenberg.org/files/1232/1232-h/1232-h.htm.

Meyer, Mialton. *Robert Maynard Hutchins: A Memoir*. Berkeley: University of California Press, 1993.

Monica McKayhan.com. "About Monica McKayhan." http://www.monicamckayhan.com/about.html.

Moore, Alex. "Parents Call Cops on Teen for Giving Away Banned Book; It Backfires Predictably." *Death and Taxes*. April 28, 2014. http://www.deathandtaxesmag.com/219767/parents-call-cops-on-teen-for-giving-away-banned-book-it-backfires-predictably/.

Moran, Jeffrey P. *Teaching Sex: The Shaping of Adolescence in the 20th Century.* Cambridge, MA: Harvard University Press, 2000.

More, Sir Thomas. *Utopia.* http://www.gutenberg.org/files/2130/2130-h/2130-h.htm.

Nancy Garden.com. http://www.nancygarden.com/books/teens.html.

"Natashya Wilson of Halequin Teen." Interview by Carlie Webber. August 2009. http://librarillyblonde.blogspot.com/2009/08/guest-post-natashya-wilson-of-harlequin.html.

Nilsen, Alleen Pace, James Blasingame, Kenneth L. Donelson, and Don L. F. Nilsen. *Literature for Today's Young Adults.* New York: Pearson, 2013.

NYTimes.com. "Norma Klein, 50, a Young-Adult Novelist." http://www.nytimes.com/1989/04/27/obituaries/norma-klein-50-a-young-adult-novelist.html.

Oswalt, Angela. "The Development of Sexual Orientation." Sevencounties.org. http://www.sevencounties.org/poc/view_doc.php?type=doc&id=41179&cn=1310.

Pattee, Amy. "The Secret Source: Sexually Explicit Young Adult Literature as an Information Source." *Young Adult Library Services* (winter 2006): 30–38.

Persson, Roland S. "Experiences of Intellectually Gifted Students in an Egalitarian and Inclusive Educational System: A Survey Study." *Journal for the Education of the Gifted* 33, no. 4 (2010): 536–69.

Peter, Jochen, and Patti Valkenburg. "Adolescents' Exposure to Sexually Explicit Material on the Internet." *Communication Research* 33 (2006): 178–204.

Phy, Allene Stuart. *Presenting Norma Klein.* Woodbridge, CT: Twayne, 1988.

Richardson, Theresa R. *The Century of the Child: The Mental Hygiene Movement and Social Policy in the United States and Canada.* Albany: State University of New York Press, 1989.

Romance Writers of America. "RITA Awards." http://www.rwa.org/p/cm/ld/fid=532.

Rubinstein, Frankie. *A Dictionary of Shakespeare's Sexual Puns and Their Significance.* New York: Palgrave Macmillan, 1995.

Russell, David L. *Literature for Children.* 5th ed. Boston: Pearson, 2005.

Scieszka, Jon. *Guys Read.* Guysread.com.

Scott Westerfeld.com. *Peeps.* http://scottwesterfeld.com/books/peeps/.

"Sexual Fables: Homer's Women." http://sexualfables.com/homers_women.php.

Shechner, Tomer. "Gender Identity Disorder: A Literature Review from a Developmental Perspective." *Israel Journal of Psychiatry and Related Sciences* 47, no. 2 (2010): 42–48.

Sheehy, Geoff. *A Teacher's Writes: One Teacher's Thoughts on Life, Literature, and Learning.* Blog. http://ateacherswrites.wordpress.com/2009/03/04/how-to-teach-shakespeare-to-high-school-students-a-few-basics-from-one-who-does-it.

Smith, Michael, and Jeffrey Wilhelm. *Reading Don't Fix No Chevys: Literacy in the Lives of Young Men.* New York: Heinemann, 2002.

"The Social Hygiene Movement." *American Journal of Public Health.* 3, no. 11 (November 1913): 1154–57.

Sparknotes. "No Fear Shakespeare, *Romeo and Juliet.*" nfs.sparknotes.com/romeojuliet.

Stall, Sylvanus. *What a Young Boy Ought to Know.* 1897. Public Domain.

Stiefvater, Maggie. "I Navigate Readers' Emotions like a Small Ship through a Rocky Strait." *Guardian.* October 8, 2013. http://www.theguardian.com/books/2013/oct/08/maggie-stiefvater-music-teen-fiction-mood.

Stone, Tanya, L. "Now and Forever: The Power of Sex in Young Adult Literature." *Voice of Youth Advocates* 28, no. 6 (2006): 463–65.

Sullivan, Ed. "Going All the Way: First Time Sexual Experiences of Teens in Fiction." *VOYA* 26, no. 6 (2004): 461–63.

Swier, Richard. "Poll: Florida Middle School Students Reading Child Pornography." http://watchdogwire.com/florida/2013/07/02/florida-middle-school-students-reading-child-pornography/.

Tenenbaum, H. R., and Campbell Leaper. "Parent-Child Conversations about Science: The Socialization of Gender Inequities." *Developmental Psychology* 39 (2003): 34–47.

Trites, Roberta Seelinger. *Disturbing the Universe: Power and Repression in Young Adult Literature.* Iowa City: University of Iowa Press, 2000.

Tvtropes.org. "Utopia." http://tvtropes.org/pmwiki/pmwiki.php/Main/Utopia.

Williams, Gordon. *Shakespeare's Sexual Language: A Glossary.* New York: Bloomsbury Academic, 2006.

Wind, Rebecca. "New Studies Signal Dangers of Limiting Teen Access to Birth Control Information and Services: Researchers and Medical Experts Urge New Congress and State Legislatures to Heed Data." January 18, 2005. https://guttmacher.org/media/nr/2005/01/18/index.html.

Wolak, Janis, Kimberly J. Mitchell, and David Finkelhor. "Unwanted and Wanted Exposure to Online Pornography in a National Survey of Youth Internet Users." *Pediatrics* 119 (2007): 247–57.

World Health Organization. "What Do We Mean by 'Sex' and 'Gender'?" http://www.who.int/gender/whatisgender/en/.

Index

8 + 1: Stories by Robert Cormier, 151
1984, xi, 77, 79, 80

abortion, 44, 46
abstinence-only programs, 14, 27, 121
"The Acuteness of Desire", 148–149
adolescence, 1–2
adolescent, x
adultery, 27, 28, 29, 30, 35n20
"The Age of Consent", 143
AIDS, 14, 103. *See also* HIV; STD;
     venereal disease
Alighieri, Dante, 28–29
The A-List, 104
allegory, 28, 29
Anatomy of a Boyfriend, 115–117
And Both Were Young, 102
Anderson, Laurie Halse, 19, 32
Anna Karenina, 29–30
Annie on My Mind, 110–112
Anthem, 76
Are You in the House Alone?, 47–48
Asher, Jay, x, 133–135
Athletic Shorts, 151
Austen, Jane, xi, 102

Beginner's Love, 65–67
birth control, 13, 48, 50, 71, 121

Blume, Judy, 59–62, 63, 117, 157
Brave New World, 76
Breaking Dawn, 91, 95
Burgess, Melvin, 138–142, 143

canon, 17–19, 125
canonical, 18, 33, 34, 156
The Canterbury Tales, 24–25
Cart, Michael, x, 146
The Catcher in the Rye, 54, 126
Cavanna, Betty, 102
challenges, 19; ALA list of, 156; causes
     for initiating in young adult
     literature, 157–158, 159;
     consequences of, 161; definition,
     155–156; in *Alice* series, 69, 70; in
     canonical literature, 156–157; in
     young adult literature, 157;
     protecting against, 164–165; top ten
     children's and young adult book,
     2001–2013, 161–163
Champion, 98
"Chat Up Lines", 143
Chaucer, Geoffrey, 24–25
Cleary, Beverly, 102
Cohn, Rachel, 126
Committee of Ten, 17
contraception, 14, 61, 62, 121

Cormier, Robert, 151
Crutcher, Chris, 151

Daly, Maureen, 102
The Dark and Hollow Places, 81, 83, 84–85
dark Romantic, 27
The Dead-Tossed Waves, 81
Delirium, 77, 77–79, 80
The Divine Comedy (*Inferno*), 28–29
Doing It, 138–142
Donovan, John, 50
Drexler, Rosalyn, 55
du Jardin, Rosamund, 102
dystopia: definition, 75–76, 95; procreation in, 76, 77, 78, 79, 81, 89; sex in, 76

Eclipse, 91–92
Edwards, Margaret, 37–38, 39
Eleanor and Park, 112–114, 126
Eliot report, 17
emerging adulthood, 2
Emery, Anne, 49–50
Eyerly, Jeanette, 41–42, 43, 95

Felsen, Henry Gregor, 39–41, 42, 43, 49
Fifteen, 102
Flaubert, Gustave, 25–27
Focus on the Family, 14
The Forest of Hands and Teeth, 77, 79–81, 84
Forever, 59, 60–62, 64, 115, 117
Free Not to Love, 49–50

Garden, Nancy, 110–112
gay, 5; in *Annie on My Mind*, 110, 111, 112; in *Grasshopper Jungle*, 85, 87, 88; in *I'll Get There, It Better Be Worth the Trip*, 50, 51; in *Openly Straight*, 130, 131, 132. *See also* homosexuality; lesbian; LGBTQIQ
gender: Hubler's study of, 6; identity, 4; influence on sexual identity, 5;

influences on females, 7; redefining of roles in YA literature, 63; Scieszka's findings on literature and male's perception of, 7
A Girl Like Me, 41–42, 43, 95
The Giver, 76, 81–83
Going on Sixteen, 102
Grasshopper Jungle, 85–90
Gray, Keith, 142–146
Great Books of the Western World, 18
"Green Screen", 145–146
Griswold v. Connecticut, 13

Halevy, Julie, 52–54
Hall, G. Stanley, 1, 38
Hamlet, 22–23
Hawthorne, Nathaniel, 27–28
Head, Ann, 42–44, 95
Heller, Mary Jo, 163
HIV, 14, 16n15. *See also* AIDS; STD; venereal disease
Homer, 31–32
homosexuality, 5, 51, 110, 146, 156; as a reason for book challenges, 161–162. *See also* gay; lesbian; LGBTQIQ
Hunter, Evan, 55–58
Huxley, Aldous, 76

I Am the Beautiful Stranger, 54
identity development, 2–4, 121; sexual, 4–8
The Iliad and the Odyssey, 31–32
I'll Get There, It Better Be Worth the Trip, 50
in loco parentis, 163
Indigo Summer, 105
The Infinite Moment of Us, 117–121
Intellectual Freedom Committee, 155
Intertwined, 105–106
It's Ok If You Don't Love Me, 63–65, 115

Johnson, Angela, 149
juvenile, x

Kimani Tru, 105
Kinsey, Alfred, 13, 38
Klein, Norma, 62–67, 115
Konigsberg, Bill, 130–132

Last Summer, 55–58
Legend series, 97
L'Engle, Madeline, 102
lesbian, 112, 130. *See also* gay;
    homosexuality; LGBTQIQ
Leveen, Tom, 126–129
Levithan, David, 126
LGBTQIQ, 5, 7, 52. *See also* gay;
    homosexuality; lesbian
Losing It, 142–146
Love and Sex: Ten Stories of Truth, 146
love triangle, 91, 93, 96, 105, 106
Lowenthal, Michael, 148–149
Lowry, Lois, 76, 81–83
Lu, Marie, 97, 98

Machiavelli, Nicolo, 75
Madame Bovary, 25–27
manicpixiedreamgirl, 126–129
marketing, x, xi; censorship and, 158;
    of young adult romance novels, 103
Masters and Johnson, 38
masturbation: dangers of, 12–13; in *The
    Absolutely True Diary of a Part-
    Time Indian*, 158; in *Anatomy of a
    Boyfriend*, 116; in *Intensely Alice*,
    71
Mesrobian, Carrie, 136–138
Meyer, Stephenie, xi, 90, 91–96
McKayhan, Monica, 105
More, Sir Thomas, 75
Mr. and Mrs. Bo Jo Jones, 42–44, 95
Myracle, Lauren, 117–121

narrator: alternating, 97, 98, 108, 113,
    133, 135, 165; Hawthorne as, 28;
    judgmental, 42; Lolita type, 54;
    multiple, 138; older, wiser, 56;
    preachy, 129, 142; responsible, 43;
    stilted prose of, 52; third-person, xi,

    39, 40; unnamed, 150. *See also*
    point of view
new adult, x, 52
New Moon, 91
new realism, 42
Nick and Norah's Infinite Playlist, 126

Oedipus and Antigone, 30–31
Oedipus complex, 31
Office of Intellectual Freedom, 156
Oliver, Lauren, 77, 77–79, 80
Openly Straight, 130–132
Orwell, George, xi, 77, 79, 80

Pascal, Francine, 103
Peck, Richard, 47–48
Peeps, 83–85
Perfect Summer, 103
Pike, Aprilynne, 106–107
point of view: in *A Girl Like Me*, 42; in
    My Darling, My Hamburger, 46; in
    The Scarlett Letter, 28; in *Shiver*,
    108; in *Then Again, Maybe I Won't*,
    60; of female characters in early
    YA, 38. *See also* narrator
pornography: definition, 122; in *Sex
    and Violence*, 136; *Speak* as,
    159–160
Practically Seventeen, 102
pregnancy: and fear of discussions
    about sex, 33; and sex education, 13,
    14; as a consequence of sex in YA
    fiction, 38, 121, 157; in *Alice in
    Lace*, 68; in *Beginner's Love*, 66; in
    Breaking Dawn, 94; in *Free Not to
    Love*, 49, 50; in *A Girl Like Me*, 42;
    in *Mr. and Mrs. Bo Jo Jones*, 42, 43,
    44; in *My Darling, My Hamburger*,
    44, 45, 46; in *The Scarlett Letter*,
    27; in *Two and the Town*, 40, 41; in
    Wings, 107; in *The Young Lovers*,
    53; Naylor on, 71
premarital sex, 38, 48, 95
Pride and Prejudice, xi, 102
The Prince, 75

Prodigy, 97
prostitution, 11, 12, 24, 29, 89
Puritan, 27, 28, 123n29

Rand, Ayn, 76
romance novel: categories, 101;
    Harlequin, 104–105; history of,
    102–104
Romance Writers of America, 101
Romeo and Juliet, 20–22, 33
Rowell, Rainbow, 112–114, 126
Ryan, Carrie, 77, 79–81, 83, 84–85

Salinger, J. D., 54, 126
The Scarlett Letter, 27–28
"Scoring", 144
"Secret Shelf", 147
Seventeenth Summer, 102
Sex and Violence, 136–138
Sex in the Library, 163
sexual: attitudes, 6, 7, 15, 27, 29, 64,
    138, 165; practices, safe, 121
sexuality, 4, 7, 8, 33, 37, 61, 62, 67,
    102, 121, 157
Shakespeare, William, 20–24, 33, 96,
    156
Shiver, 107–109
short story, 151
Showalter, Gena, 105–106
Smith, Andrew, 85–90, 145–146
Snadowsky, Daria, 115–117
social hygiene movement, 11, 12
social identity theory, 3
Sones, Sonya, 147
Sophocles, 30–31
Speak, 19, 32. *See also* pornography,
    Speak as

Stall, Sylvanus, 12
STD, 14, 61, 121. *See also* AIDS; HIV;
    venereal disease
Stiefvater, Maggie, 107–109
Storms, Aarene, 163
Sweet Valley High, 103

text connections, x, 27
Then Again, Maybe I Won't, 59–60
Thirteen Reasons Why, x, 133–135
Tolstoy, Leo, 29–30
Twilight, xi, 90, 91–96
Two and the Town, 39–41, 42, 43, 49

utopia, 75, 76
Utopia, 75

Valentine, Jenny, 143
venereal disease, 11, 12–14. *See also*
    AIDS; HIV; STD
verisimilitude, ix, x, 126, 142
Victorian era, morality in, 11–12, 63

"Watcher", 149
Westerfeld, Scott, 83–85
What a Young Boy Ought to Know, 12
What My Mother Doesn't Know, 147
Wings, 106–107

young adult: characteristics of literature
    for, x–xi, 75, 142; definition, x; term
    first introduced, 37
*Young Adult Literature: From Romance
    to Realism*, x
The Young Lovers, 52–54

About the Authors

Bryan Gillis is an associate professor of English education and literacy at Kennesaw State University and the director of the KSU Conference on Literature for Children and Young Adults. Bryan has more than thirty years of experience in education, having taught in elementary, middle, and high school classrooms in Phoenix, Arizona, before moving to Georgia. Bryan's publications to date include *Chris Crutcher: A Stotan for Young Adults* (with Pam B. Cole) as well as numerous articles on reading and writing pedagogy. Bryan is the proud father of two sons, Kyle and Mitch, and loving husband to wife Nancy.

Joanna Simpson is an associate professor at Grand Canyon University in sunny Phoenix, Arizona. Joanna had ten years of experience teaching high school English to inner-city students before she moved into higher education. Joanna's research includes gifted education, critical literacy, young adult literature, and differentiated instruction. When she is not reading or writing, Joanna can be found in the swimming pool with her children, husband, and dogs.